Discovery Travel Adventures™

HAUNTED HOLIDAYS

D1317393

Laura Foreman
Editor

John Gattuso
Series Editor

Discovery Communications, Inc.

INSIGHT GUIDES

Discovery Communications, Inc.

John S. Hendricks, *Founder, Chairman, and Chief Executive Officer*
Judith A. McHale, *President and Chief Operating Officer*
Michela English, *President, Discovery Enterprises Worldwide*
Raymond Cooper, *Senior Vice President, Discovery Enterprises Worldwide*

Discovery Publishing

Natalie Chapman, *Publishing Director*
Rita Thievon Mullin, *Editorial Director*
Mary Kalamaras, *Senior Editor*
Maria Mihalik Higgins, *Editor*
Kimberly Small, *Senior Marketing Manager*
Chris Alvarez, *Business Development & Operations*

Discovery Channel Retail

Tracy Fortini, *Product Development*
Steve Manning, *Naturalist*

Insight Guides

Jeremy Westwood, *Managing Director*
Brian Bell, *Editorial Director*
John Gattuso, *Series Editor*
Siu-Li Low, *General Manager, Books*

Distribution

United States
Langenscheidt Publishers, Inc.
46-35 54th Road, Maspeth, NY 11378
Fax: 718-784-0640

Worldwide
APA Publications GmbH & Co.
Verlag KG Singapore Branch, Singapore
38 Joo Koon Road, Singapore 628990
Tel: 65-865-1600. Fax: 65-861-6438

© **1999** Discovery Communications, Inc., and Apa Publications GmbH & Co Verlag KG, Singapore Branch, Singapore. All rights reserved under international and Pan-American Copyright Conventions.

Discovery Travel Adventures™ and Explore a Passion, Not Just a Place™ are trademarks of Discovery Communications, Inc.

Discovery Communications produces high-quality nonfiction television programming, interactive media, books, films, and consumer products. Discovery Networks, a division of Discovery Communications, Inc., operates and manages the Discovery Channel, TLC, Animal Planet, and Travel Channel. Visit Discovery Channel Online at http://www.discovery.com.

Although every effort is made to provide accurate information in this publication, we would appreciate readers calling our attention to any errors or outdated information by writing us at: Insight Guides, PO Box 7910, London SE1 8WE, England; fax: 44-171-403 0290; email: insight@apaguide.demon.co.uk

No part of this publication may be reproduced in any form or by any electronic or mechanical means, including information storage and retrieval devices or systems, without prior written permission from the publisher, except that brief passages may be quoted for reviews.

Printed by Insight Press Services (Pte) Ltd, 38 Joo Koon Road, Singapore 628990.

Library of Congress Cataloging-in-Publication Data
Haunted Holidays / Laura Foreman, editor.
    p. cm. — (Discovery travel adventures)
    Includes bibliographical references (p.   ) and index.
    ISBN 1-56331-832-6
    1. United States Guidebooks. 2. Haunted places — United States Guidebooks. 3. Ghosts — United States Miscellanea. I. Foreman, Laura. II. Series.
E158.H33   1999
917.304'929–dc21
                    99-26031
                        CIP

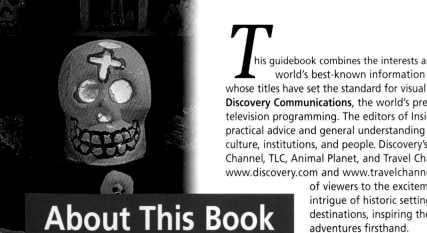

*T*his guidebook combines the interests and enthusiasm of two of the world's best-known information providers: **Insight Guides**, whose titles have set the standard for visual travel guides since 1970, and **Discovery Communications**, the world's premier source of nonfiction television programming. The editors of Insight Guides provide both practical advice and general understanding about a destination's history, culture, institutions, and people. Discovery's networks – Discovery Channel, TLC, Animal Planet, and Travel Channel – and its websites, www.discovery.com and www.travelchannel.com, introduce millions of viewers to the excitement of wild animals, the intrigue of historic settings, and the thrill of unusual destinations, inspiring them to experience life's adventures firsthand.

About This Book

This book reflects the work of dedicated editors and writers who, if not personally acquainted with ghosts, are familiar with ghostly lore and knowledgeable about supposed spectral lairs. **John Gattuso**, of Stone Creek Publications in New Jersey, worked with Insight Guides and Discovery Communications to conceive the series and select the intriguing photographic images. Gattuso looked to **Laura Foreman**, a New Orleans writer and editor with numerous books to her credit, to serve as project editor. "I hold generally with the notion that skepticism is the chastity of the intellect," says Foreman, who helped produce 14 volumes of Time-Life Books' *Mysteries of the Unknown* series. "Nevertheless, I love a good ghost story – and stretching my imagination to speculate on what might lie beyond our mundane reality."

The writers shared her liking for ghost stories, as well as sympathy for history's serious investigators of the paranormal. An award-winning science writer, **Carl Posey** notes that there "was a time when the cutting edge of science was about the supernatural." An editor and the author of six novels and several nonfiction books, Posey affectionately recalls those innocent times as "science's good old days." Of course, ghosts are said to prefer bad old days – wartime in particular. In writing about Civil War specters, **George Daniels**, a former senior editor of *Time* magazine, called on knowledge he acquired as executive editor of Time-Life Books overseeing production of the *Civil War* series. "I never felt the presence of any ghosts on the Virginia battlefields," says Daniels, "but we do have a ghost in our house." His wife once spotted her late mother, along with two other shades, in the refurbished pantry of their Martha's Vineyard home. "She was sure," he says, "that her mother was showing her fellow ghosts what we'd done to the house."

Peter Jensen, a Del Mar, California, freelancer who's collaborated on many travel books, also cites his wife's "experience with several" ghosts as contributing to his own fascination with the paranormal. But Jensen, who wrote "Ghosts of the Old West," notes that "my key credential is that people have paid me to wander the West for the past 20 years or so, and I've found myself in some quite lonely places in some quite lonely months." As a Harvard student, **Tim Appenzeller** got acquainted with some lonely places himself, "the rocky coasts and forests where New England ghost stories unfold." Now a writer and editor for *Science* magazine, Appenzeller works on stories about hard science, but, he notes, "I learned about the aspects of the world that are beyond the reach of reason when I was a writer for Time-Life Books' *Enchanted*

World series." Fellow *Science* editor and Harvard grad **Eliot Marshall** is well versed in the ghostly lore of his hometown, Washington, D.C., and the surrounding area. "Edgar Allan Poe is one of my favorite ghosts in this part of the world," Marshall says. "I've never met him, though he seems to visit Baltimore regularly."

Mark Brewin learned about big-city hauntings during his days as a graduate student at the University of Chicago and later at the Annenberg School for Communication at the University of Pennsylvania in Philadelphia. "If you're interested in a big city's history," he says, "you have to be interested in its ghosts." Living near the biggest city of all, freelance writer **J. Jennings Moss** was well situated to write about New York revenants, although his "interest in other worlds" began on the West Coast. Growing up in California, he haunted, as it were, the ghost-rich Winchester House in San Jose. The house is also familiar to **Christian Kinney**, a Santa Monica, California, book editor and aspiring screenwriter who wrote about the ghosts of Los Angeles and San Francisco.

Roberta Conlan, a freelance writer based in Washington, D.C., was born and reared in Honolulu, where she developed a taste for island ghost stories. Retelling them here, she says, made her homesick for her lovely state. Another writer with a strong sense of place, **Janisse Ray** lives on her great-grandfather's farm in Baxley, Georgia. An award-winning poet, she aspires to a ghostly encounter. "Sometimes in the middle of the night I go sit on a backwoods stretch of railroad track where a ghost has been seen many times," she says, "hoping for a glimpse."

Thanks to Michael Castagna for assistance on Travel Tips, and to other members of Stone Creek's editorial team: Nicole Buchenholz, Bruce Hopkins, and Edward A. Jardim.

Illuminated skulls (opposite) are used in the celebration of Mexico's Day of the Dead, when departed souls are believed to visit the living.

Spirit photographs (above) like this obvious fake were used in the late 19th and early 20th centuries to convince nonbelievers of the existence of ghosts.

Graveyards such as these in Yorkshire, England (below), and Jerome, Arizona (following pages), are rife with supernatural energy.

Table of Contents

SECTION THREE: HAUNTED DESTINATIONS

MAPS

In Search of Ghosts

Some years ago, a learned prober of paranormal matters remarked that the question "Do you believe in ghosts?" was highly ambiguous. It could mean any number of things. But, he went on to say, "if we take it to mean, 'Do you believe that people sometimes experience apparitions?' the answer is that they certainly do. No one who examines the evidence can come to any other conclusion." ◆ This confident assertion that people really do see ghosts would be wholly unremarkable, of course, if it came from your run-of-the-mill talk-show psychic or New Age crystal-gazer. In fact, it came from an eminent (and very skeptical) fellow named Henry Habberly Price, a professor of logic at England's hallowed Oxford University. Price and most of his colleagues in the ghost-hunting Society for Psychical Research – hard-headed investigators all – came away from years of study of the subject with the same conclusion: Something is Out There. ◆ The researchers didn't always

Do ghosts exist? The attraction of the unknown makes believers of us all.

agree on the nature of the Something: pure projections of febrile imaginations, said some; effluvial residue of past passions, said others. But for people who've actually seen ghosts, theorizing on the nature of the phenomenon is merely so much academic twaddle. They need no studies or theories to be convinced. They believe. And so do many others who, while they haven't per-sonally pierced the veil to the Great Beyond, feel in their bones and viscera that spirits of the dead do indeed walk among us, sometimes as solid as the earth they cling to, sometimes as fragile and tenuous as belief. ◆ True believers, polls say, are a minority; but then, true believers don't have a corner

Apparitions like the one depicted in this manipulated photograph are rare, but the mere possibility of such an encounter is chillling enough for most ghost hunters.

Preceding pages: *Danse macabre*, a common motif during the Middle Ages, represented the power of death; an incubus crouches atop his victim in Henry Fuseli's *Nightmare;* haunted Fort Concho in San Angelo, Texas.

on the market when it comes to curiosity about ghosts or interest in them. Arguably, it doesn't matter so much whether haunting spirits are fact or fiction, as long as they have something to offer. And they do. Even the most cynical skeptic can suspend disbelief long enough to enjoy the delicious *frisson* that comes with a good scare, with merely imagining a confrontation with some mysterious, ethereal specter emerging from the gloomy mists of death with harrowing tales to tell. Ghost stories touch in all of us the child's need to believe in things unseen, the adult's need to know things unknowable.

And even the skeptics might well concede that dead souls have it all over the living in one regard: They're hardly ever boring. Almost every ghost comes with a story, a juicy romance or intriguing mystery – of passions thwarted, hearts broken, hopes dashed, crises unresolved, of death in duels or by murder most foul, of unfinished business, undelivered messages, unpunished wrongs, profound sorrows, deathless dreams. For pure entertainment and good company, one could do worse than hang out with ghosts.

So why not go find some? You probably won't even have to travel far, since ghosts seem to be everywhere in America, tangled in the roots of the nation's history. They rise from the stony soil of New England and hover in the humid, scented nights of the Deep South, gathering in the shadows of Savannah's squares and Charleston's mansions or vanishing into hidden French Quarter courtyards in New Orleans. They swell the population in New York City's crowded canyons and wail in the winds that howl across the empty deserts of the West. They haunt historic halls in Philadelphia and Williamsburg and gangster dens in Chicago. They dwell in the waterfalls and lava flows of beautiful Hawaii. They weep in cemeteries and march invisibly across blood-drenched fields of battle.

You'll know them when you see them, when you hear their moans and sighs or feel their icy touch. Or perhaps you'll know when they see you.

They're out there. They're waiting – for you.

Halloween decorations (above and right) recall ancient European beliefs about the return of departed souls on Hallows' Eve.

A ghostly radiance (opposite) enshrouds a statue in London's Brompton Cemetery.

◆

The Ghostly Tradition

◆

Ghosts are eternal in at least one sense: They have always been with us, terrifying our ancient ancestors and persisting through the millennia to intrigue more enlightened minds. Before beginning your own search for revenants, it's useful to know how others have envisioned them.

To anyone who's ever experienced the chilling sensation that an unseen someone, or something, is hovering nearby, there's no question that ghosts are real. But even if this were not so – even if ghosts did not exist – we would probably have invented them. They are, if nothing else, a basic human response to the mystery of death. ◆ We can imagine our most ancient ancestors, faced for the first time with grief and loss, grappling with the unacceptable notion of extinction. Finding it too hard to bear, they must have formulated beliefs that allowed for the dead to linger in this world, still accessible to the living. Along with easing sorrow, such beliefs would have offered hope: If our dead loved ones survive in spirit form, then so might we; death – the manifestly terrible corruption of the body – need not extinguish the soul. ◆ It must have occurred to those long-ago people soon enough, however, that postmortem existence **Ghosts may or may not** was an idea that cut both ways. The spirits can comfort, **exist – but whether** but they can also threaten – lingering forever, **they're real or not, we** fearsomely and maliciously immortal. One can **seem to need them.** imagine a Neanderthal man strutting triumphantly away from a fatally clubbed enemy, only to pause, wondering for the first time in history whether that crumpled form might yet have his revenge. And then, this prototype haunted humanoid might have tiptoed back and covered the body with stones, just to be on the safe side. ◆ The same dichotomy that must have troubled our ancient forbears is still with us: We long for ghosts as a comfort and as proof of an afterlife, but we also dread them. ◆ The nature of our reaction lies in part in the nature of the particular ghost. Everyone knows stories of protective and helpful ghosts, the ones that offer

The Day of the Dead, a Mexican holiday, is a time for tending graves and praying for the souls of lost loved ones.

Preceding pages: A stone carving of Thomas à Becket at supposedly haunted Toddington Manor in England.

Casper (right), the famously friendly ghost, visits actress Christina Ricci in the 1995 film.

The grave (below), according to some believers, is not a final resting place but a gateway to the Other Side.

The image of Death as a skeleton on a pale horse (opposite) is among the Four Horsemen of the Apocalypse in this Albrecht Dürer woodcut from about 1500.

sage advice to the living, or show up just in time to warn of impending disaster. There are even cuddly parodies of ghosts – the friendly cartoon Casper, for instance, or the sheet-draped youngsters who show up annually with the Halloween ultimatum, "trick or treat."

Even frightening revenants can delight us, as long as we don't have to confront them personally: They can make us safely afraid. Believers and nonbelievers alike are apt to recall fondly the

delicious shiver of childhood fear that went with hearing a good ghost story, and the most skeptical adult may not be immune to the well-told ghost tales of M. R. James or Shirley Jackson or to the film versions of Henry James' "The Turn of the Screw" or Peter Straub's *Ghost Story*. In these cases, the listeners or readers or viewers know, after all, that the ghosts are not real. Similarly, Elizabethan audiences – many of whom accepted the reality of ghosts without question – probably enjoyed watching Banquo's blood-smeared ghost show up at dinner to rattle his old friend Macbeth, or the ghost of Hamlet's father drift out of the mist to deliver his bad news. Plausible or not, these ghosts were somebody else's problem.

Why Ghosts Are Frightening

But spectral pleasures notwithstanding, the idea of actually encountering a ghost – even the notion that spirits of the dead truly exist – is enough to make most of us shudder.

Perhaps this is because

ghosts remind us of our own mortality. Or maybe we fear their power, the force that comes from a knowledge no living mortal can match: They have penetrated the ultimate mystery, death itself, and they know what lies beyond. If they turn out to be our enemies, they're enemies with clout.

Perhaps we fear them because these creatures of another realm are so alien to the living, so utterly different from us. On the other hand, perhaps we fear them because they're not.

One person who holds the latter view is a man who should know: Stephen King, the novelist who's made a multimillion-dollar industry out of pinpointing with uncanny accuracy what scares us. In his *Danse Macabre*, a book-length essay on the horror genre, King proposes that ghosts are Freudianly frightening because they're just like us – the dark, untrammeled, irrational side of us all.

"We fear the Ghost for much the same reason we fear the Werewolf," King writes. "It is the deep part of us that need not be bound by piffling Apollonian restrictions. It can walk through walls, disappear, speak in the voices of strangers. It is the Dionysian part of us ... but it is still us."

So terrifying are these postmortem alter-egos, in fact, that King classifies the Ghost as the most potent of the four supernatural archetypes (the others being the Vampire, the Werewolf, and the Thing Without a Name). The Ghost, says the master of horror, is "really more than symbol or archetype, it is a major part of that myth-pool in which we all must bathe."

Ghostly History

As King's mention of archetypes suggests, we modern humans are hardly the first to test the myth-pool's waters. In primitive societies, signs of humanity's early notions of ghostliness are still on the surface, showing where we all have been. The tribes of inland New Guinea still believe that the last breath of the dying is a spirit that takes the form of a bird. The same belief is suggested in the 15,000-year-old cave paintings near the French town of Lascaux. In fact, the whole aboriginal world was populated with spirits – of humans, animals, the heavens, even rivers, stones, and trees. When life fled, it fled into that teeming universe of spirits; it embarked on a journey that wasn't headed for oblivion but for some domain beyond our own.

The Egyptians ramified that simple journey into an excursion not by a single entity but by a tripartite one: the bird-like *ba*, or heart-soul, fluttering away from the body at death, but never far away; the mysterious *ka*, which could survive the death of the physical body by taking up residence in a statue or some other effigy; and the *akh*, the part of the human soul that could take any form and revisit the living as a ghost.

In ancient Greece, the soul became less elaborate – more spartan, you could say. There was, as Homer reported, a body-soul that animated the corporeal self, and a free soul, a kind of objective life force. At death, the free soul departed, leaving the body a dune of "senseless earth." But there remained the *eidolon*, or image of the self, which roamed the earth aimlessly until the body was cremated. Only then could this essential,

substanceless self – this ghost – turn toward the underworld abode of the dead. Given the stakes, the Greeks were quick to cremate.

The idea of the ethereal drifter is still with us, despite the fact that human understanding has become so broad and complicated that most mysteries have evaporated in its glare. We know that birds are not the revived spirits of the dead; we know that life is not entirely breath or blood, that rocks reveal their souls only to geologists, stars only to astronomers. In our culture, the body has become somewhat renewable; organs can be replaced, and we can ameliorate or cure more maladies than ever. Even so, there remains that persistent tug of doubt, that suspicion that no matter how much we know, some mysteries may go forever unplumbed. And in this dwindling no-man's-land of the mind, there is still room for ghosts.

The Ghosts We Love

In truth, our favorite ghosts are the ones most at home in the mind, those who've kept themselves as multiform and evanescent as thought itself. The others – the ones that rattle chains or jiggle tables or fluoresce in the darkness with moans and groans – are not the stuff of true terror and can easily be faked. To be properly haunted, we need something that no one can explain: a woman in white, the human form in flight, apparitions in the shape of their real-world counterparts, or long-dead celebrities coaxed to speech by the

Premature burial (above), as depicted in this 19th-century painting by Antoine Wiertz, was a widespread fear in Europe in the days before doctors had fully unraveled the mysteries of bodily death.

Anubis, the jackel-headed Egyptian god who guides the dead to judgment, is pictured in the tomb of the artist Sennedjem (left).

Death escorts a young woman to her grave (opposite).

sensitivities of living ones. The ghosts we love are the ghosts we create with our imagination.

Like the grief and fear and love and loathing that produce them, ghosts are stamped with such properties as we suppose them to have. Fiction gives us what we'd like to be the real thing, and it tells us what to expect in the way of hauntings. Where we expect retribution, we see fearsome ghosts, like the vengeful shades that haunt Shakespeare's Richard III. Amateur murderers, fictional or real, are visited by the spirits of their victims, or think they are. Only the killer in Poe's "The Telltale Heart" can hear the throbbing of his victim's heart, but to him the sound is thunderous.

Ghosts are nowhere more satisfactory than in motion pictures, where specters find stone walls transparent and work all sorts of wonders. Who wouldn't want to have someone around as amusing as Charles Laughton's chubby, chicken-hearted Canterville Ghost? What lonely young woman wouldn't want to buy a seaside cottage, like Mrs. Muir's, and find it haunted by the irascible sea captain created by Rex Harrison? What woman would shun the tender protection of her lover's spirit, refusing to play – à la *Ghost* – Demi Moore to his Patrick Swayze?

And the ghosts manufactured by creative minds need not be appealing to be compelling. Think of the awesome evil that pervades the Overlook Hotel in King's *The Shining* or that animates a home in an elite urban enclave in Anne Rivers Siddons' novel *The House Next Door*.

The Ghosts We Create

Those of us who feel truly haunted have no need of these fictional beings; there's already some presence that behaves and feels like a proper ghost, something that overtakes us, fills our lives, our minds, with apprehension or replenished grief.

Ancestors may come back, like Hamlet's father, urging the living to avenge some secret wrong. Victims may materialize to finger their murderers, and the scent of lovers persists long after they're gone. The battle-weary men of every war have seen their fallen comrades' ghosts, who march with them and protect them; and they've anxiously sensed the presence of the spirits of fallen enemies, their shattered selves returned to haunt the victors. The only sure thing about ghosts is their reliability: They guarantee that the living reap what they sow.

Sometimes it's impossible to say where the line of demarcation falls between the real and the imaginary, between the living and the restless dead. Our ghosts are sometimes spun from the subconscious stuff that dreams are made on, as Shakespeare said, and it is when we dream, awake or sleeping, that those specters come to us. What can be the difference between a recurring dream of a lost loved one and a haunting?

Whatever they are, real or fancied, ghosts do not call us; we summon them, drawn by some age-old impulse that no infusion of rationality can entirely dispel. Ghosts may be the spirits of the dead, or only the spirits of the human mind, the animated entities born of the terror and mystery and inevitability of dying. Either way, it's as if death were a still pond whose profound, dark depths cannot be seen, but whose untroubled surface is a mirror. When we look into the mirror of death, ghosts are what we see.

E.H.L.

The idea that the energy of life just vanishes into nothingness in death has never been comfortable for us humans – or very logical. Such potent energy must go somewhere: to Paradise, perhaps, or the Underworld, or some purgatorial holding pattern, or the interstices between the stars. It must revive secretly on some other side of existence. And there, many have long supposed, the spirits traverse eternity, reaping whatever good or ill they sowed in life. ◆ Such an explanation accounts nicely for what happens to an individual's life force. But not all energy that has gone on to its post-mortem dimension seems content to stay there. Unfinished business, hatred left unquenched, revenge uncompleted, one's murderer gone free, lost or unrequited love, the need to warn or scare or save one's survivors – there are so many compelling reasons not to rest that one would expect the ether to teem with souls still not quite decoupled from life. And so they seem to

From Spiritualism to quantum physics, the quest persists to find out exactly what haunts us, and how, and why.

hover about us, occasionally visible, often subtly perceptible, just out of earshot, but nevertheless there, palpable enough to prompt never-quite-answered questions about who they are and what they want. ◆ The questions about the fate of the life force have been asked for thousands of years. In the 18th and 19th centuries, however, it appeared at times that science was on the verge of providing some definitive answers. Energy of all sorts was much on people's minds then: electrical energy, magnetic energy, how the two transferred back and forth, how energy was transformed into light and heat. Energy never vanished, it seemed, it merely changed forms. So it might be with the energy of life, some scientists speculated: Perhaps life

This spirit photograph, taken around 1890 and obviously staged, is typical of the chicanery that crept into Spiritualism in its waning days.

was another manifestation of energy, as indestructible as electricity or sunlight, and as quick to take another form.

It made sense, and it carried the advantage that the whole business of an afterlife might be viewed objectively, not through the distorting lenses of superstition or metaphysics. And if one could quantify the existence of human energy after the body's death – ghosts and spirits, as it were – why couldn't one get in touch with them? Why couldn't science open a line to the Other Side?

Science and the Supernatural

The idea smacked somewhat of hubris; the science of the time (and of today, for that matter) was as yet ill-equipped to unveil nature's most closely held secret: the mystery of death and what lies beyond it. Even so, there were pioneers willing to try. And if they fell short, some were equally willing to cloak their efforts in enough pseudoscientific mumbo jumbo to at least confuse the issue.

One of these was Franz Anton Mesmer, the 18th-century Austrian physician whose theory of "animal magnetism" – a natural magnetic energy he believed to exist in all living creatures – suggested the possibility of sensing objects and events beyond one's waking ken.

Mesmer was wrong about nearly everything except the technique of hypnotizing, or "mesmerizing," subjects. Still, his incorporation of magnetism into his spiel imparted a certain learned aura to his work and to the otherworldly pranks of a legion of Mesmerists who sprang up on both sides of the Atlantic. Emanuel Swedenborg, a renowned Swedish scientist who was a contemporary of Mesmer, offered a philosophical counterpoint to the Austrian's mind-bending hocus-pocus. The hidden worlds to which Mesmer claimed to send his hypnotized subjects were familiar ground to Swedenborg, who reported the frequent company of Jesus, a host of spirits, and even God. He framed the afterlife into six spheres of Spiritualism, which spirits traversed from the lowest (life on Earth) to the highest (unknowable to us).

About equal parts brilliant and deranged, Swedenborg, like Mesmer, helped fertilize the occult ground of what would become, in the 19th century, the Spiritualist movement.

The Good Work

Andrew Jackson Davis, born in 1826 in upstate New York, carried the Mesmer and Swedenborg ideas onward but mixed with the peculiarities of a frail, miserable boy born to an illiterate zealot of a mother and an alcoholic dad. Davis had a grand facility for falling into trances during which he had visions and visitors. One of them was Galen, the ancient Greek physician, who passed on to Davis a healing staff and steered him toward the business of clairvoyant medicine.

Davis did so much to prepare the way for Spiritualism that he's been called the movement's John the Baptist, and, indeed, he seemed to foresee its advent. "About daylight this morning," he wrote

Elizabethan occultists (opposite) invoke a spirit of the dead in this 18th-century English engraving.

Franz Anton Mesmer (above) pioneered hypnotism, along with more arcane theories involving clairvoyance and spirit realms.

Emanuel Swedenborg (left) claimed contact with all sorts of spirits, including God, Christ, and Plato.

on March 31, 1848, "a warm breathing passed over my face and I heard a voice, tender and strong, saying, 'Brother, the good work has begun....'"

The Fox Sisters

The good work was, in fact, a fraud concocted by two bored girls, Margaretta and Catherine Fox. Living poor in a ramshackle house in Hydesville, New York, 13-year-old Maggie and 12-year-old Kate no doubt found life such a vacuum that they felt impelled to fill it. Thus, one night in March 1848, the Fox family was jarred awake by the sounds of knocking powerful enough to shake the flimsy dwelling. They couldn't find the cause.

The next night the ominous racket revived, as it did each night thereafter until March 31 – the day of Davis' epiphany about the good work beginning – when Mrs. Fox confronted the mysterious sounds. She snapped her fingers and told the sound

to reply. It snapped back. The mother asked the entity to rap 10 times, and again it complied. Finally, she asked it to rap out the ages of her six children, and it did. Convinced that she had made contact with an occult agency of some kind, Mrs. Fox carried the tale out into upstate New York, and, without really meaning to, she lit the fuse for a metaphysical movement that would sweep the world.

The Fox girls became world famous for a time; it was quite some time before their mysterious rappings were traced to their true source: the curious ability of the sisters to pop their toe joints with resounding force. Both Kate and Maggie died in 1892, bloated with alcohol and bleached by despair. They were laid to rest in potter's field, from which, it is generally supposed, their exhausted spirits never wandered.

But the spiritualistic conflagration they'd sparked flared like wildfire. According to one contemporary tally, some 30,000 mediums were at work in America within five years of those first Hydesville rappings. "It came upon them like the small-

pox," one English scholar observed. A carnival of séances ensued in which spirits, working through mediums, were said to make tables move, produce lights, voices, bells – illusions of every description.

In time, most of the mediums were exposed for the frauds they manifestly were. There were a few, however, whose effects could not be explained then, and cannot now, without invoking the supernatural. It was on the gossamer wings of such magic as theirs that Spiritualism really took flight.

Levitations and Luminosities

Daniel Dunglas Home (pronounced Hume) emerged from the Connecticut outback only two years after the Hydesville rappings of 1848. To some he was a medium with superhuman gifts, and even his detractors conceded that he must be a magician of a very high order. He thought nothing of scrubbing his face with hot coals, he could elongate his body, and he could make himself – as well as heavy tables – levitate weightlessly. Most important, the spirits he summoned arrived with physical attributes and sometimes appeared in their full, luminous form.

During one famous séance in London, Home astonished his companions by appearing to exit from one third-floor window, drift through the air outside, and then step back through another window.

Featherweight

How much does the soul weigh? Duncan MacDougall posed this question in 1907 and came up with an answer that at least satisfied himself.

"If personal continuity after the event of bodily death is a fact," he wrote, "if the psychic functions continue to exist as a separate individual or personality after the death of brain and body, then such personality can only exist as a space-occupying body."

MacDougall, a physician in Haverhill, Massachusetts, observed in the publication *American Medicine* that if the spirit occupies space, "the question arises: Has this substance weight, is it ponderable?"

The question echoed the scientific thinking of the time. To explain the behavior of light and other electromagnetic waves, scientists of the Victorian era had hypothesized a substance called ether, which was transparent, weightless, and otherwise undetectable but also universally pervasive. MacDougall postulated that the ubiquity of ether made it an unlikely candidate for the stuff of souls, which must be weighable. Ah, but how to take its measure?

To the modern ear, MacDougall's response has a chilling simplicity: The soul could be detected "by weighing a human being in the act of death." Accordingly, he obtained a bed "arranged on a light framework built upon very delicately balanced platform-beam scales." MacDougall selected moribund patients exhausted by the rigors of disease, so their deaths would occur with little or no muscular movement.

The first subject was a tubercular man who lasted three hours and 40 minutes. At the moment of death, the beam dropped "with an audible stroke hitting against the lower limiting bar." MacDougall crowed: "In this case, we certainly have an inexplicable loss of weight of three-fourths of an ounce. Is it the soul substance? How other shall we explain it?"

Five more subjects died on MacDougall's balanced bed, with mixed results. The second lost only half an ounce at death, but moments later this increased to just over an ounce and a half. Number three lost half an ounce at death, and an additional ounce a few minutes later. Number four, a woman in diabetic coma, may have lost three-eighths to half an ounce; MacDougall wasn't sure because "there was a good deal of interference by people opposed to our work." Number five lost three-eighths of an ounce at death very suddenly, as in the first case. The sixth subject died before MacDougall could adjust the scales.

As a man of science, MacDougall knew he needed to verify that the lost weight was the departing human soul, not something else. As a control, he carefully executed 15 dogs ranging in weight from 15 to 70 pounds and made his point. The animals gave up no weight at the moment of passage, which was as MacDougall expected, because he believed dogs have no soul.

In the end, MacDougall believed he had assayed the human soul as an entity weighing between three-eighths of an ounce and one and a half ounces. His results, he wrote, would quantify the fact that the soul survived and offer proof of an afterlife "worth more than the postulates of all the creeds and all the metaphysical arguments combined."

An angel and devil (below) vie for the soul departing from a dying man in this 19th-century illustration.

Andrew Jackson Davis (opposite, above) had visions and practiced clairvoyant medicine – an art later ascribed to another famous American psychic healer, Edgar Cayce.

D. D. Home (opposite, below) floats above astonished onlookers at one of his séances. Levitation was the renowned Connecticut medium's trademark feat.

D. D. Home had many critics who thought him both effeminate and fraudulent. But, while his performances brought him patrons, Home never charged for his séances and was never proved to be a trickster. It made him a hard act to follow, and in fact, Spiritualism itself nearly died after he retired; most of his successors were too easily exposed as charlatans.

The White Crow

Indeed, by the end of the 19th century, séances had become so fraught with elaborate chicanery that they were convincing only to the most credulous. Ironically, it was about this time that some of history's truly remarkable mediums appeared with tools that were not rappings and bogus full-body illusions but a kind of wise, penetrating psychological connection with the spirit world.

Leonora Piper, for example, came from a very commonplace Boston background but seemed to have real psychic powers – a fact attested to by many researchers of the paranormal who investigated her over a number of years.

Mrs. Piper's most famous investigator was the great Harvard psychologist William James, founder of the philosophical system called Pragmatism and also a founder of the American Society for Psychical Research. James was well aware that most mediums were fakes. After studying Mrs. Piper, however, he wrote, "if you wish to upset the law that all crows are black, you must not seek to show that no crows are: It is enough if you prove one single crow to be white. My own white crow is Mrs. Piper. In the trances of this medium, I cannot resist the conviction that knowledge appears which she never gained by the ordinary waking use of her eyes and ears and wits."

Her séances were as tranquil as sleep. She would sink

Leah Fish (above) drapes protective arms around sisters Margaretta and Catherine Fox, whose mediumship, though it later proved fraudulent, popularized the Spiritualism movement. A Rochester physician tries to catch the sisters in fakery (left).

into a trance that seemed to sever utterly her connection with the world of the living, then meet one of her ghostly spirit guides: an Indian girl named Chlorine, J. S. Bach, Henry Wadsworth Longfellow, Cornelius Vanderbilt, actress Sarah Siddons, a loud, profane French doctor named Phinuit.

These, and a host of "controls" who came later, would relay messages from the dead, even letting them speak for themselves through the medium. So consistently did Leonora Piper exceed the nominal boundaries of her knowledge, experience, and education on these otherworldly excursions that even the most skeptical observer was forced to conclude that her powers were real and formidable.

Pearl and Patience

Another medium with seemingly inexplicable powers was Pearl Curran, a thoroughly ordinary St. Louis housewife of no particular gifts until one day in 1913 when, while playing with a Ouija board, her life changed. To Mrs. Curran's astonishment, the board spelled out this message: "Many months ago I lived. Again I come – Patience Worth is my name."

Patience, who claimed to be a Quaker woman born

Leonora Piper (right) was a Boston medium whose psychic talents convinced even the most skeptical investigators.

in 17th-century England, was soon dictating lengthy messages through her newfound medium, first with the Ouija board, then directly. The words tumbled out as fast as Mrs. Curran's husband could write them down, forming themselves over the years into plays, novels, and poems that enjoyed a wide readership in the United States. The settings of these works ranged from medieval England to first-century Palestine – times and places of which Pearl Curran herself seemed wholly ignorant.

One of Mrs. Curran's several psychic investigators was Professor Charles Edward Cory of Washington University. Cory had no doubt the medium was honest, but he suspected she was suffering from dissociative personality; he believed, in other words, that Patience was a secondary personality that Mrs. Curran had manifested unconsciously to provide an outlet for repressed literary gifts. But another respected investigator disagreed. Walter Franklin Prince, a member of the American Society for Psychical Research, thought that Patience constituted "respectable evidence" for the survival of the soul.

Science and the Soul

Since the days of Mrs. Piper and Mrs. Curran, science and mediumship have gone their separate ways, the latter dissolving into the often-suspect claptrap of channeling and psychic hot lines, the former searching for spirits in wholly new directions.

These days, the serious scientists speculating on the soul's possible survival tend to be, of all things, physicists. Their mystical turn of mind is doubtless linked to quantum mechanics itself, the science describing the cosmos as a mysterious

Thomas Edison
(above) ponders one of his works in progress. The prolific inventor proposed building a "spirit machine" to talk with the dead.

Automatic writing
(opposite), reputedly the work of spirits communicating through a medium's hand, appears on a slate in this picture from the archives of England's Society for Psychical Research. Part of the message is in Greek.

Extreme Long Distance

Can we get through to the dead on the telephone? Don't laugh, it's been considered. One who gave it some serious thought was no less than that great do-it-yourself handyman Thomas Alva Edison. Even as a boy, Tom was interested in electricity, trying to manipulate pulsations for unreal purposes. Meanwhile, his parents, Sam and Nancy Edison, dabbled in Spiritualism.

So it's perhaps not shocking to learn that the Wizard of Menlo Park came to believe that communication between the living and the dead was possible. After dreaming up a slew of wonderful inventions – an electric lamp, a phonograph, a motion picture projector – he broached a scheme that was right out of the Twilight Zone. Edison announced, in the October 1920 issue of *Scientific American*, that he had concocted a transcendental telephone scheme. Alas, he himself passed into other realms before anything came to fruition, and he took all knowledge of his spirited intentions with him. This longest of long-distance connections never got off the ground, so to speak, to reach the status of the Wizard's 1,093 patents.

He wasn't the only true believer. In the 1950s some pioneering attempts to record ghostly voices were made. An inquisitive Swede named Friedrich Jurgenson detected, in 1959, what has come to be called electronic voice phenomena, or EVP. These are audible intrusions of phantom sounds in recordings.

Jurgenson was an opera singer, a painter, and a filmmaker. One day, while listening to tapes of birdsongs he had recorded near his country house, he heard something else on playback: an unfamiliar Norwegian voice describing the songs of night birds. Other recordings brought in other voices. They told Jurgenson how to record more voices from the Other Side. Jurgenson publicized his experiments in a 1964 book, *Voices from the Universe*.

The next leap forward was taken by a German psychologist-philosopher, Konstantin Raudive. He became so engaged in the search for EVP that the phantoms came to be called Raudive Voices. According to Raudive and other researchers, the voices usually relay their terse messages ungrammatically and sometimes too cryptically to be easily understood. They may range, says Sarah Estep of the American Association-Electronic Voice Phenomena, from faint, indecipherable whispers to sounds understandable with the help of headphones to messages that are loud and clear without a headset.

One of the most ambitious EVP efforts to date involved Spiricom, a device designed by a retired engineer, George Meek, and an electronically savvy medium, William O'Neill. Meek and O'Neill claimed to be instructed by a discarnate scientist they called Doc Nick. Designing a Spiricom is one thing; building such a device is another. No one has succeeded.

Although the living have not been able to develop a telephone line to the Other Side, spirits have reportedly established a central exchange of their own. Sometimes they ring up to say hello, or to remember Mom on Mother's Day, or mark some anniversary. Often the connection is suffused with static and a murmur of ambient voices, like those transatlantic calls in the 1930s.

The discarnate may reach out, it seems, but only in the most exceptional cases. When they do, it is always only briefly, a quick communiqué, before their distant voices fade and the line from the Other Side goes... dead.

mesh of being and nonbeing in which tiny, invisible bits called quanta – the building blocks of the universe – behave in exotically erratic and unpredictable ways.

All creation is joined "in a state of unending flux of enfoldment and unfoldment," says the University of London's David Bohm, a leading authority on quantum mechanics and also a student of Eastern mysticism. Bohm asserts that human consciousness is part of a unity that includes the whole universe. If such oneness is indeed the case, it's logical to assume that somewhere in that universe, disembodied souls exist.

Another physicist influenced by Eastern thought is Brian Josephson, a Nobel laureate and professor at England's Cambridge University. "One is not the same as one's body," says Josephson, who defines the soul as a nonphysical "organizing center" of the self. He is convinced that this organizing center survives death.

Mind, Brain, Soul

Other scientists approach the soul by speculating on whether human consciousness is separable from human flesh: Is the mind merely what the brain does? Or is it more, and other – an entity that can exist independent of the brain and survive the brain's death? One renowned thinker who argues for the second proposition is Australian neurophysiologist

Sir John Carew Eccles, another Nobel Prize winner. "I cannot believe," says Eccles, "that the wonderful gift of a conscious existence has no further future, no possibility of another existence under some unimaginable conditions."

Eccles has an ally in Sir Karl Popper, the eminent philosopher of science. Popper posits the existence of three worlds: a material one containing the brain and all other material objects, an abstract world in which the mind dwells, and a world that holds all the mind's achievements, all the fruits of civilization. These worlds interact constantly, but they are essentially separate; the mind, therefore, enjoys an existence independent of the brain.

No End in Sight

Inquiring minds, including some of the best minds around, do indeed want to know. But this side of the grave, will we ever really understand what death is and what the spirit is and whether it survives after the

body dies? The best minds seem to think not.

Physicist Josephson contends that physical science will never, by itself, unravel all reality's secrets, although he concedes that mystical insight may open new pathways for rational thought.

Neurophysiologist Eccles is even more modest about the prospects, although – good scientist that he is – he allows for all possibilities. "I don't want to claim that I have some extraordinary revelation telling me the answer" says Eccles. "I keep everything open. I keep so many doors open because I am, as it were, a lost soul trying to find my way in the unknown."

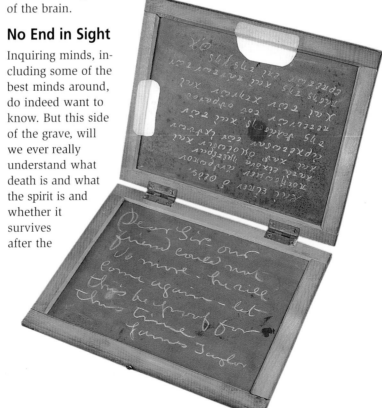

MODERN SPIRITUALISM

BY
J. N. MASKELYNE.

SPIRITS

A MOONLICHT TRANSIT OF VENUS

LONDON: FREDERICK WARNE & C

n Victorian times, when Spiritualism was all the rage, almost every medium worthy of renown had a sort of signature gimmick. ◆ The famous Daniel Dunglas Home, for instance, was best known for levitation, for he seemed to float above the heads of sitters at his séances with majestic disdain for gravity. French medium Marthe Beraud was best at extruding copious gobs of a mystical goo called ectoplasm from a variety of bodily orifices. And earthy Eusapia Palladino, child of Neapolitan streets, was remarkably sexual, displaying a look that one bemused researcher described as "voluptuous ecstasy" as she made chairs skitter mysteriously across the floor and solid objects vanish into air. That same researcher, British anthropologist Eric Dingwall, also chronicled that after sittings, Eusapia would sometimes "throw herself into the arms of men attending the séance and signify her desire for more intimate contacts in ways which could hardly be misinterpreted except by the most innocent." ◆ Then there was Agnes Guppy of London, whose celebrity rested with her "apports" – objects that materialized out of the air during séances, supposedly dropped by spirits. Mrs. Guppy could produce apports by the bushelful on cue and on request. When one of her sitters once asked for a sunflower, for instance, a six-foot-tall specimen clunked obligingly down on the séance table with roots and soil still attached. ◆ Mrs. Guppy's most famous apport, however, was herself. One night as she sat at home doing household accounts, the story goes, she had no sooner written the word "onions" than she was suddenly

If the spirits of the dead do walk the Earth, they must be dismayed by the fakery that abounds among some who claim to call them forth.

Airborne Agnes Guppy is the subject of an 1876 magazine cover commemorating her purported spirit-driven flight across London. She is said to have landed on a rival medium's séance table.

transported to a séance in progress two miles away. The feat was no less remarkable for its lack of grace: Mrs. Guppy, a lady of wondrously elephantine proportions, made a thunderous landing.

Science and Spirit

Needless to say, such marvels drew scrutiny from psychic investigators, among them some of the era's foremost scientists, men eager to turn nebulous notions of the afterlife into matters concrete and quantifiable. These men tended to align themselves pro and con in assessing various mediums. For instance, Alfred Russel Wallace, the great naturalist who had worked out a theory of evolution independently of Charles Darwin, was an avid supporter of Mrs. Guppy's claims. But John William Strutt, a Nobel Prize-winning physicist, found the medium's venomous nature most unspiritual. "Mrs. Guppy I don't think I could stand," Strutt once wrote, "even in the cause of science." Many of his colleagues were of a similar mind – enough of them, in fact, to drag Mrs. Guppy down from the heights (literal and figurative) that she'd once enjoyed.

Other mediums were not so easily dislodged. That was the case with Florence Cook, a young London medium whose signature shtick was the apparent ability to materialize the full form of a dead pirate's daughter named Katie King. Despite numerous allegations of fraud – mostly from those who noted the resemblance between the living Florence and the dead Katie – Miss Cook supplanted Mrs. Guppy as the darling of London's Spiritualists. It was an outcome most galling to poor, portly Agnes, who hated her slim and pretty successor.

Charges of trickery notwithstanding, Florence excited the investigative interest of Sir William Crookes, perhaps the most respected physicist and chemist of his day. After observing five months' worth of Cook's séances, Sir William pronounced her the genuine article. Alas, the endorsement fell rather flat among rumors that the engaging young medium and the esteemed man of science had become lovers.

Magicians Join the Fray

As time went on, Spiritualism began to lose its luster as one medium after another was either exposed as a hoaxer or widely suspected of being one. Palladino, Guppy, Cook, Beraud, and many lesser lights dimmed. Some were exposed by scientists, but now another enemy of mediums was on the prowl, one generally harder to fool than those men who espoused rationalism in their work but were sometimes amazingly gullible otherwise: It took a trickster to spot a trickster, and magicians were good at it.

So it was that by the early 1900s, mediums came to fear those who liked to disrupt sittings with shouts of "Fake!" But there was one particular stranger who soothed them with his very ordinariness. Behind the little fellow's beard and spectacles shone a believer's face. Reassured, the medium would carry on, and soon apports would pelt, or ectoplasm ooze.

Then, as the séance hit its stride, the stranger would leap from his chair and whip away the disguise. Without it, he was immediately recognizable. Pointing a finger accusingly at the medium, he would use the name by which the whole world knew him. "I am Harry Houdini," he would exclaim, "and you are a fraud!" It was the worst

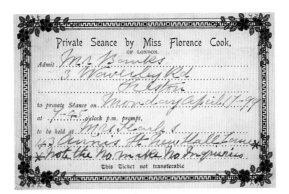

Private Seance by Miss Florence Cook,
OF LONDON.

Admit *Mr Banks*
3 Waverley Rd
Nelston
to private Séance on *Monday April 17-99*
at *7-45* o'clock p.m. prompt,
to be held at *Mrs Searle's*
43 Avenue Rd New Hall Lane
Note the No. make no inquiries
This Ticket not transferable

An invitation to a Florence Cook séance (left) meant a chance to see the materializing of an apparition (opposite), pictured here with psychic investigator William Crookes.

Ectoplasm (below), a supposedly supernatural substance, oozes from the ear of Mina

news a medium could get. The master magician and greatest escape artist of all time was also the scourge of mediums everywhere. He would attend their séances incognito until they trapped themselves with some trick that the master found utterly transparent.

Born Ehrich Weiss, the

son of a Wisconsin rabbi, Houdini had embarked on his search-and-destroy mission after his beloved mother died in 1913. He visited many mediums, hoping to make contact with his mother, but finding instead only trickery of a very inferior sort. Disappointment turned to rage, rage to action.

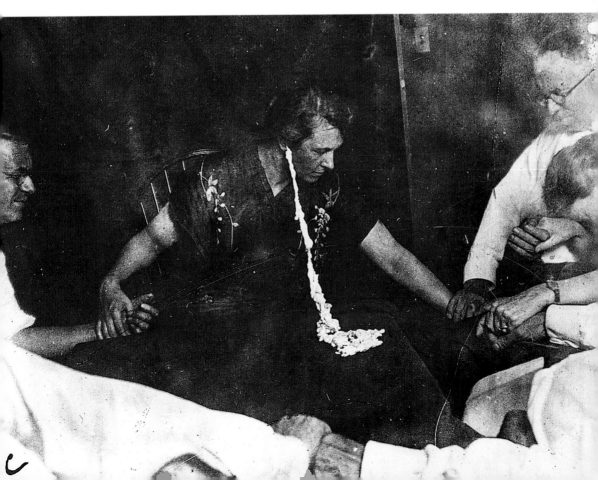

But what moved Houdini was not entirely his futile search. Magicians were the natural enemies of phony mediums who turned the innocent deceptions of stage magic into cruel fraud. Mediums gave magic a bad name. The world's top magicians became debunkers of mediumship. Harry Kellar, dean of American magicians, and John Maskelyne of Britain joined the battle. But none had the angry fervor of Houdini, the greatest debunker of all time.

Amazing Margery

Usually the mediums were easy prey, their clumsy magic childishly simple. Usually, but not always. A case in point: Mina Crandon, the Witch of Lime Street.

Her presumed psychic potency had been discovered in 1923 when her husband, Boston physician Le Roi Goddard Crandon, developed an interest in mediumship and arranged a small séance at their Beacon Hill home. For a time, nothing happened; then the heavy wooden séance table began to thrash about. Crandon had the guests leave, one by one, but the table continued hopping. Finally, only Mina and Le Roi remained, and still the table moved. She was the medium!

Both were much taken by this discovery. Mina, at 30, liked having a skill that so delighted her 44-year-old husband. The Crandons held regular séances through the summer, and she became better and better. From spooky knockings and bursts of light she moved on to apports and self-playing musical instruments. She then added a spirit guide, her rough-tongued dead brother, Walter. He was a good choice: No one believed his vulgarities could have come from Mina.

Her husband, thrilled by this development, wrote to Sir Arthur Conan Doyle. The famed author of the Sherlock Holmes crime mysteries was a committed Spiritualist who was quick to believe whatever spectral contact was reported any-where. Doyle immediately accepted Mina as authentic, then ratified his endorse-ment with a sitting in

Strange Bedfellows

Sherlock Holmes meets Harry Houdini. Sounds improbable, but it happened, back in 1920, and they really hit it off.

It was not exactly Holmes, of course, but his alter ego, Arthur Conan Doyle. The creator of the world-famous sleuth went to Portsmouth, England, to see the equally famous American illusionist in action. They met and took a liking to each other.

Harry and wife Bess visited the Doyle estate and charmed Sir Arthur's children with their bag of magical tricks. Doyle, in return, visited the Houdini home in New York. They made an incongruous pair, the serene British surgeon-author with his walrus mustache and upper-crust stature looming over the smaller, high-strung, powerfully built American. In fact, they were bound by differences, but not those of appearance.

Doyle was a lifelong champion of all things psychical; Houdini was their nemesis and scourge. But they shared a keen interest in the supernatural, and both, in their disparate ways, were true believers. "Who was the greatest medium-baiter of modern times?" Doyle asked in one of his Spiritualist essays. "Undoubtedly Houdini. Who was the great physical medium of modern times? There are some who would be inclined to give the same answer." In Doyle's view, a man without supernatural powers could not do what Houdini manifestly did.

Their strangest encounter came in 1922. Doyle was making his second American tour since the Great War, and in Atlantic City he and his wife were visited once again by Houdini. Lady Doyle invited the magician to participate in a séance, and Houdini understood that she intended to raise the spirit of his mother, Cecilia Weiss, who had died nine years earlier. Houdini's acute skepticism had been curdled into hatred by psychic frauds, but, knowing the Doyles to be sincere, he kept an open mind and accepted the invitation.

To make conditions more favorable to the maternal spirit's appearance, the June 17 séance was limited to Houdini and the Doyles. Lady Doyle sank into a trance holding a pencil ready to write on a pad of paper. Suddenly she went rigid, as though possessed; her pencil drew the sign of the cross. Sir Arthur asked: Was this the spirit of Houdini's mother? Lady Doyle rapped the table three times. Then her pencil flew into motion. "Oh my darling, at last I'm through." The message went on and on, until finally the pencil dropped from Lady Doyle's fingers.

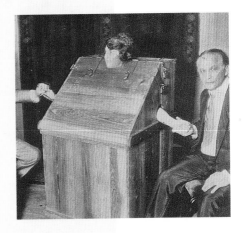

An ardent debunker, Harry Houdini (opposite, seated on left) demonstrates a parlor trick used by Spiritualists to dupe unsuspecting clients.

Arthur Conan Doyle (above) was an avowed Spiritualist, a true believer in the power of mediums.

Harry Houdini (below) immobilizes The Amazing Margery's left hand in a 1924 séance; Margery sits in a "fraud-proof" box that he helped invent.

Afterward, the Doyles thought that the visitation, which they believed was genuine, should have cured Houdini's skepticism. For his part, Houdini wondered why a Hungarian Jew like his mother would use the sign of the cross, or master English after death, or say nothing about June 17 being her birthday. He politely kept quiet.

The two men parted on good terms that night, but six months later Houdini openly expressed his conviction that the experiment had failed. Doyle thought Houdini churlish for ignoring what he truly believed to be proof positive of Spritualism. Henceforth, the spirits that had united them would keep them apart. The next time Sir Arthur Conan Doyle and Harry Houdini met, it would not be as friends who differed but as bitter adversaries in the strange case of The Amazing Margery.

England. He also commended her to J. Malcolm Bird, an associate editor at *Scientific American*.

The magazine was then offering $2,500 to any medium who could prove genuine to a blue-ribbon investigating committee, a six-man group consisting mostly of skeptics – the most skeptical of all being Harry Houdini. The Crandons welcomed the gauntlet. In a note to Doyle, Le Roi Crandon wrote that they would "crucify" Houdini.

The investigation of Mina – now known as Margery the Medium, or just The Amazing Margery – got under way in November 1923. Five members gradually came to view Mrs. Crandon in a favorable light. By spring, the committee was ready to hand her the $2,500 prize. Incredibly, however, this position had been reached without consulting the missing sixth member, who was on tour. Houdini learned of it from a headline: "Houdini the Magician Stumped."

Houdini vs. Mina

The famed magician sped to Boston and discovered that the committee's findings had been compromised in no small measure by Mina's allure. Indeed, when he first visited her in July 1924, he felt some of her magnetism himself. She was, he sensed, a natural like himself, born to trickery. Besides, she was very attractive. Legend has it that Houdini asked her to disrobe to prove that she concealed no hoaxing paraphernalia on her person. When she complied, he gallantly observed that if she couldn't raise the dead, no one could.

But, he concluded, she could not: Her tricks were slick, he conceded, but tricks nevertheless. In the end, Mina Crandon did not receive $2,500 from *Scientific American*, and Houdini's efforts made doubters of some of her formerly faithful. Still, she strode from the battle intact and with the support of such celebrity believers as Conan Doyle.

Margery added new refinements to her act, including the extrusion of a grosser form of ectoplasm said to resemble animal lung tissue. But Eric Dingwall, the researcher who'd earlier reported on Eusapia Palladino's sensual shenanigans, thought he could see fine wires from which the ectoplasmic limbs dangled, and he opined that Margery discharged false ectoplasm hidden in various body cavities.

With this and other assaults, belief soured into doubt. Soaked in alcohol, widowed in 1939, Mina, the Witch of Lime Street, turned toward the Other Side.

The Channelers

The heyday of spirit mediums is long past, but some magicians continue to ferret out fakery. Foremost among them is Toronto-born James

Polish psychic Stanislawa P. (opposite) produces ectoplasm in a 1913 photograph.

The Amazing Randi (center), magician and founder of the skeptical James Randi Educational Foundation, is dedicated to exposing fortune-tellers (above), spoon-benders (below), and other suspected psychic frauds.

Randi, who, like Houdini, embarked on a lifelong crusade to expose phony psychics, fraudulent psychokinetic spoon-benders, and other hoaxers. The Amazing Randi, as he is known professionally, has even offered a million dollars to anyone who can demonstrate to his satisfaction paranormal abilities of any kind. So far, no one has collected.

Among the purveyors of the paranormal who excite Randi's ineffable contempt are channelers, the present-day successors to the mediums. There are certain differences between the two breeds. Whereas the old-time mediums purported to deal solely with spirits of the dead, for instance, channelers invoke all sorts of spirits – not just of the dead, but of aliens, or the inner self, or of creatures never incarnate at all. Randi finds such distinctions trifling. Channeling, he says, "is just Spiritualism

that's been stuck in the microwave for a few months to warm up."

Even so, he might admit that many channelers make more money than the mediums ever did, and they don't have to work as hard. Eschewing taxing physical stunts – no ectoplasm or apports – a channeler may merely sit quietly and act as the alleged conduit for dead rock stars or denizens of Alpha Centauri. Aside from saving energy, this approach also makes fraud harder to prove: Who can say, in fact, whether John Lennon's spirit is speaking through a channeler? One either believes or not.

Channelers became popular in the 1970s and peaked in the 1980s. One typical exemplar of the breed, albeit a phenomenally successful one, was J. Z. Knight, a one-time homemaker and cable-television executive from Washington

state. Claiming to channel Ramtha, a 35,000-year-old warrior spirit from the lost continent of Lemuria, Knight attracted enough support to buy a multimillion-dollar mansion and to stable her purebred Arabian horses in barns lit by chandeliers.

Ramtha's brand of cosmic knowledge was generally vague, cryptic, and couched in wrenching syntax. He described himself, for example, as "that which is termed servant unto that which is called Source, to that which is termed the Principal Cause, indeed, unto that which is termed Life, unto that which is termed Christus – God experiencing that which is termed Man, man experiencing that which is termed God – am I servant unto also."

It's perhaps no wonder that, in the 1990s, "channeling is pretty well faded," as Randi notes.

He, among others, seems relieved.

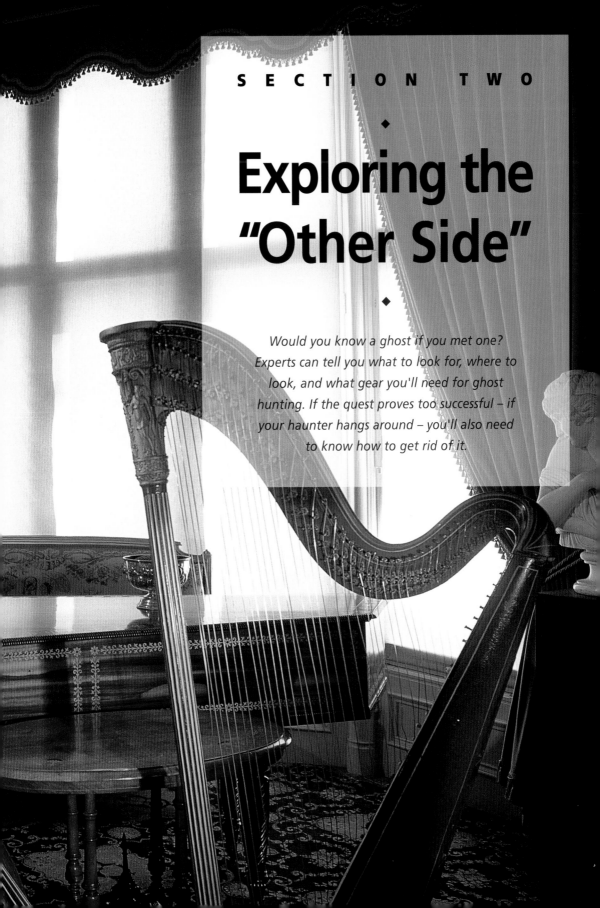

Exploring the "Other Side"

Would you know a ghost if you met one? Experts can tell you what to look for, where to look, and what gear you'll need for ghost hunting. If the quest proves too successful – if your haunter hangs around – you'll also need to know how to get rid of it.

CHAPTER 4

Ghosts are easy to define, hard to explain. Almost everybody agrees on the basic proposition that ghosts are spirits of the dead. But that deceptively simple definition is just a gateway to a thorny thicket of questions, some of them the most profound that humans ever ask. ◆ What exactly is a spirit? Is it the same thing as a soul? Does such a thing really exist? And if it does, can it survive the death of the body? In what form? Why do the dead haunt the living – or just some of the living? Why do some people apparently see ghosts, others not? Are ghosts vengeful? Kindly? Sad? Should we fear them? Avoid them? Seek them out? ◆ The answers depend largely, of course, on whom you ask – and when. People who believe in ghosts or claim to have encountered them – a minority that hovers between 10 and 20 percent, according to most polls taken over the years – are quick to speculate on the nature and significance of spirits. For unbelievers, on the other hand, ghosts are merely the stuff

While some people sense ghosts or see them, others are driven to sort them out, to discover what they really are.

of idle chitchat, the quaint fantasies of credulous minds. But this wasn't always so. There was a time, beginning about a century and a half ago, when some of the world's finest intellects (skeptical intellects, mostly) pursued the subject of ghosts in deadly earnest. It was for them, one might say, a matter of eternal life or death. ◆ The mid-19th century was a turbulent time in the Western world. In Europe, old empires and entrenched caste systems were headed toward catastrophic change. The Industrial Revolution was making working-class lives increasingly miserable, and socialism was

The unquiet dead are said to wander a graveyard overlooking an Arizona ghost town.

Preceding pages: Ghosts exhibit a surprising attraction to music. Some are drawn to the strains of a familiar tune, others return to play a beloved instrument.

rising in response. America, meanwhile, was foundering on the question of slavery.

And everywhere organized religion was under attack for a seeming indifference to all the social ferment. Then, in 1859, naturalist Charles Darwin published *The Origin of Species*, setting forth the theory of evolution through natural selection, Traditional faith shuddered to its very foundations. If man were only an animal among animals, as Darwin powerfully suggested, there was no reason to suppose that humankind occupied any favored place in the universe, no reason to believe we have souls, or that some blessed afterlife exists to receive them.

While venerable creeds quivered, new ones began to form, and hope focused with particular passion on science. If this was a chaotic age, it was also a creative and inventive one. The telegraph was born, railroads sent tendrils out over continents, and – most exciting of all – electricity seemed to offer miracles of a new and palpable sort.

It was in this climate, then, that certain profound thinkers set out to bring order. They would rescue Christianity, if they could, with scientific methods. They would prove the existence of the soul and an afterlife, if such indeed could be proved. They would, in short, hunt ghosts.

The First Ghost Hunters

It was in England in the 1880s that a group of Cambridge University scholars formed the Society for Psychical Research (SPR) to fix a cold and skeptical eye on paranormal phenomena. Not given to mysticism, these dons were thoroughly systematic. They would collect information, collate, analyze, theorize, test. They began with ghosts.

A trio of SPR founders – Edmund Gurney, Frederic W. H. Myers, and Frank Podmore – interviewed about 6,000 people regarding their experiences with ghosts. In 1886, they published their results in *Phantasms of the Living*, a two-volume tome of 1,400 pages. There, Myers coined the word "telepathy," postulating that some ghosts were really telepathic impulses, which percipients – the people who see or sense ghosts – took to be phantoms. "Instead of describing a 'ghost' as a dead person permitted to communicate with the living," he wrote, "let us define it as a manifestation of persistent personal energy."

Eleanor Balfour Sidgwick, a mathematician and the principal of Cambridge's Newnham College, speculated that inanimate objects might absorb and store psychic impressions from the living in the same way that stones gather heat energy from the sun. When the impressions were radiated by the object – the figurative hot stones – their energy, she thought, might be perceived as ghosts. The strength of the apparition, Sidgwick believed, depended on the emotional magnitude of the psychic imprint, the amount of stored energy, and the percipient's sensitivity.

Ghostly Intentions

Phantasms of the Living was the first great leap into the paranormal unknown. Based on its findings, the Cambridge group began classifying different types of ghosts. Motive seemed to be one differentiating feature.

"We were struck," said Gurney, "with the great predominance of alleged apparitions at or near the moment of death. And a new light seemed to be thrown on these phenomena by the unexpected frequency of accounts of apparitions of living persons, coincident with moments of danger or crisis." As people experienced death or some other extreme condition, he suggested,

their psyche became more adept at projecting itself in ghostly guises.

Nor was crisis the only motive. Some apparitions brought balm for the grief of loved ones; others, comfort for the dying. Some apparitions appeared to remind the reincarnate of their previous lives, or to give a future family a preview of a reborn person on the way.

Ethereal Theories

Myers kept his belief that human existence didn't end at death, but he saw flaws in his telepathy hypothesis. In *Human Personality and the Survival of Bodily Death*, published in 1903, he theorized that apparitions were a kind of knot of energy emanating from the agent but strong enough to alter the percipient's space. As for the actual substance of ghosts, Myers proposed that specters existed not as material beings but as "metetherial" – a kind of fourth-dimensional creature linked here and there to our ordinary three-dimensional domain.

Some years later, SPR president Henry Habberley Price, an emeritus professor of logic at Oxford University, echoed Myers with the notion of a "psychic ether," which he described as "something intermediate between mind and matter." He believed that thought and other types of mental activity generated an image that survived on another plane even after the death of the thinker. While

A bereaved husband (left) receives an astral visit from his wife in this 1894 lithograph.

The Society for Psychical Research was established in England by Edmund Gurney (top), Frederic W. H. Myers (center), and Frank Podmore (bottom).

A rooster's crow sends ghosts scrambling back to their graves (left) in this 1908 illustration of Shakespeare's *A Midsummer Night's Dream.*

invisible to most folks, such images might be perceived as ghosts by psychic sensitives.

Ghostly Taxonomy

G. N. M. Tyrell, who became SPR president in 1945, devoted 40 years to ghost research. Tyrell, who held degrees in physics and mathematics from London University, is credited with formulating the four categories of phantoms that are still generally recognized today: crisis apparitions, apparitions of the living, postmortem apparitions, and continual, or recurring, apparitions. Drawing on modern psychology, Tyrell proposed that ghosts came out of a confluence of creative energy from the unconscious minds of both the agent and the percipient. He called the result an "apparitional drama," or "sensory hallucination."

Researcher Andrew MacKenzie also postulated a link between apparitions and the subconscious mind. Examining a number of reported hallucinatory experiences, he found that most of them came when the percipient was tuning out the external world and concentrating on something else. At such times, MacKenzie reckoned, the barriers between the conscious and unconscious come down. The resulting flow from our unknown mental interior sometimes seems to be a ghost.

Inside the Mind and Out

The pioneering work of Tyrell and MacKenzie can still be seen in the work of present-day psychical researchers like William G. Roll, a prominent American parapsychologist. Like them, he explains hauntings as an interactive drama between haunter and observer, as he calls the percipient, but he proposes that the phenomena occur along a sliding scale.

Haunting visions or sounds can be related to a particular situation or event, which, Roll contends, seems

"to leave an imprint in the environment that lots of people can respond to." But he sees no need for such carrier substances as psychic ether. "All we need to say is that there is no sharp distinction between mind and matter, and that the processes that go on in the human brain may also go on in the human environment. To me the main interest of these phenomena is that they suggest body and mind and matter are not as clearly distinguished as we have been led to believe, that mind is enfolded in matter, that there is meaning in matter, that the physical environment has mental qualities that come from the people who have lived in that environment."

Those qualities imprinted on the environment compose the ghostly side of Roll's equation. The percipient composes the other. Hauntings move on a sliding scale between them, driven by whichever factor – the spectral or the personal – is more active. If the power lies toward the environmental end, the imprint should be so deeply etched that anyone can discern it. At the far end on the percipient side of the scale, the observer creates the ghost out of nothing – that is to say, he or she makes it up.

Roll says that the latter type of haunting seems to follow emotional stress; it is often seen, for example, in strife-torn marriages. Then, according to Roll, the percipient creates "an objective reality" to fill a void. "It's like a dream that has become real," he explains, "a strong need that somehow has created a situation that satisfies it. My impression is that memories will be drawn out in response to needs. And it is just as likely to happen in a new duplex as in an old mansion." Anything, including oneself, can be haunted.

Ghostly Behavior

Today, speculation about ghosts has largely passed out of the academic realm. Most ghost hunters are hobbyists who are serious about their subject but not necessarily making it their life's work. Their language is more casual than that of the academicians, and their scientific tastes tend more toward psychology than physics. For instance, Troy Taylor, the founder and president of the American Ghost Society, finds it useful to divide phantom encounters into two types: the intelligent haunting and the residual haunting.

The intelligent haunter, according to Taylor, is "the personality of a once-living person who stayed behind in our world instead of passing over to the Other Side." Such ghosts are self-aware and are able to interact with the living. The residual haunter, on the other hand, is merely "an imprint that is left on the atmosphere" of a haunted site. It is the spirit of an event, rather than a person-

ality, that plays out over and over in phantom form.

As to the nature of intelligent ghosts, Taylor reports that generally, they're "very sad. We have to remember that many of them are very confused over what has happened to them." Some, he says, don't even realize that they're dead. Ghosts are never evil, he contends, although they do project in their phantom forms whatever personalities they had in life: benevolent, caring, angry, bitter.

David Oester and Sharon

Ectoplasm streams between a medium and a spirit (above) in this lithograph of a séance.

Three enchanting spirits (below) startle a midnight rambler in this early-19th-century engraving.

Gill, cofounders of the International Ghost Hunters Society, agree. "A ghost is a mirror of who he or she was in life," they say. "If they were happy campers in life, they will be happy campers in death. The reverse is also true. If they were angry and mean in life, so too in death." Whatever their natures, the spirits remain earthbound "because of unfinished business, unresolved issues, or because they have a comfort level and choose to remain here. In many cases, the soul or spirit has negative earth emotions that were not released while living, and now these negative emotions are creating an anchor that will hold them back until they can release these negative emotions."

Times have changed. Pondering a ghost's "unresolved issues" seems a far less pressing task than trying to validate religion by proving that spirits exist. Now and then, though, an echo of the old urgency can still be heard: "Ghosts are really the evidence," say Oester and Gill, "that religion should lean toward as proof of an afterlife."

Is My House Haunted?

Ghosts come in many forms. It all depends on their type and especially on why they might want to haunt you. Some may be confused. An unexpected death, for example, may give rise to spirits who don't quite realize yet that they've passed into the other world.

If you suspect that your house is haunted, look for phenomena like the mysterious disappearance of objects, the occurrence of cold patches in the air, and the powerful sense of being watched by the dead. As a guideline for hauntedness, the White Crow Society defines a paranormal episode as a seemingly inexplicable event that disrupts the day-to-day life of an individual. Because this is a fairly broad definition and could be used to describe anything from a bad day at the office to a disastrous hair day, most services offer phone consultations to help the hauntee sort things out.

Traditional signs of a prankster spirit include the sound of footsteps where no one can be seen, doors opening and closing, moving objects, strange odors, or disembodied voices. Generally speaking, such ghosts are simply having fun, acting out against the living. Many researchers believe that poltergeist activity is in fact created by the mind of someone in the house, usually an adolescent girl, applying her psychic powers to rattle her elders. Proof positive of a poltergeist is when teacups and saucers begin to fly spontaneously from shelves, or children and family pets levitate. Such unambiguous signs of haunting require urgent professional help.

In determining whether you are haunted or merely stricken with the jitters, exhaust all natural explanations before calling in the experts. Is that high-pitched keening a ghost or an animal? Has a wild thing trapped itself in the basement, or has a cat had kittens there? Are the claws scraping at the windows actually unpruned rosebushes?

And keep in mind that ghosts, like realtors, tend to chant: location, location, location. If your home is old and stands near such ghostly waterholes as cemeteries, churches, prisons, hospitals, and battlefields, your chances of being haunted go up. A house without a history is not a home to restless spirits.

Hauntings can be as subtle as a passing scent or muffled footstep, or as obvious as a full-bodied apparition, as in this depiction (below) of a ghostly guest.

Female spirits (opposite) seem to have an affection for white gowns. The "woman in white" is a common figure in ghost lore and literature.

Playing host to a ghost is not necessarily a bad thing. Ghosts seldom present any physical threat to the living, after all, and they tend to be self-absorbed, more concerned with their own problems than with causing trouble for anybody else. Resident spirits can even be comforting, provided they belong to benevolent ancestors or departed friends, or even to a charmingly sorrowful soul who's just looking for company. ◆ Viewed with a coldly commercial eye, a haunting can even have practical value. Harmless but interesting haunts add a certain romantic cachet to a house – especially in cities such as Savannah or New Orleans that take particular pride in their past – and that cachet can enhance property values. Similarly, the odd phantom footstep or spectral sigh, assuming there's an eerie story attached, **If ghosts are getting you** can make the difference between a mediocre bed- **down, you might** and-breakfast and a booming destination **try a little tenderness –** hotel. ◆ All that having been said, how- **or maybe the Internet.** ever, most of us would probably prefer to confine our households to the living, simply because ghosts are scary. Faced with the chilling certainty that some stranger is invisibly among us, its nature unknowable and its motives and intentions unknown, our first reflex is to scream. But to whom? ◆ To a priest, is one answer. In times past – and sometimes even today – spirit infestation was deemed a religious problem, best solved by religious means. There has never been a society, primitive or modern, pagan or Judeo-Christian, that lacked the necessary technicians, whether witch doctors or shamans or clergy. Tibetan Buddhists still use a rite called *shedur* that involves summoning a protective goddess to oust an offending

Searching for spirits. Harold Ramis, Dan Aykroyd, and Bill Murray portrayed high-tech ghost hunters in the 1984 comedy *Ghostbusters*.

example, showed such power that they could drive out evil spirits by the force of their prayers alone, or by the laying on of hands.

As Christianity spread, however, and paganism waned, demonic possession became rare. "It is only Catholic missionaries laboring in pagan lands," according to the *Catholic Encyclopedia*, "who are likely to meet with fairly frequent cases of possession." Still, all reports of possession must be taken seriously and closely investigated, but only by those who have led brave and blameless lives and have prepared themselves through prayer and fasting – clergy who have immunized themselves against demonic invasion.

spirit. And, of course, the Roman Catholic Church still occasionally employs the ancient rite of exorcism.

Some purists argue that exorcism aims to oust demons, not ghosts. But other experts dismiss this distinction as mere semantics, contending that a ghost, broadly defined, is any alien spirit that impinges on the world of the living, not just a spirit of the dead. Demons qualify, therefore, and demonic possession is the invasion of a soul by some foreign entity rather than the invasion of a dwelling. Indeed, the most ancient human problem with spirits has not been so much with the haunting of property as the haunting of souls, and these spirits, by definition, were evil.

The Catholic Church perfected its rite of exorcism early, in the 4th century, and it has changed little since. Originally, the rite was built into baptism and could be applied both to the faithful and to those outside the Church as necessary. But not all ecclesiastics could be exorcists; a certain charismatic quality was needed. Some priests, for

Soothing the Sorrowful

A priest need have no special qualifications, however, to bless a dwelling that may be troubled by restless spirits. He may visit a home and offer prayers for those who live there. Sprinkling of holy water and filling various rooms with incense also may be useful.

Malicious spirits sometimes can be persuaded by these techniques to move on. If they resist, however, it's possible that they're not malicious at all. Most ghosts, it is said, cling to Earth because they're troubled souls, not evil ones.

Some experts believe that ghosts respond to exorcists not because the spirit is afraid of the talismans of

TJUAJJAL

belief, but because clergy tend to be good listeners, with an aura of emotional tranquility. In fact, the negative energy of a full-blown exorcism may only enrage the ghost, especially if it's already angry.

Most ghosts are not mad, merely sorrowful. It isn't that they don't want to leave; their sadness holds them where they are. More than any other kind of haunter, sorrowful ghosts reflect the living; all they lack is a body. Because they are so close to us, it's often easier to live with them as they endlessly relive the moments that define their grief. Let them brood. And should they become too much, they generally will depart if asked politely.

Unresolved Issues

The ghost hunters now summoned by the haunted tend to be less interested in driving away spirits than in understanding them, helping them work through the inner conflicts that keep them forever restive. There is little room for troupes of bungling, khaki-clad "ghostbusters" and their high-tech ecotoplasm collectors in the real world of paranormal investigations. The idea is not to bust ghosts but to counsel and comprehend them, to offer a compassionate solution to their emotional problems. Like their living counterparts, ghosts have issues of abandonment, self-esteem, loneliness, and anger to resolve. The language of ghost hunting has altered to reflect this understanding and uses the

Possession is the most sinister kind of haunting. Ukobach (opposite, above and below) and Beelzebub (above), seen here as the Lord of the Flies, are just two of the demons believed to invade the bodies of human hosts.

Richard Burton shields Linda Blair from demonic locusts (below) in *The Exorcist II: The Heretic*.

vocabulary of holistic therapy, not that of confrontation and spectral war. Today's professionals must be there for them.

They also must be there for hosts whose kinder, gentler approach hasn't budged the spirit. These intransigent ghosts are the plague-rats among haunters, ghosts in whom the touching melancholy of other apparitions seems to have curdled into terrible rage. They aren't working through anything familiar to the living, nor do they search for lost love; they want only to entwine themselves as destructively as possible with the lives of their hosts.

Some of these are downright messy, besides. Being haunted quickly loses its appeal when decapitated ghosts drip blood on a white carpet even when the stain vanishes a moment later. Slime is devilishly difficult to get out of suede. A house haunted by such negative spirits is a miserably unhappy house.

Store the China

And then there are the poltergeists (German for "noisy spirits"). These demonic whirlwinds of the spirit world seem always to need attention from the living and are willing to go to any extreme to get it. Some modern ghost hunters say poltergeists are not real ghosts and that the mischief usually attributed to them is actually caused by psychic energy emanating from a troubled member of the household, especially young people. Whatever the source, however, paranormally flying crockery and slamming cabinets can be problems that need

immediate solutions.

Once a poltergeist is sensed, the first step might be to store the family china and other breakables outside the home. These prankster spirits often seem to have a sense of fun that can make them lively company as long as they're treated well. They are like pet raccoons, marvelous to watch, often funny, and wondrously destructive.

If you don't find them amusing, however, the most important tactic for getting rid of them may be to look inward. Most investigators now believe that ghosts, including poltergeists, are drawn to the projections of the human unconscious. Thus, before trying to expel an angry ghost or rowdy poltergeist, a certain amount of introspection is in order. Haunted hosts are often just people under a lot of stress or jangled by a recent emotional ordeal, so they radiate a powerful negativity, a dark flame that draws spectral moths. Before calling anyone, one must change that aura and deprive the ghost of its negative beacon.

Calling in the Ghost Hunters

If the dark beacon attracting the ghost is external instead of internal – something to do with the property rather than the host – a trip to the library might reveal what happened there that would leave a ghost-drawing psychic imprint. A murder? A suicide?

A memorable injustice or failed romance? Old houses virtually glow with forgotten violence.

To help erase this psychic residue, you may need to call in the professionals. Their tactics will vary according to the nature of the ghost and the nature of the hunter. Some excel at tracking, some are eager for discovery.

Among professional services, the White Crow Society offers expert help to those whose homes or souls are haunted by demons,

Troubled children are often at the center of poltergeist phenomena, as in this 1849 engraving (above) of a haunting in France.

Hovering furniture (opposite, above), typical of poltergeist activity, is depicted in an 1849 engraving.

Hollywood's *Poltergeist* (opposite, below) showed what could happen when the living violate the resting place of the dead.

spirits, or poltergeists. The society's name was taken from famed Harvard psychologist and psychic investigator William James, who, on finding one medium he believed to be genuine, remarked that it takes only

Tips for the Living

For the patient ghost-host, who feels more sympathy than fear for a restless, haunting spirit, there is always the option of coming to terms with the ghost. But if the haunter must be ejected from the premises, here are a few simple suggestions:

● Plants can heal more than earthly ills. A hedge of lavender or lilac will make the house more pleasant for you and more uncomfortable for the disembodied. Burning sage or incense also clears the air. If you can wield a shovel, planting rowan, elder, or willow trees can be a strong external deterrent to the negative energy of ghosts. A word of caution, however: Once planted, the trees cannot be cut without incurring the risk of a matching paranormal disturbance.

● Environmental change – and not on a global scale – can render ghosts unhappy enough to flee. Simply changing your physical surroundings can make spirits crazy, especially if the changes bear some subtle psychic touch. For example, burning white or blue candles will help clear a room of specters, as will the addition of objects invested with religious power, such as crosses and Bibles.

● Something new may force a gentle exorcism, for ghosts gather like a squadron of bats in the drawers and shelves and crevices of antique furniture and books. These objects can preserve the psychic fingerprints of previous owners for years. If there is a strongly negative experience attached to something, chances are good that a ghost is there, too. If you think one of your antiques is haunted, find out the history of the piece. Don't hesitate to get rid of it if it has a ghost that is unwilling to leave. If you can't bear to get rid of the antique, clean it and use it. That generally does the trick.

● Benign neglect may fill your attic with ghosts, for nothing hatches them like idle things and unvisited places. Check your attic or basement for things that can be cleaned up and used or thrown away. If the ghost doesn't take the cue, perhaps it can be accommodated: Okay, you can stay, but only in the third drawer of the attic bureau. Ghosts are as ready as the next nonperson to deal.

● Your psychic state is the key to confrontations with a ghost. It's important to remember that spirits can sense your emotional pitch as keenly as dogs scent fear. Try to keep a positive attitude when confronting one. Reassure it, tell it that you understand and want to help; then ask it to leave. Even with the help of professionals, your best defense against ghosts is to keep your own negative energies well banked. The merest flicker of your dark side can bring them flapping back into your life.

one white crow to prove that not all crows are black.

The International Ghost Hunters Society, a storehouse of information on ghost hunting and hauntings, has a large collection of ghost photographs posted on the Internet – a kind of spectral rogues gallery to help the haunted identify what's plaguing them. Besides photographs, the society has posted tips on equipment usage and ghost-hunting strategies, along with four dozen goose-bump-inducing recordings said to be the voices of the dead. There is information about annual conferences, and a newsletter for do-it-yourself ghost hunters. For those seeking additional aid, the society provides links to other useful sources on the Internet and elsewhere. Let the buyer beware, however. A good ghost hunter is as hard to find as a really convincing ghost, and charlatans have always been drawn to the spirit world.

Even if you have good professional help, "laying the ghost" – the unfortunate but traditional term for getting rid of one – can be a long and complicated process. Eventually, you may have to decide whether your spectral guest is more welcome than the hunters pursuing it.

Intuition and Patience

Because ghosts generally require patience and understanding more than the shock of an all-out exorcism, a good ghost hunter must be intuitive to a fault, a person whose own psychic abilities allow contact with the spirit on an emotional plane. No one wants an angry banishment that could result in more ghost trouble down the line. But the client's instincts are also central here. Generally, anyone sensitive enough to have a paranormal problem reads underlying psychic vibes well enough to find the right ghost hunter for the job at hand.

Once a professional has been called in, the investigation unfolds step by step in a logical fashion. First, an interview examines the hauntee's report, with

Aromatic plants like lavender (opposite, left) and religious objects like crucifixes (opposite, right) make houses less amenable to ghosts.

The *Ghostbusters* logo (right), though cute, suggests an inappropriate enmity toward ghosts. Modern ghost hunters see themselves more as counselors of confused souls than as their enemies.

the experienced hunter wielding skepticism like a machete. Few reputable practitioners would undertake an investigation before ruling out every possible natural scenario, turning to the paranormal only as a last resort. Then photographs are taken of the site, and perhaps drawings are made. If the haunt has a discernible pattern, the investigators may want to stay on site for a while to map it. Given the intrusive nature of the inquiry, you should never embark on a paranormal investigation lightly, or with investigators who are not sympathetic companions. Hunters who are too ready to believe, or too skeptical to accept what their senses tell them, should be replaced immediately: Ghosts sneer at their psychic inferiors.

Whatever the type of spectral presence, its removal should be undertaken with compassion and understanding, or at worst with tough love. Despite their restless, worrisome ways, ghosts are more like us – more like the living – than not. They have beliefs, hopes, fears, concerns, and expectations that must be respected. And they have vast experience. Many ghosts are believed to have been roaming the world for centuries.

Sometimes they may be gentled into a tolerable domesticity. But now and then they are so dark, so angry, so destructive that they have to be forced to leave. Time is on their side, however, and they know it. Having one's ghosts removed, even with today's conciliatory methods, may take a good long time. Patience is the key. Patience is what we should be thinking when we finally decide to pick up the telephone and ask for professional help.

hosts would be hard enough to hunt just because they have no bodies. But they are not merely discarnate, they're famously indirect in their approaches to the living. Now and then you'll hear of one that haunts in full human form, an amiable ghost, perhaps, that eats and dances and talks with the living as if there's nothing unusual about popping up in the wrong dimension. More often, however, they appear to humans by hints and signs rather than in the protoplasmic flesh. They produce strange and inexplicable noises, smells, and visions: the sound of weeping, or phantom conversations, or footsteps in an empty hall; sweet floral scents or noxious odors; shadowy forms or eerie blobs of light. Sometimes they're even more oblique in their manifestation. You perceive them as a sudden coldness in the air, or a general sense of **The ineffable and invisible** restlessness, irrational and pervasive, or as an **can be hard to find.** atmosphere densely humid with melancholy **You need to know where** or fear. ◆ Indeed, hunting ghosts is like hunt- **to look and how.** ing H. G. Wells's Invisible Man, looking not for the unseeable whole but for the visible footprint in the snow. Ghosts are like elusive birds, and ghost hunters are like determined birders, hurrying to sites where this or that species has been reported, hoping to claim even the merest intimation of these spectral *rara avis*. ◆ Like birders, ghost hunters look first for favorable locations. Ghosts may settle around silver, which they favor, but disperse where blocked by running water, which they're said to abhor and fear to cross. They're believed to congregate around such oases of death as battlefields and cemeteries, hospitals, and the sites of violent crime. But they may turn up at the scene of some long-ago act of violence, attracted,

Prisons, hospitals, and hotels, like this one in Austin, Texas, are thought to attract ghosts because of the intense human dramas played out within their walls.

experts believe, by the dense psychic imprints etched on the surroundings.

Crossroads were once popular gathering places for specters because witches, criminals, and traitors were executed at such junctions. Ghosts also like hotels and schools because of their thick strata of psychic residues. And spirits, attracted by the intense emotions expressed on the stage, seem to like theaters. Among actors it's axiomatic that any theater worth the name must be haunted. The curse that seems to haunt almost every production of *Macbeth* (among other plays) has done nothing to dispel that notion.

Homebodies

Sometimes ghosts don't flock to a place but simply live there because they always have. Haunted houses are usually inhabited by former residents, although now and then a spectral newcomer may do the haunting.

Some spirits appear to be pinned eternally in place by some violent event – often grief of unrequited love, while others may return simply to recapture a sweet happiness they once experienced there. In one English manor, an aristocratic ghost reportedly drops in to use the current lord's fine library.

More recently, investiga-tors of the paranormal have theorized that ghosts are not drawn so much by a particular location as by something at that location. Many believe this something is a so-called portal, or doorway, from our three-dimensional world into worlds of another dimension.

These ghost gateways are like the hypothetical worm holes that are believed by some cosmologists to link different universes. So what appears to be a haunted house may be just a kind of spectral turnstile to and from the Other Side.

Beginning the Hunt

Like all expeditions, ghost hunting is largely preparation. Every report of paranormal activity must be examined with an eye to finding a natural explanation. An underground stream or fault line might produce the strange noises attributed to restless spirits, for example, and houses may tremble not from a terrible entity within but because they sit atop abandoned mine shafts. Only when all other explanations have failed should a hunt begin.

The aspiring hunter's most important items of equipment are a sensitivity to the paranormal and a skeptical but open mind. No amount of gear can compensate for what the hunter brings in the way of natural ability, and no amount of yearning will produce a sighting to a hunter whose mind is closed to all but a few possibilities. Ghosts are generally inclined to shun overly skeptical or unimaginative company. Nor do they favor hunters who arrive reeking of alcohol. Tobacco should also be put aside. Smoke skews the sense of smell and may look like a ghost on film.

Ghost-Hunting Gear

As for a physical kit, the modern investigator's prime imperative should be: Keep it simple. Going out to explore reported paranormal phenomena isn't much different from going out as a reporter to cover a fire, and it requires the same basic equipment. Like any good reporter, the hunter has to take notes and make diagrams, so a notebook and writing implement are primary. And because the hunt is generally nocturnal, a flashlight is essential.

Beyond the basics, the hunter's outfit really depends on the expected type of prey. A camera isn't needed for a spirit that manifests itself only with noise, and there's no point recording the silence of a floating white veil. Again, spares are important: film for the camera, tape for the recorder, and batteries for

Gadgets and Gizmos

Because all living things are surrounded and animated by a spectrum of energy, many paranormal investigators believe that the denizens of the Other Side may likewise crackle with some form of electromagnetism. A glowing specter, for example, might be composed of pure light, while others might emit radiation at other wavelengths. Another, invisible ghost might cut a rippling wake through the geomagnetic field or visually distort its background. Still others might produce sudden cold spots.

With these presumed ghostly properties in mind, ghost hunters have adopted a broad array of remote sensors. Some are quite ordinary. Compasses, for example, are said to skew toward concentrations of paranormal energy; their needles will spin if placed directly over the source. More elaborate devices, such as electromagnetic field meters and Geiger counters, detect energy emissions that are thought to be generated by spirits.

Where the ghost signal is a sudden chill, some hunters recommend a digital thermal scanner, which provides instantaneous readouts of air temperature. Anomalous pools of low temperature may mark the spot where spirits have drawn energy from the air in order to manifest themselves. Infrared night vision devices are also popular. They permit the investigator to see relatively warm objects in almost total darkness – in effect, to see the Unseen.

Such high-tech gadgets can be cumbersome and costly and sometimes produce false readings. In the end, there's no substitute for a keen observer with a skeptical but open mind.

A compass (left) is said to whirl in the presence of supernatural energy.

Night-vision goggles (below) and thermal scanners are among the new high-tech tools employed by ghost hunters.

The well-equipped ghost hunter doesn't forget practical items such as a tape recorder and flashlight (opposite), useful for capturing ghostly voices or taking notes in the dark.

everything electronic.

As on the veldt and in the jungle, the hunter is bound by certain rules of engagement. Where the quarry may ignore boundaries, the investigator must not. Care should be taken not to trespass on private property, and those who violate this rule – especially in the company of a disgruntled spirit – probably deserve what they get. A good hunter gets permission to enter the premises

before, not after, being challenged at gunpoint by a jittery owner.

Hunts should never be undertaken on *terra incognita* but in an environment whose present and past have been closely studied beforehand. A trip to the library is probably a good idea before a trip to the site. Moreover, hunts should not be conducted by just one hunter; any sightings will need the corroboration of a witness.

Examining Witnesses

An investigator's most important partner is the person who reported the phenomenon in the first place. Reports should be checked against external facts; a stormy night remembered by the witness can be verified by weather records, for example. Every possible natural cause should be eliminated before a ghost hunt is considered.

While taking these data, however, the good hunter also keeps in mind that no two people remember events in precisely the same way, and he or she must be careful not to influence what is reported. A chance remark, the wrong body language, an inadvertent intrusion can trigger all sorts of bogus memories and responses. Investigators must also be delicate in explaining away reported phenomena (the ghostly rattle that turns out to be a tree branch rubbing an attic window), so as not to seem to be calling the witness a liar.

Not that no one lies. Ghost hunters have learned, often the hard way, that liars and lunatics are to be avoided – albeit courteously – at all costs. Nothing destroys a ghost hunter's reputation faster than the hot pursuit of a ghost spun by a liar. Certainly any self-respecting spirit would think twice about manifesting itself to someone who was so easy to deceive.

Finally, no matter what comes out of the expedition, a ghost or some natural phenomenon, the veteran hunter writes up a report, which becomes part of the body of knowledge for all explorers of the paranormal. For all you know, a hunt that seems to yield nothing may turn out to be a key step in the continuing exploration by the living of the unquiet dead.

Photography can be used to hoodwink the gullible or mount a convincing case for the existence of specters. The ghostly figures in these images of Raynham Hall (left) and Eastry Church (below), both in England, were captured unwittingly by the photographers.

Ghost hunters with a taste for adventure can travel to such far-off haunts as Ballaghmore Castle in Ireland (opposite), but they're just as likely to find ghosts close to home.

Ghost Image

The camera doesn't lie? Fact is, cameras were telling visual fibs long before computers made altering photos an easy possibility. Still, because photography was supposed to be beyond reproach, it has long been a key tool of the ghost hunter.

The first spirit photograph was taken by William Mumler in 1861. Mumler was a jeweler's engraver in Boston who stumbled on the potential of the camera to capture spirit images on the large glass plates of the day. As he developed a photograph he'd made of himself, he saw materializing next to his image what appeared to be a portrait of someone dead. Coming as it did when Spiritualism was at full throttle, Mumler's discovery quickly found applications among mediums and serious probers of the paranormal. But the ability of spirit photographers to cook up multiple exposures and to manipulate images in the developing baths was too rich a vein for charlatans to ignore. The photography fad, like mediumship itself, soon dissolved into fraud.

Serious investigators still use cameras, but their equipment is much improved. Electronic cameras and extremely fast film have turned that venerable art into something closer to a science. A modern camera sees far more than does the human eye. In fact, many ghost images are never seen until the film is developed. The anomalies often appear as orbs or vortices of light or as an opaque white fog. While many of these can be explained optically, some remain a mystery.

To avoid the oft-heard challenge that ghostly images are merely products of flawed film or developing, serious photographers of the paranormal generally have multiple sources for their film, carry more than one camera, and have the films developed using different processes. Some load their second camera with infrared film, which permits them to photograph entities at wavelengths longer than visible light. But ghost hunters urge caution here. Almost everything emits some infrared energy, guaranteeing that every frame may be full of spooks – but not necessarily of spirits.

◆

Haunted Destinations

◆

Fortunately for ghost hunters, specters are said to be at home in all parts of America. So in settling on a destination, you can choose among a variety of climates, landscapes, and historical attractions, from New England to the Deep South, from East Coast to West.

New England

CHAPTER

7

SALEM WITCH MUSEUM

OPEN
DAILY
10AM-5PM

People visit New England for its past. They go to Boston to follow the Freedom Trail past the Old North Church and Paul Revere's house, to Plymouth to see where the Pilgrims set up house in a new land, to Lexington and Concord, where the first shots of the American Revolution were fired. Yet in few corners of New England is the past more eerily present than in a place far from the usual tourist destinations, in the woods of northeastern Connecticut. Its unlikely name is **Bara-Hack**. ◆ The words are Welsh for "breaking of bread," but there's nothing cozy or hospitable about what lies up an old cow path next to **Mashomoquet Brook**. Bara-Hack has been abandoned for more than a century, and nothing is left of its houses but gaping dark cellar holes. A low, fieldstone wall encloses a small cemetery, its tombstones weathered nearly blank and tipped this way and that by frost heave. ◆ The town and the people who lived there are long dead, but Bara-Hack is not quiet. The hauntings began when the town was still thriving, its small factory making looms and spinning wheels. It was early in the 19th century, before abolitionism swept New England, and the factory owners kept slaves. The town had already had its first deaths, and the slaves saw how the spirits of the dead would not rest, roosting instead at dusk in an elm tree near the cemetery and silently watching the bustle of village life. ◆ Since then the character of the haunting at Bara-Hack has changed, and it's the village itself that will not slip silently into history. Over the years, visitor after visitor has reported hearing sounds in the woods, sounds easy to mistake at first for the stirring of leaves, then

Along the back roads and byways of picturesque New England, all is not as quiet as it seems.

Salem Witch Museum in Salem, Massachusetts, commemorates the witch trials of 1692; the town is still inhabited by the spirits of accused witches.

Preceding pages: An Arizona bridge haunted by La Llorona, the "sobbing woman" of Mexican lore.

museums, and New England is saturated with history. Waves of historical events have swept over the damp, rocky seacoasts, woodlands, and stony fields, and each wave has left a flotsam of unquiet spirits.

Witch's House

One of the cruelest episodes of New England's past, the Salem witch trials, left a ghostly legacy not far from the old seaport in a colonial farmhouse called **Witch Hollow Farm** in **Boxford**, Massachusetts. A foursquare, clapboard-sided colonial house erected in 1666, it was the childhood home of Mary Tyler. After her marriage, Mary moved 15 miles to **Salem**, where she was accused of witchcraft in 1693. She escaped the gallows by confessing and repenting.

Though little is known of her life afterwards, it seems safe to assume that it was blighted by the false accusations. What is clear is that her spirit still searches for peace at the place where she spent happier days as a girl. A young woman in somber dress sometimes can be seen walking in the gardens at Boxford in the light of the full moon.

The Rockport Fisherman

Like Mary Tyler's spirit, ghosts often roam because of some wrong they suffered during life. But some, it seems, seek out the living because they're simply too sociable for the rarefied society of the dead. A Maine fisherman named William Richardson became such a ghost when he died during the American Revolution. Richardson

clear and distinct: children playing, wagons rumbling down rough lanes, cattle lowing. Somewhere, just out of sight, Bara-Hack is still speaking, and it has come to be known locally as the Village of Voices.

Nowhere else in New England does an entire vanished village intrude from the past, but the region as a whole harbors a ghostly throng. Ghosts, after all, are a kind of history that won't stay tranquilly in books and

New England cemeteries (left), some dating to the 17th century, are both scenic and spooky.

Gravestone art (opposite) is crude but poignant on many early New England headstones.

would have been remembered just for helping his neighbors in the fishing village of Goose River – now **Rockport, Maine** – when boats and men were lost at sea. But the war gave him an opportunity for heroism.

Burning houses and destroying crops, the British had been harassing the citizens of Goose River in an effort to break support for the rebels. Richardson was eager to help one day in 1779 when word came that, out beyond the rocky headlands, a British warship was pursuing a privateer. He went to sea in his fishing boat, met the privateer, led it on a course around islands and through hidden channels and eventually eluded the warship. Four years later, when the war ended and a new nation was born, Richardson threw a party. As the ale flowed, he went from house to house, a pitcher in his hand, urging the stay-at-homes to join the celebration.

But as he crossed the Goose River, he met three horsemen who took a dim view of the celebration. They were Tories, still loyal to the crown. When Richardson offered them a drink, they struck a last blow for the Empire by clubbing him to

death. The pitcher smashed, and the ale ran into the river as Richardson fell.

Two hundred years later, he's still looking for company. Couples parked at night on the quiet lanes near the river have reported seeing a strange apparition through the fogged car windows: a man in 18th-century clothes stepping from the woods with a welcoming smile on his face. In his hand is an intact pitcher, brimming with ale.

An Embittered Wigmaker

Richardson was a local hero, but on the island of **Nantucket** off the Massachusetts coast a ghost cannot rest because, for 21 years, he was an object of scorn.

By the end of the 18th century, local whaling captains were pouring their profits into Nantucket's banks. One night in 1795, however, one bank's coffers dwindled drastically as $21,000 in gold vanished. A wigmaker, William Coffin, was suspected of the crime, perhaps for no better reason than that he was ill-tempered, unsociable, and a miser. Without evidence, he could not be tried, but the suspicions remained, and whispers followed him wherever he went along the cobbled streets of the port.

His ordeal ended 21 years later, when someone else confessed to the theft. But Coffin took his bitterness to the grave – and beyond. His house still stands, and the old wigmaker has been seen sitting by the fireplace, rocking furiously, a fire blazing there even in midsummer.

Ghost on the Bridge

Sometimes history or local records leave little doubt about why a particular ghost cannot rest. Sometimes we can only surmise. That's the case for Emily, the

ghost that haunts **Gold Brook Bridge** in **Stowe, Vermont**.

No one knows just how she died, or if Emily is her true name. But the convulsive sorrow that keeps her shade from resting is obvious. The bridge she inhabits is a one-lane, covered structure from the early 19th century, its interior smelling pleasantly of dust and old pine. It's just 50 feet long, and its interior is gloomy but not pitch-black. Traffic, whether horse-drawn carriages or cars, has always had to negotiate it at a crawl. That allows plenty of time for the ghost to make herself known, and dozens

Corey's Revenge

Giles Corey was the eldest and most defiant victim of the Salem witch trials of 1692. The rich and unlikable codger was 80 years old when his neighbors accused him of witchery, and he was the only one of the accused who refused to testify before the feverish witch court. The judges sentenced him to "the press," a devilish contraption designed to extract a confession by slowly crushing its victim under a pile of rocks.

But Corey's will proved irrepressible. The rock pile grew atop his chest, but the old man only whispered defiantly, "More weight." Bones began to crack. Again, he rasped, "More weight!" until his body could no longer bear the pressure. With his dying breath, Corey allegedly placed a curse on the town and its high sheriff, George Corwin.

Corey's body was tossed into a pit at the Howard Street Burial Ground. Although his family later buried his remains on their property, Corey is said to haunt his first resting place, his mouth stretched open as if to howl or gasp or demand still more weight.

Some folks believe, however, that Corey had his vengeance. A succession of sheriffs suffered heart attacks after Corey's execution, starting with the hated Corwin, who died suddenly at age 30 after profiting handsomely from the confiscation of property belonging to "witches." His ghost, still threatening in death, is sometimes spotted near his family home on Washington Street.

Elsewhere in town, the spirits of accused witches are said to appear on Gallows Hill, site of their hangings, shortly before local misfortunes. They have also been seen at the Witch House, former home of Jonathan Corwin, one of the witch court's seven judges. – *Michael Castagna*

The Witch House (left) has a forbidding name, but its ghost, witch trial judge Jonathan Corwin, is far less harmful in death than he was in life.

A bewitched girl (below) falls to the floor during the Salem Witch Trials of 1692.

Gold Brook Bridge (opposite) in Stowe, Vermont, is haunted by the spirit of a heartbroken young woman.

of people, locals and tourists alike, have noted her manifestations over the years. Strange, beseeching cries ring out in the interior of the bridge. Light flickers from dark crannies, sometimes taking the spectral form of a woman. One drizzly evening, a motorist was appalled to see handprints on his foggy windshield as he emerged from the bridge, as if someone had pressed warm hands there while he was passing through the dark interior.

Perhaps Emily had mistaken him for the lover she waited for when she was a woman of flesh and blood. Though little is known of her story, the best guess is that she is the ghost of a Stowe girl who killed herself at the bridge in 1843. She had fallen in love with a young man whom her family rejected, so they decided to elope. She slipped away from her parents' home at night and went to the bridge, where she and her beloved had agreed to meet. Perhaps the young man had lost his nerve, or perhaps he'd deceived her and had another lover. In any case, he never appeared for the rendezvous, and after a day and night of waiting in the shadows of the bridge, she hanged herself from the rafters.

Writers at The Mount

War and tragedy have left ghosts roaming New England's stony landscape, but so has a different kind of history: the legions of writers who have distinguished the region. Some of the most famous congregate after death, as they did in life, at **The Mount**, a mansion built at the turn of the century in Lenox, Massachusetts, by the writer Edith Wharton.

Wharton's novel *Ethan Frome* told a story of blighted hopes and poverty set in the hills of western Massachusetts, but the Mount, set on 100 acres in those same hills, was a place of gentility and wealth. Wharton, a daughter of New York society, spent six years at The Mount and made it a salon that was visited often by other literary lights such as Henry James.

Those lights, it seems, have not entirely dimmed. For many years after Wharton

The Haunted Lighthouse

In Long Island Sound, between New London, Connecticut, and the eastern end of Long Island, sits a most unusual lighthouse. This is no simple tower with a barber-pole stripe. In a fit of extravagance just before the First World War, marine authorities built it to look like a three-story mansion that has floated out to sea, with the light perched incongruously on the roof. But the New London Ledge Lighthouse also has a less obvious quirk: It is manned by a ghost.

True, the light and foghorn are automated, as at every other lighthouse in Long Island Sound. But the keepers who vacated the New London light in 1987 knew they didn't have to rely entirely on machines to keep it running smoothly. After all, Ernie – the ghost's affectionate nickname – had lived there for almost 50 years, a rambunctious but generally friendly companion to the keepers. As they tended the light at night and sounded the foghorn on days of fog and drizzle, he played the usual ghostly tricks, hiding coffee cups, turning radios and televisions on and off, and stomping about in empty rooms. When the weather was fine and the keepers had time on their hands, Ernie became more mischievous, blasting the foghorn on crystal-clear afternoons and untying the boats of visiting fishermen.

All in all, Ernie seemed to understand the life of a lighthouse keeper, perhaps because in life he was one himself. In 1939, the New London Ledge Lighthouse was the scene of a tragedy, when a keeper killed himself after his wife ran off with a ferryboat captain. Certainly the gruesome manner of his death seemed likely to produce an unquiet spirit: Leaning from a window on the top floor, the distraught keeper cut his own throat with a butcher's knife, spilling blood down the side of the lighthouse. Then he plunged out the window into the waves. Although Ernie generally is taken to be the ghost of the suicide, no one knows for certain.

Nor does anyone know how Ernie is faring now that the gulls and the mindless machinery are his only companions. The same poignant question hovers over the Penfield Reef Lighthouse, down the coast at Fairfield, Connecticut. It, too, is known to be haunted, by the ghost of a lighthouse keeper who drowned in heavy seas as he was rowing to land to visit his family at Christmas. His ghost, a more sober spirit than Ernie, was said to haunt the lighthouse's records room, keeping the weather and tide readings in order. Now the readings, like the light itself, are automated, and another lighthouse ghost may be at loose ends.

Lonely outposts on a wave-battered coast, New England lighthouses such as the Nubble Light (above) in Maine, the Minots Light (opposite) in Massachusetts, and the New London Lighthouse (below) in Connecticut are beacons for both sailors and lost souls. Some are haunted by former lighthouse keepers, who seem unwilling to abandon their posts even in death.

sold the estate in 1908, the mansion housed a girls' school. Today it serves as the headquarters of a theatrical troupe. Both the schoolgirls and the actors were quick to realize that the house's first occupants have not completely decamped.

Sometimes Wharton appears alone, formidable in her high-collared dresses and upswept hair. Sometimes she's seen in tableaux with colleagues and family. Down the halls and in vacant rooms, she's been spotted talking to her secretary, a mutton-chop-whiskered gentleman with whom she's rumored to have had an affair; turning impatiently from her dim socialite husband, Teddy, whom she later divorced; deep in conversation with a man whom witnesses have identified by his waistcoat and grave demeanor as Henry James.

These are aloof ghosts, pursuing their own private affairs as if the house was still theirs. They sometimes fill empty rooms with their own spectral furniture – small ornate desks and a divan – and, in winter, drive off the drafts with gusts of warm air that dissipate as soon as the ghosts them-

selves fade. But those who see them feel privileged to have had a glimpse of spectral footnotes in New England's literary history.

Haunting the Library

It's an illustrious member of New England's literati who does the glimpsing in one cherished ghost tale. Not only did Nathaniel Hawthorne encounter a ghost, he also recorded his encounter in a letter noteworthy for its unvarnished treatment of an easily inflated topic. But encounter is too tame a word for what befell this Romantic novelist and short-story writer. Hawthorne recalled that his experience lasted "for weeks at least, and I know not but for months."

The **Boston Athenaeum**, a handsome proprietary library founded in 1807, has stood at 10½ Beacon Street since 1847. In 1842, however, the Athenaeum was situated in a mansion on 13 Pearl Street. There it was that Hawthorne, like others of the members-only reading room, would pass hours, sometimes whole days, absorbed in newspapers, journals, and rare books. One elderly gentleman, a notable Unitarian minister, was as fixed in Hawthorne's daily routine at the library as the fireplace by which the octogenarian sat. The Rev. Dr. Thaddeus Harris was, wrote Hawthorne, a "small, withered, infirm, but brisk old gentleman, with snow-white hair, a somewhat stooping figure, but yet a remarkable alacrity of movement." Seldom did the writer see the clergyman without the *Boston Post* in his hands. Indeed, a more loyal reader the *Post* never had, for the good reverend was, quite literally, the kind of person who would read the paper that contained his own obituary.

Assuming his accustomed spot in the reading room one day, Hawthorne, as always, took comfort in the sight of Rev. Harris seated near the fire. But, he recounted later, "that very evening a friend said to me, 'Did you hear that old Dr. Harris is dead?' 'No,' said I, very quietly, 'and it cannot be true; for I saw him at the Athenaeum today.'" Hawthorne soon gained incontrovertible evidence of the said passing and, strangely unperplexed by this strange incident, glumly noted that he would never again see the Reverend.

Hawthorne returned to the Athenaeum the next day, still lamenting the loss of his serenely hunched lodestar. "As I opened the door of the reading room, I glanced toward the spot and chair where Dr. Harris usually sat, and there to my astonishment sat the grey, infirm figure of the deceased Doctor, reading the newspaper as was his wont." Hawthorne collected himself and went about his routine. The reverend's specter neither looked at others in the room nor seemed detected by anyone save Hawthorne. And so things continued for a number of days.

What later amazed Hawthorne most about this fantastic interlude was his relative lack of interest or excitement during those otherwise bookish afternoons. The ghost, he wrote, "grew to be so common that at length I regarded the venerable defunct no more than any of the other old fogies who basked before the fire and dozed over their newspapers." Why this incuriosity in the presence of mystery? Hawthorne offered these speculations: "Perhaps I was loath to destroy the illusion and rob myself of so good a ghost story. Perhaps after all I had a secret dread of the old phenomenon and therefore kept within my limits with a secret caution which I mistook for indifference."

Though the Boston Athenaeum is still for members only, visitors are now permitted on the first and second floors of this august Renaissance-style building, which houses many of Boston's finest works of art. But be warned: an elevator there may rise and fall on preternatural cables. According to Jim McCabe, tour guide of New England Ghost Tours, thousands of dollars have been applied to this lingering problem. And still the elevator rises to the second floor without provocation, baffling the Athaenaeum's director of public relations (outside whose second-floor office, it

Edith Wharton (opposite) has been seen socializing with other "ghost writers" at The Mount, her former Massachusetts home. One of her phantom guests is Henry James (left), author of *The Turn of the Screw*, a classic tale of psychological horror.

The Boston Athenaeum (below) is haunted by a minister whose spirit first appeared to Nathaniel Hawthorne.

should be noted, hangs a portrait of Rev. Harris). A librarian told McCabe that a decision has been made to build a new elevator shaft. Meanwhile, a man in a brown suit sometimes appears to those who work in the basement among the library's stacks. But whenever workers approach the man, he vanishes. Did the ghost of Rev. Harris follow the Athenaeum to its present location? If so, perhaps the loss of his favorite newspaper, the long-gone *Post*, has left him surly – or just bored and pardonably prankish.

DETAILS

When to Go

The best time to visit is from June to October. Summer can be hot and humid, with temperatures usually in the 80s. Fall foliage attracts many visitors, who enjoy temperatures in the high 50s and 60s. Winter is unpredictable, sometimes blanketed with gentle snow, sometimes assailed by gloomy rain and sleet.

How to Get There

Major airports in the region are Logan International in Boston, Mass.; Portland International in Portland, Maine; and Bradley International in Hartford, Conn.

Getting Around

A car is essential for travel in the region; rentals are available at the airports. Amtrak, 800-872-7245, provides rail service between Hartford, Boston, and Providence.

INFORMATION

Connecticut Department of Economic Development

865 Brook Street; Rocky Hill, CT 06067; tel: 800-282-6863 or 203-258-4355.

Greater Boston Convention and Visitors Bureau

Prudential Plaza; 800 Boylston Street; Boston, MA 02199; tel: 800-888-5515 or 617-536-4100.

Maine Publicity Bureau

P.O. Box 2300; Hallowell, ME 04347; tel: 800-533-9595 or 207-623-0363.

Massachusetts Office of Travel and Tourism

100 Cambridge Street; 13th Floor; Boston, MA 02202; tel: 617-727-3201.

Vermont Travel and Tourism

134 State Street; Montpelier, VT 05602; tel: 800-837-6668 or 802-828-3237.

HAUNTED PLACES

Bara-Hack

About six miles southeast of Pomfret, Conn., off Highway 97 near Mashamoquet Brook State Park.

The foundations and cemetery are all that remain of this erstwhile factory town, which reputedly buzzes with spectral life.

Boston Athenaeum

10 1/2 Beacon Street; Boston, MA 02108; tel: 617-227-0270.

This famous library may be haunted by Rev. Dr. Thaddeus Harris. The ghost of Rev. Harris was observed for many days by Nathaniel Hawthorne in the previous location of the Athenaeum. Today, a mischievous elevator and brown-suited specter feed speculation about the Reverend's ghost. The Athenaeum's first two floors, which contain many noted works of art, are open to the public.

Coffin House

Coffin House Restaurant, Union Street; Nantucket, MA 02554; tel: 508-228-2400.

Wigmaker William Coffin, a suspect in the 1795 bank robbery of $21,000 from a Nantucket bank, haunts his old house, now a restaurant.

The Mount

Shakespeare & Company, P.O. Box 865; Lenox, MA 01240; tel: 413-637-3353.

Once the home of Edith Wharton, later a boarding school for girls, the Mount now houses Shakespeare & Company, a theater troupe that performs plays and conducts tours of the house in summer. Ghostly activity runs the gamut from sightings of Wharton and Henry James to the sound of giggling schoolgirls.

Witch Hollow Farm

474 Ipswich Road; Boxford, MA.

The ghost of a woman accused of witchcraft in 1693 has been seen strolling the grounds of her childhood home. Please do not disturb the occupants of this private residence.

LODGING

PRICE GUIDE – double occupancy

$ = up to $49 $$ = $50–$99
$$$ = $100–$149 $$$$ = $150+

Captain Lord Mansion

P.O. Box 800; Kennebunkport, ME 04046; tel: 207-967-3141.

A female ghost in 19th-century attire has been spotted on a spiral staircase in this old and stately mansion. Guests enjoy 16 large and luxurious rooms, each with private bath, all but one with gas fireplace. $$–$$$$

Maple Hill Farm

365 Goose Lane; Coventry, CT 06238; tel: 203-742-0635.

This farmhouse was built in 1731 and is said to be haunted by a ghost who occasionally appears in a white gown. Four large guest rooms are furnished with antiques. The grounds sprawl across seven acres with gardens, horses, and a pool. $$

Sise Inn

40 Court Street; Portsmouth, NH 03801; tel: 800-267-0525 or 603-433-1200.

Beware! Guests in Suite 214 of this Queen Anne-style inn may experience stolen keys and icy floors. Built in 1881, the house is haunted by an impish spirit who occasionally scatters ice on the floor and purloins the key, and once forced a potted plant off a coffee table. The inn's 34 guest rooms feature Victorian decor. Each has a private bath; some have whirlpools, saunas, Grecian soaking tubs, and separate living rooms. $$–$$$$

Victorian Inn

Box 947; 24 South Water Street; Edgartown, MA 02539; tel: 508-627-4784.

Situated on Martha's Vineyard, this restored whaling captain's house is a classic Victorian with 14 guest rooms, private baths, and a four-course gourmet breakfast. Occasionally making an appearance in the guest rooms is an amorous ghost, a bearded man who once cozied up to a woman in bed. Another time he spent half the night sitting on someone's chest. $$$–$$$$

TOURS

Graveyard Tours

Heritage Trails Sightseeing Tours; P.O. Box 138; Farmington, CT 06034; tel: 860-677-8867.

Guided tour to Colonial and Victorian graveyards in historic Farmington examine gravestone carvings unique to New England. Cemetery ghosts include a Native American carrying the body of a deer on his shoulder and the founder of a girls' school. The tour is followed by dinner in a haunted inn. September through October, or by prior arrangement.

Haunted Footsteps Ghost Tour

8 Derby Square; Salem, MA 01970; tel: 978-745-0666.

Costumed guides explore Salem's supernatural history by lantern light, offering a "spirited" perspective on Colonial Massachusetts. May through November.

New England Ghost Tours

P.O. Box 812128; Wellesley, MA 02482; tel: 781-235-7149.

Excursions to haunted and legendary sites delve into the realm of the supernatural, with on-the-spot examinations of the most intriguing ghosts in Massachusetts. Walking tours and bus tours available. Sites include Boston, Concord, Groton, Littleton, and Salem.

Excursions

Hale Homestead

2299 South Street; Coventry, CT 06238; tel: 860-742-6917.

For hundreds of years, American schoolchildren have learned Nathan Hale's reputed last words: "I regret that I have but one life to lose for my country." What few people know, however, is that the 21-year-old spy, caught and hanged by the British, may have given something additional to his country: his ghost. Hale was born in 1755, the sixth of 12 children; some members of his family may still inhabit their snug farmhouse. Locals have long reported ghost activity in and around the house. Dudley Seymour, an attorney who purchased the homestead in 1914 and devoted himself to the popularization of Nathan Hale, claimed to have seen the ghost of Deacon Hale, the hero's father, peering out a window. The ghost of a servant sometimes sweeps the upper hall. Nathan's ghost, on the other hand, may account for the sound of someone pacing the floors.

High Point

Belfast, Maine

Boaters have reported hearing the clank of shackles and an unearthly moan around this overlook on the Maine coast, about 50 miles south of Bangor. The chilling sounds are said to come from the spirit of Barbara Houndsworth, a potion maker who was sentenced to death in the 17th century for practicing witchcraft. Just as she was to be hanged, however, a stone mysteriously struck the town clerk on the forehead. Houndsworth used the commotion to slip away. The villagers made after her, but a sudden torrent ended their pursuit. No sooner had she escaped than the doomed woman slipped on a rock and fell into the sea.

The Palatine

Block Island Chamber of Commerce, Drawer D; Block Island, RI 02807; tel: 401-466-2982.

Block Islanders have caught sight of it for more than 200 years: an incandescent ship skimming through the distant darkness like a torch dropped down a bottomless pit. The *Palatine*, a Dutch ship packed with immigrants, sailed toward Philadelphia in 1752. Faced with spent rations, the crew mutinied, leaving a murdered captain and helpless passengers in the wake of their lifeboats. The *Palatine* ran aground on Block Island, where islanders pillaged and set fire to her. According to legend, a madwoman remained on deck as the waves carried the ship back to sea. A laughing sound borne by the waves may be little more than the wind – or it may be this unsinkable wraith.

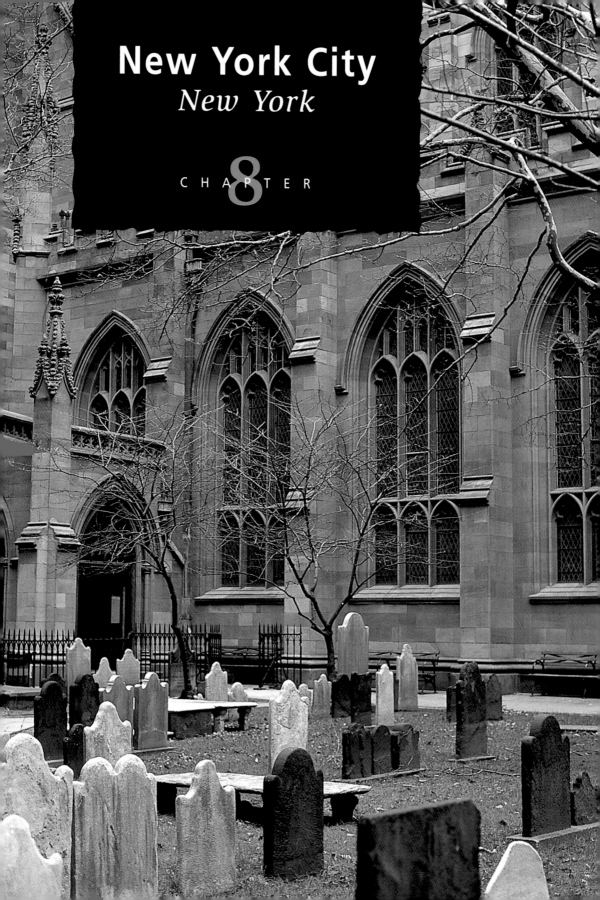

New York City
New York

CHAPTER 8

T here are certain spots where the human and spirit worlds converge, and New York City is one of them," says the Reverend Daniel Neusom, pastor of New York's First Universal Spirit Church. This is probably not surprising in a place with such a tumultuous history – a raucous colonial seaport that grew helter-skelter into the nation's largest and most dynamic city. It's a proper *mise en scène* for brooding spirits. ◆ Take, for example, the most famous catastrophe in maritime history: the sinking of the *Titanic* in April 1912. When survivors reached New York, it appears that some of them may have been accompanied by the spirits of their doomed shipmates. These haunted survivors were people who disembarked from the rescue ship *Carpathia* with no loved ones to greet them. They were offered temporary lodging at the Institute of the Seaman's Friend, a five-story building on the northern edge of Greenwich Village. ◆ They settled into the small

From Peter Stuyvesant to Dylan Thomas, three centuries of restless spirits haunt Manhattan.

rooms, grateful to be alive, but then began to feel that they were not alone. The building's creaking elevator, ordinarily manned by an operator, seemed to be rising and falling by itself. Shrieks and wails were reported emanating from hallways in the dark of night. Some of the survivors concluded that the *Titanic*'s dead had indeed accompanied them to New York and established residence at the Institute. ◆ Today the imposing red-brick building that was once home to the Institute houses the **Hotel Riverview** and the **Jane Street Theater**, but it looks much the same as it did in 1912. What were resting places for weary sailors are now some of the cheapest rooms in New York. In the threadbare lobby, the bas-relief of

The cemetery at Trinity Church
in lower Manhattan is the final
resting place and favorite haunt of
Alexander Hamilton.

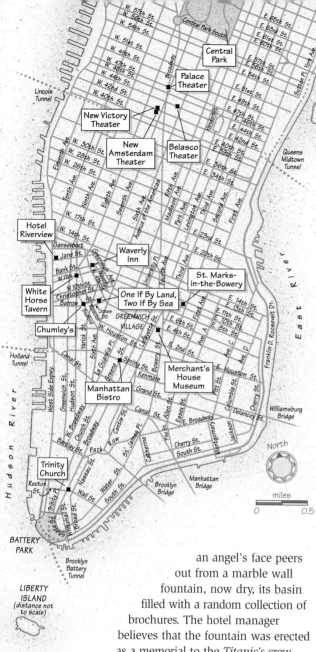

after Stuyvesant bitterly surrendered the colony to English intruders, who promptly renamed the place New York, his peg-legged apparition supposedly was seen wandering about the charred ruins of what had been his executive mansion.

The fire occurred in 1774. The mansion was eventually replaced by a church, **St. Mark's in the Bowery**, and over the years people have said they heard the thumping of a wooden leg along the grounds, or church bells pealing without the aid of a bell ringer. In a city he ruled for a quarter of a century, Peter Stuyvesant seems to be omnipresent long after his physical departure.

The Body in the Well

And then there is the strange case of Gulielma Sands, whose body was discovered by two boys in 1799 at the bottom of a well in a hilly farming area of New York. Soon after her death, New York's planners eyed this ground for expansion, and by 1825 the hills were gone and the neighborhood (now called SoHo) was Manhattan's most densely populated. The well still exists, in the basement of the **Manhattan Bistro**, a quaint French restaurant on Spring Street. Apparently, Gulielma is still there, too. There have been several sightings at the restaurant of a spectral woman with long hair and a soiled dress.

Deadly Duel

Gulielma Sands was the fiancée of Levi Weeks, who was accused of her murder. Weeks, the brother of a wealthy contractor,

an angel's face peers out from a marble wall fountain, now dry, its basin filled with a random collection of brochures. The hotel manager believes that the fountain was erected as a memorial to the *Titanic's* crew, but it's hard to tell for sure: The words on the bronze plaque laid in the floor beneath it have been rubbed clean over the years. Only a ghostly blur remains.

Pegleg Pete

Ghostly legends go all the way back to the New Amsterdam of Peter Stuyvesant, the Dutchman who ruled the colony with an iron fist and a wooden leg. Almost from the time of his death in 1664, there were reports of his lingering presence. A century was aided in his defense by two individuals who didn't otherwise get on well together: Aaron Burr and Alexander Hamilton. Weeks beat the rap, and his two prominent defenders went on to their fateful encounter.

Burr and Hamilton had been ambitious young men, less than a year apart in age, who hoped for key roles in the new republic. Their rivalry was born early; Burr and Hamilton started their political careers supporting competing factions. By the time of Gulielma's death, Hamilton had finished a stint as the nation's first secretary of the treasury and Burr was about to run for president. Hamilton's support of Thomas Jefferson guaranteed that Jefferson would win the top office and that Burr, who became vice president, would be Hamilton's enemy for life. The feud peaked in 1804 after Hamilton made disparaging remarks about Burr, who thereupon challenged him to a duel. The duel was fought in New Jersey, with pistols the weapons of choice, and Hamilton was mortally wounded.

Aides rushed the stricken Hamilton across the Hudson River to Manhattan and the Jane Street home of his doctor, John Francis. After Francis did what little he could, Hamilton was moved down the street to his own home, where he died the next day. Legend has it, however, that Hamilton never left the Francis home. A ghost in 18th-century dress reportedly has been seen there since the mid-1900s. Hamilton's remains are interred downtown, in the lush cemetery that surrounds **Trinity Church**, a majestic Gothic Revival structure at Broadway and Wall Street, where his ghost is said to hover near his pyramid-topped white tomb.

St. Mark's in the Bowery (right, below) was erected on the site of a mansion once occupied by Peter Stuyvesant (right, above). The volatile, peg-legged ruler of New Amsterdam has been heard walking the grounds of his former home.

Alexander Hamilton's shade might find solace in the fact that Aaron Burr leads an even more restless afterlife. Burr owned a large property in what today is Greenwich Village. His carriage house now houses an elegant restaurant called **One If By Land, Two If By Sea**, where the ghostly Burr is said to pull chairs from under people and to break dishes.

Such cantankerousness might be explained by the fact that Burr had a rather unpleasant life. His once-promising political career was aborted by charges that he treasonously tried to provoke a war with Spain. Though cleared, he moved to Europe for four years. He returned only to heartbreak when, in December 1812, his daughter Theodosia was lost at

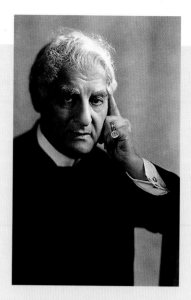

Shades of Broadway

No man, it seems, should have been more comfortable in a theater than impresario David Belasco. He was, after all, a famous producer, and he owned two theaters on Broadway. But legend has it that both of these New York emporiums – the Republic and the Stuyvesant – were downright hostile to their proprietor. Objects would fall from the rafters and land on him, knocking him unconscious on a couple of occasions. It's even said that Belasco died backstage at the Republic in 1931 after a crowbar dropped from a gallery and hit him on the head.

Impresario David Belasco (right) haunts not one but two Broadway theaters.

The Palace Theater (below) is visited by a tightrope walker who gave his last, fatal performance here in the 1950s.

Aaron Burr (opposite) fires at bitter rival Alexander Hamilton in this depiction of the 1804 duel.

Not true. He fell victim to falling objects, but never fatally. Belasco died at home after several heart attacks. Some swear it's true, though, that his spirit haunts both theaters.

The Republic is now the **New Victory**, one of the grand renovated theaters on 42nd Street. Theatergoers late in leaving after the curtain falls have sometimes reported feeling a cold chill that they attribute to Belasco.

His presence is stronger, however, in the former Stuyvesant Theater, which was renamed the **Belasco** in 1910. Above the theater, with its Tiffany glass and Everett Shinn murals, was an elegant private apartment where Belasco entertained a long procession of actresses and showgirls. Some stagehands and construction workers at this West 44th Street edifice say they've heard footsteps coming from Belasco's deserted apartment. Then there are the inexplicable sounds of the private elevator that Belasco used to whisk his mistresses to his lair – an elevator that was dismantled long ago.

Perhaps, even now, the impresario has female companionship: A second apparition is seen at the Belasco, a red-haired woman in a white negligee. Some believe her to be the shade of a stripper who hanged herself in the theater's basement.

There may be other ghosts on Broadway. Across the street from the New Victory is the **New Amsterdam Theater**, another gloriously restored showplace. Before the renovation, theater personnel reported seeing the ghost of a weeping woman in a white dress trimmed with silver. She's believed to be Olive Thomas, a star of the Ziegfeld Follies, which were produced for years at the New Amsterdam. Thomas was Flo Ziegfeld's mistress. When she died in a Paris hotel room in 1920, she was buried in a white gown trimmed with silver.

Patrons of the **Palace Theater** at Broadway and 47th Street have spotted the ghost of a tightrope walker swinging from the rafters. He could be Louis Borsalino, an acrobat who plummeted to his death in the Palace in the 1950s. And workers at the **Lyceum**, who've heard strange noises there, speculate that Daniel Frohman, the producer who built the 1,000-seat theater in 1903, may never have left it.

Oddly, when Frohman opened the Lyceum, he brought with him a young man he'd discovered in San Francisco in 1882, and appointed him stage manager and house playwright. In time, the underling became his own boss and developed his own legend. His name was David Belasco.

sea. Burr, it is said, still stands at the seawall of the Battery, gazing out into New York Harbor in search of Theodosia's ship.

The Widow Burr

There's yet another legend involving Burr. Toward the end of his life, at 77, he married a woman younger than he was by two decades. She was Eliza Jumel, a social climber with a shady past who lived on a spectacular estate close to Manhattan's northern edge. Rumor had it that Mrs. Jumel murdered her first husband, Stephen, in the house in 1832, a year before tying the knot with Burr.

Her second venture into matrimony did not last long either. Burr tried to get control of her considerable fortune, and in July 1834 she filed for divorce. The decree came through on September 14, 1836 – the day Burr died. Eliza Burr died in her fine home in 1865, and it is said that she haunts it still. The only surviving pre-Revolutionary War home in Manhattan, the place is now a museum called the **Morris-Jumel Mansion**.

On a field trip there in the early 1960s, a group of schoolchildren was admonished to be quiet by the flickering specter of an elderly woman standing on a balcony.

The Pirate in the Pit

About the time Madame Jumel switched husbands, two American soldiers stationed at Fort Wood on **Bedloe's Island** were searching for the buried treasure of pirate William Kidd. The notorious Captain Kidd, who had lived in New York for four years before his execution in 1701, had reportedly buried a treasure chest on Bedloe's Island. Armed with a psychic's map and a divining rod, the two soldiers made their way to the indicated site and started digging. They did indeed find a chest, but as they were about to lift it, a flash of light and a horrifying vision rose from the pit – or so they claimed.

The terrified soldiers screamed, prompting sentries to investigate. The sentries later swore that they, too, saw the ghost – that of a dead pirate buried beside the treasure. Since 1886 the site has had a permanent

Barflies

Both the living and the dead hang out in New York's West Village, it seems, and not just on Halloween. Like poet Dylan Thomas, said to be forever hoisting a few at the White Horse Tavern, other shades are reputed to congregate in the neighborhood's restaurants and bars.

Among the restaurants said to be haunted is the **Waverly Inn** at 16 Bank Street, whose colorful history might well be conducive to ghostly presences. Built in 1844, the place served as a tavern, a bordello, and a carriage house. In 1920 it became a teahouse, whose famous patrons included poet Robert Frost. It's been a restaurant ever since.

The shade of Welsh bard Dylan Thomas (above) still visits the White Horse Tavern (left), where he downed his last shot of whiskey.

The Morris-Jumel Mansion (right) is inhabited by the specter of Aaron Burr's last wife, the notorious Eliza Jumel Burr.

Fire broke out at the Waverly Inn just before Christmas in 1996, and investigators probing its cause were perplexed. They identified the spot where they thought the fire had started but found nothing. Asked about the restaurant's history of alleged spirit sightings, a fire marshal told the *New York Times*, "Ghosts don't start fires – we don't think."

Hannah Drory isn't so sure. Drory bought the restaurant four years before the fire. She remarked that Room 16 was undamaged by the blaze. Legend has it that Room 16 was the favorite spot of the anonymous ghost believed to haunt the Waverly Inn, making its presence known in different ways. Some patrons and employees have seen the apparition of a man wearing clothes dating to 1900. Others have heard odd sounds coming from places where no person sat or stood.

And then there's **Chumley's**, a neighborhood pub at 86 Bedford Street. The proprietor, Henrietta Chumley, loved the spare layout of the place, but what she liked even more was the liquor selection behind the bar. One day in 1960, Henrietta drank herself to death, though it took a while for anyone to notice. She fell asleep laying out a game of solitaire and never woke up. Ever since, the tavern's lights sometimes go on by themselves, and the jukebox plays on its own. Some say it's merely Henrietta summoning up a tune, as in the good old days.

guard, the Statue of Liberty, on what is now called **Liberty Island**.

Sheltered Sisters

Jane and Rosetta Vandevroot probably never saw the famous statue. They were so sheltered by their wealthy, overprotective father that they could venture unescorted to only two places, a favorite restaurant and the ice-skating pond in **Central Park**. Their father believed that all the men who approached

his beloved girls were fortune-hunters and scared them off. Even after he died, the sisters remained single and stuck to their limited routine until their deaths within months of each other. Witnesses still report seeing two elderly women in 19th-century dress cut ghostly figure eights on Central Park's frozen pond.

Another young woman, Gertrude Tredwell, suffered a similar fate at the hands of a tyrannical father. She was born in 1840, the youngest of Seabury Tredwell's eight children, in a four-story home on East Fourth Street near **Washington Square**. Alas, Gertrude fell in love with a young Roman Catholic. The Tredwells were strictly Episcopalian, and any thought of marriage to a Catholic was forbidden by her father. A shattered Gertrude vowed never to wed. She watched as her siblings married and left the house, and she tended her parents as they died. In 1933, at the age of 93, Gertrude herself passed on, leaving a home that had changed little in her long life.

A distant relative bought the house and turned it into the **Merchant's House Museum**, where Gertrude may still be dwelling in spirit. Some people have reported seeing a prim woman in a plain brown dress playing the piano. A museum volunteer once reported feeling a pencil she was holding move of its own accord, forming the words "Miss Tredwell is here" in an unfamiliar scrawl.

Poetic Spirit

As with the rest of New York City, the spirit population has grown apace since Gertrude Tredwell's day. Shades of the rich and poor, the obscure and prominent, are said to mingle in their democratic netherworld throughout the great metropolis. Many share a bond of self-destruction: swift suicides who leaped from skyscrapers, slow suicides who drank themselves to death, none more famously than Dylan Thomas.

The brilliant but sodden Welsh poet made four trips to the United States in the early 1950s and was a familiar patron of the **White Horse Tavern** on Hudson Street in Greenwich Village, once a Prohibition speakeasy. On his last trip, in 1953, Thomas spoke of seeing the gates of Hell, and thereupon downed 17 or 18 shots of whiskey at the White Horse. He went into a coma, and within days he was dead. The bar consecrated a room to his memory, for the staff says he still visits and leaves half-empty shot glasses strewn about from time to time to mark his spectral passage. One can almost hear the refrain: "Do not go gently into that good night..."

DETAILS

When to Go

The most pleasant times to visit are spring and fall. Summer tends to be muggy; the average temperature in July is 77°F. Winter can be quite cold, with occasional snowfall, icy winds, and temperatures dipping below freezing.

Getting There

Three airports service New York: John F. Kennedy International, 15 miles southeast of Manhattan; La Guardia International, eight miles northeast of Manhattan; and Newark International, 16 miles southwest of Manhattan, in New Jersey. Gray Line Air Shuttle, 212-757-6840, offers service from the airports to Manhattan hotels. Amtrak trains service Pennsylvania Station.

Getting Around

Subways are the city's quickest and cheapest means of transit. For subway and bus information, call the New York Transit Authority, 718-330-1234. Taxis are available just about everywhere. Car rentals are available at the airports but are inadvisable unless you plan to travel outside the city.

INFORMATION

New York Convention and Visitors Bureau

2 Columbus Circle; New York, NY 10019; tel: 212-484-1222.

HAUNTED PLACES

Belasco Theater

111 West 44th Street; New York, NY 10036; tel: 212-239-6200.

Impresario David Belasco lived above this theater, formerly the Stuyvesant Theater. An alleged philanderer, Belasco died in 1931 but reportedly has thrown many riotous parties as a ghost.

Chumley's

86 Bedford Street; New York, NY 10014; tel: 212-675-4449.

Poor Henrietta Chumley drank herself to death here in 1960 while beginning a game of solitaire. Various anomalies have been attributed to her ghost.

Manhattan Bistro

129 Spring Street; New York, NY 10014; tel: 212-966-3459.

The ghost of a murdered women is said to haunt this restaurant.

Merchant's House Museum

29 East 4th Street; New York, NY 10003; tel: 212-777-1089.

The ghost of a former resident has been seen playing the piano at this 1830 brownstone.

Morris-Jumel Mansion

1765 Jumel Terrace; New York, NY 10032; tel: 212-923-8008.

This historic mansion is said to have five ghosts. The most notable specter is that of Eliza Jumel, divorced wife of Aaron Burr.

New Amsterdam Theater

214 West 42nd Street; New York, NY 10036; tel: 212-282-2900.

The spirit of Olive Thomas, who starred in the Ziegfeld Follies, was seen here. Tours of the theater are available on Monday, 11 A.M. to 5 P.M. Tickets may be purchased at the box office.

One If By Land, Two If By Sea

17 Barrow Street; New York, NY 10014; tel: 212-228-0822.

The former carriage house of Aaron Burr is now a beautifully restored Greenwich Village restaurant. His ghost is said to smash dishes and swipe chairs from under patrons.

Palace Theater

1564 Broadway; New York, NY 10036; tel: 212-730-8200.

Toeing the line between this world and the next requires great skill. The ghost of a tightrope walker, seen performing at this theater, must certainly have an advantage.

St. Mark's in the Bowery

131 East 10th Street; New York, NY 10003; tel: 212-533-4650.

Four ghosts haunt this 1799 church, including that of Peter Stuyvesant, the Dutch governor of the town before it was handed over to the British.

Trinity Church

74 Trinity Place; New York, NY; tel: 212-602-0800.

Alexander Hamilton was buried at this Gothic Revival church after being shot and killed in a duel with Aaron Burr. His spirit is said to haunt the area surrounding his tomb.

Waverly Inn

16 Bank Street; New York, NY 10014; tel: 212-929-4377.

The ghost of a man dressed in turn-of-the-century attire has been spotted at this restaurant.

White Horse Tavern

567 Hudson Street; New York, NY 10014; tel: 212-243-9260.

Welsh poet Dylan Thomas drank himself to death at this Greenwich Village tavern. His ghost still knocks back whiskey from unattended shot glasses.

LODGING

PRICE GUIDE – double occupancy

$ = up to $49 $$ = $50–$99
$$$ = $100–$149 $$$$ = $150+

The Castle at Tarrytown

400 Benedict Avenue; Tarrytown, NY 10591; tel: 914-631-1980.

This turn-of-the-century stone castle just north of New York was modeled after Norman fortifications in Great Britain. Like many of its august sister castles, this edifice may be haunted. A Welsh man, there to inquire about lodging, recently claimed to have spotted the apparition of a lady jumping from a window in the castle's 75-foot tower. Meticulously renovated, the luxurious inn overlooks the Hudson River. It has 21 rooms and 20 suites, each with private bath, some with fireplace. $$$$

Chelsea Hotel

222 West 23d Street; New York, NY 10023; tel: 212-243-3700.

Dylan Thomas stayed here, and this is where Sid Vicious killed girlfriend Nancy Spungeon. The elevator stops, mysteriously, on Ms. Spungeon's former floor, supposedly so the ghost of Mr. Vicious can step off. Singer and songwriter Schizo said, in 1994, "I think all the ghosts have been helpful. I never wrote any music before, but since I'm here I wrote 40 songs." $$–$$$$

Hotel Riverview

113 Jane Street; New York, NY 10014; tel: 212-929-0060.

Ghosts of the *Titanic's* ill-fated passengers may haunt this basic, inexpensive hotel. $–$$

Martha Washington Hotel

30 East 30th Street; New York, NY 10023; tel: 212-689-1900.

The crotchety spirit of an elderly lady is said to occupy a twelfth-floor room in this women's hotel. The hotel has 451 simple rooms. $$–$$$

TOURS

Tombstone Tours

Tel: 718-760-8662.

"We put the fun back into funerals," claims this Manhattan outfit, whose tours of famous murder scenes and haunts are conducted in the "world's most luxurious hearse."

Excursions

Rockefeller State Park

P.O. Box 338; Tarrytown, NY 10591-0338; tel: 914-631-1470.
Visitors may take in more than the beautiful views of the Hudson River. Spooky stories have been associated with the area since the Dutch first settled it. Washington Irving set his classic tale of the Headless Horseman here. The *Flying*

Dutchman, a legendary phantom ship, has been spotted on the river, as has the ghost of a young Dutchman named Van Dam, who disappeared during a midnight revel and is now seen floating in a rowboat. Don't forget to visit the ruins of Rockwood Hall, once the home of John D. Rockefeller's brother William.

The Conference House

Conference House Museum; Hylan Boulevard; Tottenville, NY 10307; tel: 718-984-2086.
Built in 1688, this two-story manor in Staten Island was the home of Christopher Billopp, a British naval captain. The building was host to an unsuccessful peace conference during the American Revolution between British commander Lord Howe and a delegation that included Benjamin Franklin and John Adams, but some people argue that ghosts give the house its enduring appeal. One legend has Billopp jilting his fiancée, who then died of a broken heart. Her ghost is sometimes heard moaning. Screams in the house may relate to an altogether different woman. Billopp, in a fit of anger, is said to have murdered a servant girl on a staircase leading to the attic.

United States Military Academy

West Point Visitor Center, Building 2107; West Point, NY 10996; tel: 914-938-2638.
Set high above the magnificent Hudson River, West Point has its share of ghost stories. One autumn night in 1972, four cadets in Room 4714 of the 47th Division Barracks witnessed the apparition of a sol-

dier dressed in an 1830s cavalry uniform and sporting a handlebar mustache. The ghost made several more appearances, emerging from the wall or floor and occasionally toying with robes and showers, prompting a commanding officer to rule the area off-limits. But the ghost is still said to roam the barracks and its grounds. The Superintendent's House, too, has a ghost: Molly, the specter of a 19th-century maid, unmaking beds.

Philadelphia
Pennsylvania

CHAPTER **9**

A gaggle of ghosts haunts the City of Brotherly Love, where Americans declared their independence and conceived a nation, and where they established the country's first hospital, first public library, and first real penitentiary. Apparently, some of the people who created all this history are reluctant to leave. ◆ Among the most famous specters in this "city of firsts" is that of Benjamin Franklin, a great innovator himself, who appeared to a charwoman early one morning in 1884 at the **American Philosophical Society**. As the story goes, the young woman was setting out her pails and brushes when she was bowled over by one of the Society's members as he rushed toward a bookshelf. ◆ He was an old gent, mostly bald, but with a fringe of gray hair that curled down over a collar that was as old-fashioned as his hose and knee breeches. Tiny, wire-rimmed spectacles perched on the end of his round nose, and he carried a huge stack of books in his arms.

A lively Founding Father is among the many shades said to linger in America's Birthplace of Independence.

◆ The cleaning woman was astonished, not because Benjamin Franklin, who'd just knocked her over, had been dead and buried for a good many years, but because he didn't stop to apologize. She and her mother, who both encountered Mr. Franklin's ghost frequently, agreed that his manners were usually impeccable. ◆ This incident, reported in an 1884 issue of the *Philadelphia Press* that testified to the upstanding character of the women who related it, is one of the most famous of the Franklin sightings at the Society's library, which still stands near Independence Hall on the south side of Fifth Street between Chestnut and Walnut Streets. The library is open only to members, but visitors often

Benjamin Franklin, depicted here at the University of Pennsylvania, is just one of the historic figures who return to the City of Brotherly Love.

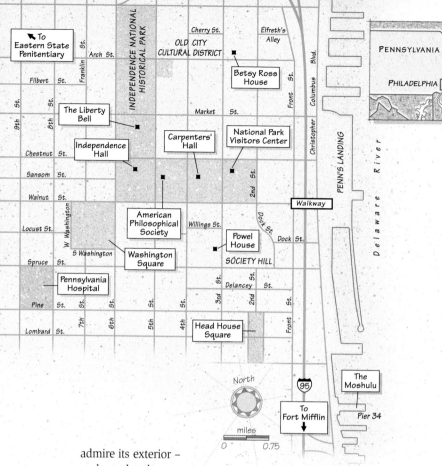

admire its exterior –
and ponder the statue
of Franklin that still stands out
front. In the 19th century, the statue was
said to detach itself from its base from time
to time and dance along the city streets.

The Seamstress' Spirit

Betsy Ross is thought to linger, too, haunting
her old home – the **Betsy Ross House** – on
239 Arch Street in the **Old City** district, not
far from Independence Hall. Some historians
now question whether the nation's most
famous seamstress did, in fact, sew the first
American flag – or whether, for that matter,
she actually lived at the Arch Street house
that's now a museum and her memorial.
But all agree that she's buried there. As to
whether she lives there still, some people
have reported seeing her sitting at the foot
of her bed, weeping.

Museum employees also have reported
hearing strange whispers coming from the
basement of the house, but some people
speculate that shades more modern than

Betsy's are responsible.
They suggest that the
whispering specter
might be the ghost of
Charles H. Weisberger,
founder of the Betsy
Ross Memorial
Association and one-
time resident of the
house. Others speculate
that the whisperer is
the spirit of a gift
shop employee who
was shot by a former
security guard and left
to die in the basement.

Ben Franklin and
Betsy Ross are among
the most renowned
Revolutionary-era
ghosts; others from that
passionate period are anonymous, although many are associated
with famous places. The most famous
place of all is, of course, the Liberty Bell's
former home, **Independence Hall**, which
stands across the street from the American
Philosophical Library that Franklin is presumed to haunt. Although National Park
Service officials don't like to talk about it,
ghosts have been reported to wander the
first floor of the Hall's central clock tower.
One evening a park ranger, about to close
up for the night, heard the building's
security alarm go off. Checking the tower to
see what the disturbance could be, he saw
a figure clad in 18th-century garb. Before
the ranger could confront the intruder, it
vanished into the air.

Lafayette in Society Hill

More Revolutionary ghosts, famous and
nameless, are said to haunt the **Society Hill**
area just south of Independence Hall. One

of these may be the spirit of Marie Joseph Paul Yves Roch Gilbert du Motier, better known as the Marquis de Lafayette.

Despite his aristocratic origins, the young French nobleman was a passionate revolutionary and antimonarchist. He came to America in 1777 to join the colonists' fight against the British Crown and became a close friend of Gen. George Washington. Lafayette would also play a role in his own country's revolution of 1789. Perhaps his love of liberty explains his long-standing attachment to Philadelphia, for although he died in 1834 and was buried in Paris, there are those who say he haunts Philadelphia still.

In 1965, the respected historian Edwin Courant Moore reported seeing Lafayette as one of several ghosts in the shape of Continental Army officers, clad in blue, walking up the stairs of the **Powel House**, a former home of one of Philadelphia's early mayors and now a well-known

The Marquis de Lafayette (left), friend of the American Revolution, was once seen with other disembodied soldiers entering the Powel House (below), a grand Georgian mansion in Society Hill.

tourist attraction in the city.

The Powel House seems to hold other shades as well. Moore's wife claimed to have come across a young lady wearing a beige and lavender dress sitting in the drawing room and fanning herself. As Mrs. Moore watched, the woman smiled at her and then slowly faded from sight.

Phantom Felons

Philadelphia's 18th-century assortment of spirits appears to include villains as well as heroes: **Carpenters' Hall**, for instance, is said to be haunted by the nation's first bank robbers.

The Hall, in the center of **Independence National Park**, was the meeting place of the

first Continental Congress in 1774. Although actual sightings of spirits there have been rare, strange sounds, smells, and other manifestations have been reported. Loud banging noises have been heard on the third floor, but when the racket is investigated, no source can be determined. A powerful stench is said to emanate from the same area, and witnesses also tell of seeing footprints in the dust unaccompanied by any flesh-and-blood bodies.

A statue of William Penn (left), Philadelphia's founder, stands in the rear garden of Pennsylvania Hospital.

Some investigators link the weird occurrences to a robbery that took place on September 1,1798, when two men walked into the Bank of Pennsylvania, then located on the first floor of Carpenters' Hall, and demanded at gunpoint exactly $162,821.16 in cash. One of the robbers was probably a man named Tom Cunningham, who had a room on the third floor of the very same building. Police arrested him, but for reasons that have never been entirely clear, they released him after only a few days.

If Cunningham did, in fact, elude justice, he didn't escape punishment. Not long after the robbery, he contracted yellow fever and died in his rented room above the bank. It was shortly thereafter that witnesses began reporting strange noises coming from his third-floor room.

Graves of Washington Square

One of Philadelphia's most enduring ghosts haunts the fashionable pathways of **Washington Square**. Now the center of an

Ghosts Afloat

The *Moshulu* is a floating restaurant moored permanently at Pier 34 in Philadelphia's Delaware River port. With her dark wood exterior and handsome dining room, the four-masted vessel is a romantic spot to eat. But diners at the *Moshulu* sometimes get more than a meal. They get a visit from another world.

In her time, the *Moshulu* was a grand sailing ship. Considered one of the fastest cargo transports of her kind, she made 54 passes around Cape Horn ferrying grain, coal, copper ore, lumber, and other goods from one side of the world to the other. In 1939, she won an international race from Australia to England. But she knew tragedy as well as glory. From her launch in 1904 until she was retired in 1940, 28 of her crewmen lost their lives on the high seas.

Strangely enough, present-day crew members and restaurant guests have heard voices murmuring in the ship's rigging, just where one might expect to find ghosts of dead sailors. Of course, an old ship rocking gently on the river might well creak and groan, but those who've heard the eerie whispers attest that these are spectral voices.

More ghosts seem to walk below deck. The staff regularly snuffs out the restaurant lanterns at evening's end, but almost as regularly it finds them lit the next morning. A number of employees working after hours claim to have seen the lanterns spontaneously begin to glow. Members of the ship's cleaning crew found the sight so unnerving that they asked to have their shift changed, so they could begin work before everyone else went home.

The clock tower at Independence Hall (opposite), former home of the Liberty Bell, may harbor 18th-century spirits.

The *Moshulu* (above), once a cargo ship, now a moored restaurant, is haunted by lost crew members.

snatchers. Even after she died, she wandered the graveyard in spectral form. It is said that her ghost still lingers in the Square.

Spirits in Solitary

If Washington Square was once a symbol of suffering, **Eastern State Penitentiary** remains so even today. The old prison, on Fairmount Avenue between 20th and 22nd Streets, was the first of its kind in the nation. It has always been a bit creepy. Back in the early 1970s, just before it closed, guards would shiver a little when they had to walk down its dim, crumbling halls.

In its prime during the 1800s, Eastern State was considered a model institution; its pioneering method of keeping inmates in solitary confinement to ponder and repent their sins was hailed by many as enlightened. But even then, the place that added the word "penitentiary" to the language disturbed some people. Charles Dickens thought its isolation of prisoners barbaric: "I believe that very few men are capable of estimating the immense amount of torture and agony which this dreadful punishment, prolonged for years, inflicts upon the sufferers," he wrote. "There is a depth of terrible endurance in it which none but the sufferers themselves can fathom, and which no man has a right to inflict upon his fellow-creature."

upscale neighborhood, the Square was once the site of mass graves. An estimated 4,000 bodies are buried there. About half were Revolutionary War soldiers. Of the rest, many were the unidentified dead or those too poor to afford a proper burial. During the 19th century, a macabre trade centered on the potter's field in the Square. Unscrupulous men would dig up bodies there for doctors and medical students in need of cadavers.

There was no one to protect the nameless and indigent dead against such predations until a Quaker woman, remembered only as Leah, began to patrol the Square at night. Her mere presence scared away the body

Some of those sufferers, and the men who watched over them, may still be serving endless sentences. Since the prison reopened as an historic monument, a number of ghosts have been seen. Sean Kelley, program director at Eastern State, recalls being told of a ghostly guard in one of the prison's abandoned towers. The witness distinctly saw the guard waving at him through the tower glass, but when he looked up again, he realized that the guard couldn't have been there; the tower had been abandoned for several years. And a locksmith working on the penitentiary's restoration reported being caught up in a sort of supernatural maelstrom while alone one evening in the prison's exercise yard. Trying to unlock a door to the yard, he watched terrified as rocks in the walls began to glow, and spectral figures and faces appeared.

William Penn's Garden

Tourists disturbed by visiting the most horrific of Philadelphia's haunted sites might seek serenity in one of its loveliest places, the beautiful garden behind the nation's first hospital, **Pennsylvania Hospital**, at Ninth and Pine Streets. Fittingly, the presiding specter there is a ghost who in life predated by a century the turmoil of revolution and war. He is William Penn, the city's founder.

Penn's statue in the hospital garden, though not as famous or nearly as large as the Penn statue atop City Hall, has the advantage, or so it is said, of being mobile. Rumors have long circulated that Mr. Penn takes to strolling the streets every now and then, just as the clock strikes six in the evening. If true, one can only wonder what the old Quaker thinks of the city now and what other famous shades might join him in his ghostly perambulations.

Haunted Fort

On the banks of the Delaware River, next to Philadelphia International Airport, stands Fort Mifflin, where American revolutionaries made a brave stand during the darkest period of the War of Independence. For six weeks in the fall of 1777, the British bombarded the fort and demoralized the American contingent. At one point, the Redcoats delivered up to 1,000 cannonballs a day.

"I endured hardships sufficient to kill half a dozen horses," Pvt. Joseph Plumb Martin of the Continental Army wrote, "our men were cut up like cornstalks." Four hundred revolutionaries – an estimated 70 percent of the garrison – died in the ordeal.

Perhaps it is one of those young American soldiers whom modern-day visitors to Fort Mifflin have seen hanging about near the artillery shed. Witnesses report spotting a callow, confused-looking soldier with gun in hand awaiting orders that will never come.

Other Mifflin ghosts relate to different periods in the history of the fort, which later served as a Civil War prison. One of the most famous is the "screaming woman," a middle-aged female in early 18th-century clothes whom a number of visitors claim to have seen in the officers' quarters. Some people say that she's the ghost of Elizabeth Pratt and that she screams out of a terrible sadness. Pratt's estranged daughter died of dysentery before they could be reconciled. Distraught, Elizabeth committed suicide shortly thereafter, and she still weeps, eternally desperate and unable to make amends.

Other visitors have spotted the ghost of a man lighting oil lamps in the barracks. A medium who went through the fort claimed the ghost was a lamplighter named Joseph Adkins. Several other ghosts reputedly haunt the casemates, including a shadowy figure that sits in a corner sewing, sometimes revealing, as he turns to look at visitors, the complete lack of a face beneath his crumpled hat.

Phantom inmates may still wander the decaying halls of Eastern State Penitentiary (opposite).

Fort Mifflin (left and below) was active during the American Revolution and Civil War, and its specters hail from both periods.

TRAVEL TIPS

DETAILS

When to Go

Prime visiting conditions exist in spring and fall, when weather is usually sunny and cool. Winters are cold, though seldom drop below 23°F. Expect hot, sticky weather from June to September. July's average temperature is 78°.

Getting There

Philadelphia International Airport, 215-492-3181, is located seven miles southwest of the city. SEPTA Airport Line, 215-580-7800, offers express rail service to downtown. Amtrak trains arrive at 30th Street Station, 215-824-1600, at 30th and Market Streets.

Getting Around

For bus, subway and streetcar information, call SEPTA, 215-580-7800. Taxis are available just about everywhere.

INFORMATION

Philadelphia Convention and Visitors Bureau

1515 Market Street, Suite 2020; Philadelphia, PA 19102; tel: 800-537-7676 or 215-636-1666.

HAUNTED PLACES

American Philosophical Society

105 South 5th Street; Philadelphia, PA 19106; tel: 215-440-3400.

The ghost of Benjamin Franklin was sighted here in 1884 and may still be hanging around. The society's library is open to the public.

Betsy Ross House

239 Arch Street; Philadelphia, PA 19106; tel: 215-627-5343.

Our nation's First Seamstress, buried at this site, may also have lived here. Her spirit has been seen crying at the foot of her bed. Sounds emanating from the basement may belong to the deceased founder of the Betsy Ross Memorial Association or to a gift shop employee who was shot to death here.

Carpenters' Hall

320 Chestnut Street; Philadelphia, PA 19106; tel: 215-925-0167.

The first Continental Congress met here in 1774, but what now congregates here has many people guessing. All manner of odd sounds and smells add to the mystery, as do unaccountable footprints in the dust.

Eastern State Penitentiary Historic Site

2125 Fairmount Avenue; Philadelphia, PA 19130; tel: 215-236-3300.

The spirits of former guards and inmates may haunt the gloomy cells of the nation's first penitentiary. Call ahead for tour schedule.

Fort Mifflin

Fort Mifflin Road; Philadelphia, PA 19153; tel: 215-492-1881 or 215-685-4192.

The ghost of a young Continental soldier has been seen near the artillery shed. The fort also harbors ghosts of the Civil War period, when it held Confederate prisoners of war.

Independence Hall

National Park Service, 3rd and Chestnut Streets; Philadelphia, PA 19106; tel: 215-627-1776.

Though Independence Hall is the birthplace of American freedom, some spirits seem trapped in this building. Park officials have described the sounds of ghosts heard wandering the clock tower. At least one specter, garbed in 18th-century attire, has been spotted.

Moshulu

735 Columbus Boulevard; Philadelphia, PA 19147; tel: 215-923-2500.

A cargo ship during her years on the high seas (1904-1940), the *Moshulu* now houses a floating restaurant. Twenty-eight crewmen were lost at sea over the years, and reports of strange noises and lanterns that ignite spontaneously may be the work of their ghosts.

Pennsylvania Hospital

800 Spruce Street; Philadelphia, PA 19106; tel: 215-829-3971.

The statue of William Penn, founder of the city, reportedly leaves its pedestal from time to time in the lovely garden behind the hospital.

Powel House

244 South 3rd Street; Philadelphia, PA 19106; tel: 215-627-0364.

This popular Society Hill tourist stop is popular among ghosts, too. Historian Edwin Courant Moore claimed to have seen the spirit of Lafayette here in 1965. Moore's wife reported an encounter with the ghost of a young lady in the drawing room.

LODGING

PRICE GUIDE – double occupancy

$ = up to $49	$$ = $50–$99
$$$ = $100–$149	$$$$ = $150+

Black Bass Hotel

3774 River Road (Route 32); Lumberville, PA 18933; tel: 215-297-5815.

This hotel and restaurant, in operation since the 1740s, is located on the Delaware River about 90 minutes from center city Philadelphia. The apparition of an 18th-century boatman has been seen several times in the cellar. Upstairs, the hotel bears tribute to its Loyalist past, with English antiques and portraits of Kings Charles I and II and James II. Grover Cleveland enjoyed lodging here during fishing expeditions. The inn has nine antique-filled guest rooms, including two suites with private baths. $$–$$$$

Logan Inn

10 West Ferry Street; New Hope, PA 18938; tel: 215-862-2300.

Built in 1722 by a ferryman and expanded several times in the 19th century, the Logan is set in a historic village on the Delaware River north of Philadelphia. Those hungry for a good haunting will want to check out Room 6, where an apparition is alleged not only to appear but to introduce a not-so-subtle fragrance of lavender. Elsewhere, the combination inn and restaurant is said to entertain the ghost of a Revolutionary War soldier. Other ghost stories abound at the Logan, whose 16 guest rooms, each with private bath, are furnished in a simple but attractive early-American style. Several have four-poster canopy beds. $$–$$$

Rexmont Inn

299 Rexmont Road, P.O. Box 127; Rexmont, PA 17085; tel: 717-274-2669 or 800-626-0942.

It's said that a ghost roams this romantic 19th-century inn set in Pennsylvania Dutch Country outside Philadelphia. Some folks believe the ghost is the long-dead niece of the original owner, Cyrus Rex, a wealthy banker and entrepreneur, although one psychic says it's Cyrus himself indulging in a bit of transvestism. Along with cross-dressing ghosts, the inn offers seven handsome guest rooms furnished in a plush but understated period style. $$–$$$

TOURS

Philadelphia Ghost Tour

5th and Chestnut Streets; P.O. Box 53713; Philadelphia, PA 19105; tel: 215-413-1997.

A walking tour of Old City and Society Hill explores the haunting tales behind these historic neighborhoods. May through October.

Excursions

Cape May

Chamber of Commerce of Greater Cape May; P.O. Box 556; 513 Washington Street Mall; Cape May, NJ 08204; tel: 609-884-5508.

"Cape May looks haunted," wrote Charles J. Adams III of this Victorian-era seaside village in New Jersey. Visitors can lodge with ghosts, museum with ghosts, even beach with ghosts. Haunted accommodations include the Queens Hotel, and the Washington and Winward House Inns. The latter's Wicker Room, located on the third floor, has witnessed several ghostly encounters with an only partially departed Irish maid. The rugged dunes of Higbee Beach are visited by two ghosts – Old Man Higbee and his elderly slave.

Lancaster

Pennsylvania Dutch Convention and Visitors Bureau; 501 Greenfield Road; Lancaster, PA 17601; tel: 800-723-8824 or 717-299-8901.

A white phantom has hovered for many years above the seats and stage of the Fulton Opera House. Built in 1852, the theater's upper balcony continues to chill some technicians, who avoid working there alone. A "ghost light" has reportedly been placed off-stage to deter spirit activity. Lancaster Cemetery may have need of such a light. There, a statue of a lovely young woman allegedly strolls the grounds, as does her ghost. So forbidding was Rock Ford, a Georgian mansion built in 1793, that vagrants refused free lodging there. Now a museum, the house is haunted by the first owner's son, who committed suicide within its walls.

New Hope

New Hope Information Center; 1 West Mechanic Street; New Hope, PA 18938; tel: 215-862-5880.

Just as this tony river town was once a noted artists' colony, so is it now a popular ghosts' colony. Sometimes the artist becomes the ghost, as is the case with Joseph Pickett. The famous painter died in 1918, but his apparition occasionally manifests itself in his former studio and sometimes roams the towpath of the Delaware Canal. Little wonder that the ghost of a Revolutionary War soldier is said to haunt the Logan Inn: Soldiers' corpses were kept in its cellar during the bitter winter of 1776–77 until the ground thawed.

Washington
District of Columbia

CHAPTER **10**

f you're going ghost-hunting in the nation's capital, by all means stop in at the White House. Lots of action there. Presidents, first ladies, staffers, visitors – all categories seem to include somebody who has bumped up against a "no-body." Literally.   ◆   Why such hyped-up spectral activity? Perhaps it has something to do with all the momentous, life-or-death decisions taken there, by all sorts of characters in larger-than-life dramas. Here, for example, Abraham Lincoln brooded in 1864, during a particularly divisive election campaign conducted against the backdrop of a war grown horrifying beyond imagination. As historian James M. McPherson observed, the experience made the Great Emancipator's life a living hell and deepened his sad countenance. It's a place that tries men's souls. And, apparently, some souls are reluctant to leave.   ◆   Among the first to sense the presence of ghosts was President Lincoln's wife. Mary Todd

Washington closets, some say, are full of skeletons– and some of those closets are in rooms full of ghosts.

Lincoln told her friends that she heard stomping and swearing in the **Rose Room**, an upstairs suite; she was certain the voice belonged to Old Hickory himself, Andrew Jackson. He'd died two decades earlier in Nashville, but the boisterous spirit of that particular chief executive apparently lingered on in his favorite party room.   ◆   Years later, Lillian Rogers Parks, a member of the domestic staff, had a sudden fright in the Rose Room. In her 1961 book, *My 30 Years Backstairs at the White House*, she tells how she felt a cold draft behind her as she sat hemming a bedspread in preparation for a visit from Queen Elizabeth II. She sensed that someone was looking down at her, then she felt a hand on the back of her chair.

The White House may be home to more than one president. Some say Abraham Lincoln and Andrew Jackson still reside there.

Without turning, she ran from the Rose Room and refused to return alone.

Perhaps the most abiding presence in the White House is Lincoln himself. Many people, including President Theodore Roosevelt, have mentioned seeing a tall, gaunt figure retreating quietly down a hall or crossing a distant room. Even people looking in from the sidewalk have noticed a shadow of Lincoln's dimensions at the center window of the Oval Office, where Honest Abe spent many days during the Civil War peering southward across the Potomac River.

President Calvin Coolidge's wife, Grace, said that she once glimpsed Lincoln in black, "with a stole draped across his shoulders" to ward off the cold. Another first lady, Eleanor Roosevelt, acknowledged only that she sensed Lincoln's "presence." But she said that a secretary on her staff had a more tangible encounter. Walking past the Lincoln bedroom one day, the secretary saw a tall man pulling on boots.

Terrified, she screamed and ran downstairs. She need not have been afraid. A dozen visitors, including Queen Wilhelmina of the Netherlands, have reported meeting Lincoln's shade at the White House. None suffered any harm.

The Octagon House

The White House is doubtless the most famous haunted house in Washington – or in all of America, for that matter – but it's hardly the only dwelling in the nation's capital where shades are said to walk. There are many, and their ghosts are often associated with tragedy. One incident involved the **Octagon House**.

The burning of the White House by British soldiers during the War of 1812 forced its occupants, James and Dolley Madison, to find new lodgings while the place was being rebuilt. They accepted an offer from Colonel George Tayloe, a Virginia friend of George Washington, and moved into Tayloe's elegant brick home two blocks west on New York Avenue. Known as the Octagon House, it was one of the few buildings to survive the British attack; it had been protected as the official residence of the French ambassador, who had rented it. Over the years, the house has sheltered

not only a diplomat and a president, but the spirits of two desperate women.

Desperate Daughters

Tragedy struck the Tayloe family before the War of 1812. One of the colonel's daughters had fallen in love with a British officer, but Tayloe had denied permission for a marriage. After an argument one night, the daughter stormed up the spiral staircase that rises to the top of the house. She never reached her room. Whether she threw herself down or slipped is not known, but the family heard her scream. She fell through the stairwell to the floor below, where she died.

One can understand why the colonel wanted to relocate for a time. What's remarkable, though, is that he decided to return to the Octagon House after the Madisons left. More remark-

able, a second Tayloe daughter died in the same place, in similar circumstances, after the war. Like her sister, she clashed with her father over marriage, but this sibling ignored her father's wishes and eloped. According to legend, she was pleading with him for forgiveness when she slipped on the infamous stairs, fell, and broke her neck. The colonel himself died not long after, and the house passed out of the Tayloes' hands in the 1850s.

For more than a century, tenants and visitors have reported strange moans, rattles,

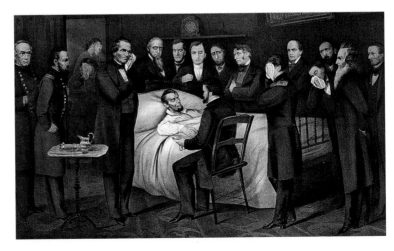

Old Hickory, Andrew Jackson (opposite, top), was heard cursing in the Rose Room long after his death in 1845.

The Octagon House (left) has another geometric distinction: a spiral staircase on which two sisters died.

Lincoln's death bed (right), as depicted by Currier & Ives.

The Exorcist Steps

At the west end of Georgetown a block beyond Key Bridge, an open stairway rises steeply from M Street to the houses perched on Prospect Street high above. In spring, members of rowing teams come here to race up the steps, building stamina for the season. But many people associate these steps with something more dreadful than wind sprints. They remember them as the instrument of murder in *The Exorcist*, William Blatty's novel about demonic possession published in 1971, followed two years later by a movie version filmed in Georgetown.

The steps make their first appearance in the story when Chris MacNeil, actor and mother of a troubled young girl named Regan, comes out the door of her house on Prospect Street. She looks to the right, glancing down a "precipitous plunge of old stone steps." As the plot develops, her daughter Regan is transformed from innocent schoolgirl to foul-mouthed fiend. Regan snarls and lashes out at everyone who offers help. And in a moment of violent abandon (off camera), Regan propels her mother's boss out the window. He is found dead at the foot of the old steps, his head rotated 180 degrees. After a grueling ordeal of her own, Regan is freed of the demon that possesses her, but only because it leaps into the body of the Jesuit priest, Father Damien Karras, who then takes a tumble down the same steps.

Blatty's story is based on a real case, as recounted by journalist Thomas Allen in his 1993 book, *Possessed: The True Story of an Exorcism*. The original incident involved a 13-year-old boy; it occurred in 1949 in Mount Rainier, Maryland, about 40 minutes' drive from Georgetown, and it caused no deaths. But the demon in Mount Rainier was quite intimidating. After the boy's family moved out of their house, the building could not be sold and ultimately had to be torn down. The family took the child to St. Louis, where, according to Allen, a team of Roman Catholic priests successfully exorcised a demon. This made such an impression on members of the family, who were Lutheran, that they all converted to Roman Catholicism.

and sights in the Octagon House, now owned by the American Institute of Architects. Some said they saw a frail woman holding a lighted candle making her way slowly up the spiral steps. No one has gotten close enough to learn which of the two doomed sisters she is.

Decatur's Duel

Directly north of the White House is Lafayette Square, named for the French marquis who poured his energy and wealth into the American Revolution. Formerly known as President's Square, it was the heart of the capital's social scene in the 1800s. It was also the locale of violent confrontations, and two men who died there continue to haunt its houses and tree-lined pathways.

One prominent resident who died in the Square was Stephen Decatur, the naval hero honored for his valor in sea battles with Britain. Decatur lived in a brick house designed by architect Benjamin Latrobe, one

of the oldest structures in the neighborhood.

Decatur's success in the Navy brought him grief as well as honor, however, for he was asked to sit in judgment on a hot-headed fellow officer, Commodore James Barron. The Navy accused Barron of allowing the British to board and remove four sailors from his ship, the *Chesapeake*. Decatur and other members of the jury found Barron guilty, and he was stripped of command. In his disgrace, Barron turned on Decatur in the following months, repeatedly challenging him to fight. Decatur brushed aside the insults for a time but finally agreed to a duel.

Rising early on March 20, 1820, Decatur faced Barron at the edge of town, in Bladensburg, Maryland. Barron was hit in the hip and survived. Decatur, struck in the side, was carried home to his family in mortal agony. He died in his house on Lafayette Square.

For decades afterward, people reported seeing a gentleman of military appearance gazing out of the old house. Some of its windows have since been bricked over, but Decatur still is said to lurk behind them, even venturing out from time to time to visit the Square. Many history-minded visitors, in turn, make the **Decatur House** a stopping point on their capital peregrinations.

The Phantom Philanderer

More shocking to society than the Barron-Decatur duel was the murder of Philip Barton Key, who also met his death in Lafayette Square. Key was the son of Francis Scott Key, author of "The Star-Spangled Banner." The younger Key, a ladies' man who was handsome and well-connected, was a frequent guest at parties in the capital. At one event, he met and fell in love with Theresa Sickles, wife of Congressman Daniel Sickles of New York and a resident of a house on Lafayette Square.

A journalist of the time reported that Key used to stroll on the sidewalk waving a handkerchief as a signal to Theresa to come out for a tryst. This arrangement ended abruptly when the congressman received an anonymous note informing him of his wife's infidelity. Sickles put a halt to the meetings, but one week later, as he looked out the window, he saw Key once again waving a handkerchief. Enraged, Sickles waited for Key to appear in the Square, then charged him with pistols drawn. Firing at point-blank range, Sickles struck Key in the chest. As Key backed away pleading for mercy, Sickles fired again, killing him.

The congressman was tried and acquitted of murder on grounds that he had suffered

Beyond Hope

Before she owned the Hope Diamond, mining heiress Evalyn Walsh McLean lived in an ornate mansion at 2020 Massachusetts Avenue. This building, now housing the **Indonesian Embassy**, was McLean's first East Coast address, a home where she spent many happy days.

Alas, her life changed for the worse after she married *Washington Post* owner Edward McLean and acquired the famous gem. Perhaps to revisit the place where her life reached its zenith, a female spirit believed to be Evalyn McLean turns up now and then at the old Massachusetts Avenue house, roaming halls and stairs.

Evalyn was not ignorant of the dark stories that shrouded the famous diamond before she bought it; she was simply unimpressed. In 1922, she acquired the icy-blue gem from a Turkish nobleman who had recently lost his title and his wealth. According to legend, the Turk had received the diamond from a dealer who died in a car accident shortly after making the delivery. The gem's former owners included a London banker named Henry Thomas Hope, who gave the stone its name, and members of the Russian and French nobility, many of whom were executed by revolutionaries. Originally, it is said to have been the eye in a statue of an Indian god.

Knowing some of these stories, Evalyn McLean reportedly had a priest bless the diamond before she wore it. But she did not forestall tragedy. Although Evalyn and Edward McLean employed a large staff, they were not able to protect their nine-year-old son, Vinson, from a freak automobile accident. Not long aferwards, the McLeans became embroiled in a bitter divorce, and in 1933 Evalyn persuaded the court to commit her husband to an asylum.

Edward died in 1941 of a heart attack. In 1946, their only daughter, Evalyn Reynolds, died of an overdose of sleeping pills. Mrs. McLean outlived her daughter by just one year. Upon her death, the jewel broker Harry Winston of New York acquired the Hope Diamond and prudently sent it to the Smithsonian Institution on "permanent" loan.

Evalyn McLean is gone, but she seems to have lost none of her glamor. Witnesses say the female figure that glides down the great staircase at 2020 Massachusetts Avenue appears in the nude.

Evalyn Walsh McLean (above) wearing the Hope Diamond; ill fortune is said to have befallen the gem's many previous owners.

Daniel Sickles (opposite, top) was acquitted of the murder of his wife's lover, Philip Barton Key, whose ghost still wanders Lafayette Square.

Halcyon House (opposite, below) was built and may still be occupied by Benjamin Stoddert, America's first Secretary of the Navy.

a "temporary aberration of the mind," the first successful use of that defense. He separated from Theresa, who died not long afterward. Key was buried but doesn't seem to have rested in peace. Scores of witnesses over the years have reported seeing his ghost striding the sidewalks near Lafayette Square, perhaps still searching for his mistress.

The House on Prospect Street

Another of the city's old, elegant neighborhoods is **Georgetown**, a working port long before the District of Columbia became the nation's capital. Its venerable mansions hold many secrets. One ancient house on Prospect Street close to **Georgetown University** was built by Benjamin Stoddert, America's first secretary of the navy. Its name, **Halcyon House**, is deceptive; some tenants have said that the nights they spent there were anything but serene. The site appears to be visited regularly by two spirits – one stout and sedentary, the other tall, thin, and cloaked in black.

Stoddert was a shipping merchant, and he designed this pre-1800 house so that the front overlooked the water traffic on the Potomac River. In later years, after his retirement from the U.S. Navy, Stoddert grew sickly and his shipping business failed. He spent his final days in an upstairs room, silently gazing toward the water, awaiting his end. He died in poverty, and the house was sold.

After several generations, Halcyon House came into the hands of an eccentric named Albert Clemons. He erected a new facade in the 1930s and carved the interior into rental apartments. Obsessed with religion and death, Clemons added stained-glass windows, a giant crucifix made from a tree, and a burial crypt. He refused to install electricity – an inconvenience for tenants. With morbid concern about his own burial, he requested in his will that at his demise, "the attending physician shall thereafter pierce or puncture my heart sufficiently for the purpose of absolute certainty of death." Clemons died in 1938, but some tenants of the house suspect that he may not have departed.

For decades, Halcyon House has been plagued by strange sights and sounds. One early newspaper account noted that servants complained of a rattling in the walls – like the sound of a branch blown by the wind

against the house – even though no trees were close enough to touch. A widow who lived there reported that for many years she'd heard muffled footsteps or slippered feet in the hallway. Another tenant told how she'd come home to the locked house to discover that her large engraving had been removed from the wall. She put it back, only to find it removed a second time. In its place was a large black "X." She moved out.

A few tenants have reported seeing supernatural visitors in Halcyon House. One is "balding, fat, short – an older person wearing a tan suit." This spirit, matching the image of Stoddert, often appeared in the front drawing room, seated in a captain's chair, looking out the window. The second intruder has been described as tall and dark, a doppelganger of Clemons. It may be responsible for the electrical problems. One woman who lived in Halcyon House calmly told a reporter in 1963 that the "lights go out, but we just turn them on again."

TRAVEL TIPS

DETAILS

When to Go

Spring and fall offer the best visiting conditions, with lots of sun and temperatures in the 60s and 70s. Summer is usually hot and muggy, with temperatures in the 80s and 90s. Winter is often raw, with occasional snowfall and ice storms, and daytime temperatures frequently below freezing.

How to Get There

Three airports service the District of Columbia: Reagan National, 4 miles south of the city; Dulles International, 26 miles west; and Baltimore-Washington International, 32 miles northeast. For bus transportation between airports and the city, call the Washington Flyer, 703-685-1400, or Airport Connection, 800-284-6066 or 310-441-2345. Amtrak trains, 800-872-7245, service Union Station.

Getting Around

For information on Metrobus and Metrorail public transportation throughout the city, call 202-637-7000. Taxis are available just about everywhere. Car rentals are available at the airports.

INFORMATION

Washington Convention and Visitors Association

Department of Commerce Building, 1st Floor, 1450 Pennsylvania Avenue NW; Washington, D.C. 20005; tel: 202-789-7000.

HAUNTED PLACES

Decatur House

National Trust for Historic Preservation, 748 Jackson Place NW; Washington, DC 20006; tel: 202-842-0920.

Look into the windows of this early 19th-century house and you may see the ghost of Commodore Stephen Decatur. The naval hero, who died in the brick townhouse following a duel, is regularly seen gazing out at Lafayette Square.

Halcyon House

3400 Prospect Street NW; Washington, D.C.

Benjamin Stoddert, the first secretary of the navy, built and named this house, which he reputedly haunts. The morbid vagaries of a later owner, Albert Clemons, may account for ongoing spirit activity. Clemons added a burial crypt to the house and left instructions to have his heart punctured after he died – a request that went unheeded. Halcyon House is now an apartment facility; please do not disturb its tenants.

Indonesian Embassy

2020 Massachusetts Avenue; Washington, D.C.

Diamonds are a girl's best friend? Maybe not. The Indonesian Embassy is the former home of Evalyn Walsh McLean, owner of the prized Hope Diamond. Upon receipt of the supposedly cursed jewel, a string of misfortunes befell this woman, now thought to haunt the staircase in a state of undress.

Octagon House

1799 New York Avenue NW; Washington, D.C. 20006; tel: 202-638-3221.

This octagonal brick house, briefly occupied by James and Dolley Madison, features a spiral staircase of grim note. Separate tragedies on this staircase claimed the lives of two sisters, and ghost activity has continued here for more than a century.

White House

1600 Pennsylvania Avenue NW; Washington, D.C. 20006; tel: 202-456-2121.

Hauntings have been reported here since President Lincoln's wife, Mary Todd Lincoln, claimed to have encountered the ghost of Andrew Jackson. Lincoln himself has been seen in the White House by both insiders and onlookers from the outside. Other ghosts include Abigail Adams and William Henry Harrison.

LODGING

PRICE GUIDE – double occupancy

$ = up to $49 $$ = $50-$99

$$$ = $100-$149 $$$$ = $150+

Hay-Adams Hotel

1 Lafayette Square NW; Washington, D.C. 20006; tel: 202-638-6600.

Here lived the famous Harvard historian and pessimist Henry Adams. Following the suicide in 1885 of his beloved wife – whom he found slouched before the fireplace – a devastated Adams erected a strange statue above her grave and specified that it be "unfathomable." The ghost of Marian, his wife, evidently disliked the absence of her name both on her tombstone and in his auto-biography, and she makes regular visits to remind us of the fact. She has been seen rocking in her former room, staring into the eyes of those who happen upon her. A chill is sometimes felt before the fireplace where her body was found. This mammoth stone house has 143 rooms, each with private bath. Amenities include a restaurant, health club, and afternoon tea. $$$$

Kent Manor Inn

500 Kent Manor Drive; Stevensville, MD 21666; tel: 410-643-5757.

This elaborate mansion, built in the 1820s, sits on a 226-acre

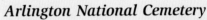

estate. It has 24 rooms of varied size, each with private bath and Victorian antiques, four with fireplace. The original owner, Alexander Thompson, reportedly died in Room 209. Thompson isn't shy about making new appearances: he enjoys moving furniture, turning on lights, and pulling hair. A restaurant, pool, paddle boats, and bicycles are available. $$$–$$$$

Old Town Inn

9503 Main Street; Manassas, VA 20110; tel: 888-869-6446 or 703-368-9191.

A fairly new hotel, this two-story brick building in historic Manassas has 56 large guest rooms with private baths, refrigerators, and microwaves. A ghost, "Miss Lucy," whose picture hangs in the lobby, strolls around, sometimes keeping a watchful eye on guests, sometimes playing pranks – unplugging appliances, messing up beds, or turning on water faucets. One couple felt a heavy presence during the night, just before the husband fell or was pushed out of bed. A restaurant and swimming pool are on the premises. $–$$

TOURS

The Curse of Lafayette Square

Mino Publications; 9009 Paddock Lane; Potomac, MD 20854; tel: 301-294-9514.

This walking tour investigates Lafayette Square, many of whose former residents were struck by a fatal curse. Their ghosts sometimes haunt the neighborhood, especially on the anniversary of their violent deaths.

Lantern Light Ghost Tour

Doorways to Old Virginia; P.O. Box 20485; Alexandria, VA 22320; tel: 703-548-0100.

A guide in colonial garb leads guests by lantern light, sharing bizarre and ghoulish tales. The tour ends in a graveyard.

Excursions

Baltimore Poe House and Museum

203 Amity Street; Baltimore, MD 21223; tel: 410-396-4866.

Edgar Allan Poe drank himself to death in Baltimore. His macabre fancies are, it seems, reflected here by various hauntings in both his former house and his burial site, Westminster Churchyard. A rotund, gray-haired female spirit reportedly occupies the house, where the writer lived from 1832 to 1835, and where strange voices and a mysterious shoulder-pressing finger are but two alleged oddities. Poe himself may account for these occurrences: Local gangs avoid the house, claiming that the ghost of "Mr. Eddie" protects it. Meanwhile, a phantom visitor has been known to leave red roses and a bottle of cognac at Poe's grave.

Arlington National Cemetery

Fort Meyer, VA 22211; tel: 703-545-6700.

Virginians are known for their keen sense of place and tradition. It's not surprising, therefore, that some of the former residents of Arlington Mansion may have returned to haunt their old abode, which was confiscated by the Federals during the Civil War. Robert E. Lee is the most notable of this elegant mansion's spirits. Guests and park employees report many oddities, including a spectral cat, queer footfalls, and the wraith-like sounds of playing children. The nearby grave of Robert F. Kennedy may be visited by the former attorney general and presidential hopeful. Pop singer Bobby Darin once claimed, with great conviction, that RFK's spirit issued him a graveside "emotional cleansing."

Old Stone House Museum

3051 M Street NW; Washington, D.C. 20007; tel: 202-426-6851.

Eleven ghosts roam the halls of this house, once a bordello, now a museum. One spirit, a misogynist named George, allegedly strangled, knifed, even raped women in a third-floor bedroom. Other ghosts roam the streets of Georgetown, including those of Gen. Edward Braddock and his troops, who were ambushed and killed during the French and Indian War and whose spectral marching has long been heard in the neighborhood. Once, during the Civil War, a Union patrol confused the sound of this ghostly regiment with that of a Confederate advance.

Williamsburg

Virginia

CHAPTER 11

ovely Williamsburg is a town not so much frozen in time as purposefully arrested in it, a village preserved in the amber of determined restoration.
Some of the townsfolk who traverse its oyster-shell, cobblestone, and brick
sidewalks often dress in garb appropriate to the era from 1699 to 1780
when this was the capital of colonial Virginia. Some live in grand, brick
homes built in Georgian or Queen Anne style, others in charming wooden
cottages painted in muted blues, greens, or grays. Sheep graze in a fenced
meadow within the town's confines, and muscular dray horses pull
wagons through its streets in the summertime. ◆ Williamsburg was
intact but largely dilapidated in the 1920s when ultrarich John D.
Rockefeller bought the old part of the town and set about restoring it,
refurbishing more than 500 buildings and **Things don't change much
in historic Williamsburg, not
for the living – or the dead.**
landscaping 90 acres of greens and
gardens. Ever since then, tourists have
marveled at the impeccable 18th-century oasis impervious to intrusions by
the mechanized modern world. The people of Williamsburg like the
changelessness of the place. So do its ghosts. ◆ No one can say just
when stories began to circulate about the **Peyton Randolph House**, one of
the oldest homes in Williamsburg. But certainly they began before this
century, possibly as far back as the mid-1800s. ◆ The house,
which is at the corner of **Nicholson and North England Streets**, a block
east of the central Palace Green, was built about 1715 by John Randolph.
Williamsburg had by then replaced Jamestown as the capital of Britain's
Virginia colony. And Randolph, a renowned lawyer, became clerk of the
lawmaking House of Burgesses, which met a short distance down **Gloucester**

The Governor's Palace, built in
1714, illustrates the abiding allure of
Williamsburg, Virginia, home to some
of the country's oldest ghosts.

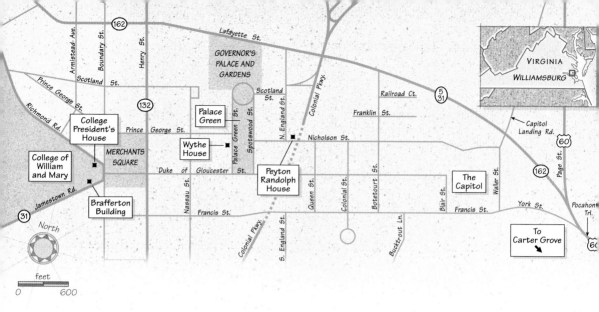

Street in the **Capitol**. For his distinguished service to the Crown, Randolph became the first Virginia-born colonist knighted by the king and was given the title Sir John. On Randolph's death, the house passed to his son, Peyton, who in 1774 was chosen by his revolutionary peers to be the first president of the Continental Congress.

The Peyton Randolph House has had many important guests, particularly in its early days when such military leaders as George Washington and the Marquis de Lafayette dined here. But it's also been home to tragedy. A child of the Peachy family, who lived here before the Civil War, fell from a tree and died. Other tenants met untimely deaths in later years. One despondent gentleman, it's said, shot himself while seated by the fireplace, and a young ex-Confederate soldier who had enrolled at the College of William and Mary expired in one of the rooms after contracting tuberculosis. There have also been several

suicides. Misfortune has hovered over the property like a cloud.

On occasion, people have heard heavy footsteps and spurs jangling at night across the second-story floorboards, possibly sounds made by the shade of one of the Virginia military men who stayed in the house. One latter-day tour guide witnessed a man in 18th-century clothing seated in a downstairs room. He vanished as she approached.

Several guests have met a mysterious old woman who seems to frequent an oak-paneled bedroom on the second floor. Her appearance was described in 1962 by Helen Hall Mason, who had stayed in the bedroom that had once belonged to Peyton Randolph. She awoke after midnight to find an old woman dressed in a long gown standing at the foot of the bed apparently summoning her. When Mrs. Mason asked the agitated figure what the matter was, the old woman remained silent. Then she withdrew.

The next day, Mrs. Mason was astonished to learn that she was not the first to experience this vision. For more than a century, her friends said, visitors to the house have spoken of seeing a hand-wringing old woman. But no one has discovered who she is or what message she wants to deliver.

After the Governor's Ball

Events that evoke deep passions – even if they remain hidden – often have consequences that last beyond the moment; sometimes they send out ripples that are felt decades later. Such is the case with a small incident that took place more than 200 years ago on Williamsburg's **Palace Green**.

It was here, one block west of the Peyton Randolph House, that a young woman in the 1770s named Lady Ann Skipwith ran seeking refuge from the grand ball then under way at the governor's mansion. Dressed in a satin gown and red, high-heeled slippers, she ran from the mansion at the top of the Green to a house halfway down its western edge, the home of George Wythe. What she hoped to escape remains a mystery. But many believe that Lady Ann – who had recently married a wealthy planter named Peyton Skipwith – may have been driven by rage and jealousy. A spirited and quick-tempered woman in her thirties, she was said to be a rival of her own sister, Jean, for Sir Peyton's love. Perhaps the two sisters clashed at the governor's ball. What is known is that many years later, after her death, Sir Peyton married that sister.

In her dash across the Green, Lady Ann Skipwith broke the strap on her slipper; she entered the **Wythe House** half-shod and raced up the wooden stairs, clumping like a peg-legged pirate. What she sought inside isn't known; perhaps she was staying the night as a guest. But the impression she made was so intense that a story arose that she had killed herself or been fatally injured on the stairs.

The tale has persisted for two centuries. Many people have reported hearing the alternating click and thump of a half-shod reveler climbing

A tombstone (left) at Bruton Parish Church seems to tell a story – but of doom or hope?

Wythe House (right) is visited by the spirit of a young lady who vied with her maiden sister for her husband's affection.

the stairs of Wythe House at midnight. And one visitor caught a glimpse of a beautifully gowned colonial woman vanishing down a hall. While Lady Ann did not in fact end her life in Williamsburg (she died much later at her home in Mecklenburg County), her spirit may have expired here. Witnesses say she's taken up permanent residence at Wythe House, and guests continue to wake late at night to the sound of uneven footsteps on the stairs – a soft tread followed by the clack of a dancing shoe.

A Soldier in the Attic

If you walk from the Palace Green toward **Merchants Square** and continue westward to the **College of William and Mary**, you come to one of the few buildings in Williamsburg still used for its original purpose: the **college president's house**. The foundations of this Queen Anne brick mansion were laid in 1732, the year George Washington was born. Except for a short period when it was taken over for military use during the American Revolution, it's been occupied without interruption by the president of the college. The years of military tenancy left a bizarre legacy, however. Repairmen working in the 20th century found the remains of a skeleton, possibly a soldier from Revolutionary times, hidden away in the attic. And many residents have

complained of hearing footsteps at night – always in the same area, on the stairs between the second and the third floor.

No one has determined the origin of the bones found in a crawl space above the third-floor ceiling. But L. B. Taylor, Jr., author of *The Ghosts of Williamsburg*, reports that the skeleton was "pressed into a brick wall," suggestive of inhumane treatment. After the skeleton was removed, the wife of the then-college president informed Taylor, it was

possible for the first time in generations to get a balky door on the third floor to stay closed. Before that, it used to open without any apparent cause.

The skeleton wasn't the only vestige of war. The place also seems to host a French soldier from the 18th century, possibly one who lived in the building when it served as a hospital. During the final weeks of the Revolutionary War, as French and American troops sought to out-maneuver the British at nearby Yorktown, General Lafayette used the president's house as a shelter for the wounded. The French were forced to evacuate in 1781 by an accidental fire, whose damage was after-ward repaired in a four-year project financed by France. But the work didn't remove all traces of those who suffered there. For generations, families staying in the house have heard the steps of a French soldier who died in a small back room making his way along a creaky stairway.

The Beat Goes On

The campus of William and Mary may appear pastoral today with its 18th-century brick buildings resting in an expanse of green. But when the college was young, life here was raw. The people of Williamsburg still lived in an uneasy peace with the neighboring American Indians, whom they'd displaced. There were attempts to integrate the two cultures, and one well-intentioned effort has left a vestige of the period: the **Brafferton Building**, just south of the college president's house. For more than two centuries, it's been haunted by the restless souls of Indian boys who were brought here and forcibly educated in the ways of the English settlers.

Brafferton was built in 1723 with a donation from Robert Boyle, a famous British scientist. Boyle had heard of the villagers' attempts to give American Indians a European education, and he wanted to provide a permanent house for the students, who'd been staying in the villagers' homes. Dozens of teenage braves came – many against their will – leaving family and familiar ways behind.

Because they repeatedly tried to escape, they were locked at night in Brafferton House. In this confinement, one group became ill with tuberculosis. Several died.

The experiment ended unhappily in 1736.

The spirits of those who suffered and died still seem to be in residence. According to legend, the ghost of one of the boys runs through the woods near the campus at night. After being confined to Brafferton, this student made a rope ladder and climbed down every night from an upper-story window. Once outside, he ran without stopping until almost sunrise, then collapsed in his room. His nighttime marathon provided a taste of freedom. One morning, however, he didn't make it back. He was found lying in the woods, dead from exhaustion.

Today, some villagers say they can still hear sighs and moans from behind the closed doors of Brafferton on some nights. And one newspaper reporter who lived in the building for a summer recalls hearing phantom footsteps when he was alone on the third floor. He's never forgotten the night when he was awakened suddenly in the wee hours by a strange sound. He realized after a moment that he was hearing the regular beat of an Indian drum. He got out of bed and rushed through the halls, checking rooms all the way down to the first floor. But the house was empty.

Costumed merry-makers (opposite, top) keep alive 18th-century games and traditions.

The campus of William and Mary (left) is haunted by an American Indian boy forced to undergo an English education.

The disgruntled ghost of Carter Grove (right, top) may be that of George Washington (below, left) or Thomas Jefferson (below, right), whose proposals of marriage were supposedly rejected here.

Carter Grove

Every ghost must have its reason for leaving the grave and intruding on the present, and some say that the spirit inhabiting the **Carter Grove** plantation on the James River is motivated by regret.

This ghost has a bizarre way of making its presence felt. People who've left white carnations in a specific room in the main house—a first-floor parlor—return later to find that the flowers have been torn to shreds and scattered all over, as though in anger. Housekeepers have investigated all the usual suspects, such as mice, by setting traps. But the traps remain empty. As a result, the staff has concluded that something or someone else is to blame.

Construction of this plantation house was begun in 1750 by one of the richest men in colonial America, Robert Carter. He died before it was completed, and the property passed to his grandson, Carter Burwell, who finished the mansion and expanded the plantation. At its high point, Carter Grove encompassed 300,000 acres and was worked by 1,000 slaves.

Burwell hired a British artisan to supervise the bricklayers and cabinet-makers, who made the home a masterwork of craftsmanship. One showpiece is the wood-paneled drawing room on the first floor, known as the "Refusal Room." It gets its name from two offers of marriage that supposedly were made here. One involves young George Washington, who is supposed to have offered matrimony to Mary Cary in this room. According to legend, the second suitor was Thomas Jefferson, who proposed to Rebecca Burwell in the same room. Both men were rejected, and neither of the two young women became a president's wife. Some people say that the angry ghost who destroys flowers in the room is one of the famous men whose proposal was rejected; others say the ghost is a lady—regretful and furious, perhaps, at what might have been.

TRAVEL TIPS

DETAILS

When to Go

Events are offered year-round at Colonial Williamsburg. The climate is temperate. Spring and fall are the best seasons to visit, when daytime temperatures are in the high 70s and nighttime temperatures in the high 40s. Summer is hot and humid, with temperatures in the high 80s. Winter temperatures range from the mid-50s to freezing.

How to Get There

Newport News/Williamsburg Airport is 20 minutes away; Richmond International and Norfolk International Airports, 50 minutes away. Shuttles are available at the airports. Amtrak, 800-872-7245, serves Williamsburg directly from Washington, Baltimore, Philadelphia, New York, and Boston.

Getting Around

An automobile is needed to get around the historic triangle of Williamsburg, Jamestown, and Yorktown. Car rentals are available at the airports. Taxis are available in Williamsburg, as is Relax and Ride, a bus service that stops at major attractions. Visitors to Colonial Williamsburg are advised to park at the visitor center and ride a free shuttle to the historic area.

INFORMATION

Colonial Williamsburg

P.O. Box 1776; Williamsburg, VA 23187-1776; tel: 800-447-8679 or 757-229-1000.

Williamsburg Area Convention and Visitors Bureau

P.O. Box 3585; Williamsburg, VA 23187; tel: 757-253-0192.

Williamsburg Hotel and Motel Association

P.O. Box 1515; Williamsburg, VA 23187; tel: 800-899-9462.

Virginia Tourism

901 East Byrd, 19th Floor; Richmond, VA 23219; tel: 804-786-4484.

HAUNTED PLACES

Carter Grove

Route 60, P.O. Box 1776; Williamsburg, VA 23187; tel: 800-447-8679.

In what became known as "the refusal room," two future presidents lost at love. In the mid-18th century, the young Mary Cary is said to have turned down a marriage proposal from George Washington. Years later, in the same room of this stately Georgian mansion, Rebecca Burwell reportedly rejected Thomas Jefferson. Since then, whenever white carnations are left in the room at night, they are found shredded on the floor in the morning.

College of William and Mary

Williamsburg, VA 23185; tel: 757-221-3169.

At least two ghosts seem to occupy the college president's house. Elsewhere on campus, the Brafferton Building is haunted by the spirits of Native American boys constrained to undergo an English education.

Peyton Randolph House

Colonial Williamsburg, P.O. Box 1776; Williamsburg, VA 23187-1776; tel: 800-447-8679 or 757-229-1000.

This early 18th-century house, once the home of a famous father and son, John and Peyton Randolph, later witnessed a number of tragic deaths, now the cause of many hauntings.

Wythe House

Colonial Williamsburg, P.O. Box 1776; Williamsburg, VA 23187-1776; tel: 800-447-8679 or 757-229-1000.

Lady Ann Skipwith, who retreated to the Wythe House after an unsettling experience during an 18th-century ball, is said to haunt the staircase, still climbing the steps wearing only one dancing shoe.

LODGING

Edgewood Plantation

4800 John Tyler Highway; Charles City, VA 23030; tel: 804-829-2480.

Built in 1849, this neo-Gothic bed-and-breakfast offers eight spacious, antique-filled rooms, each with private bath, three with fireplaces, one with Jacuzzi. The most popular room is named for Lizzie Rowland, whose father built the house. Lizzie fell in love with a Confederate soldier, who gave her a diamond ring before going to war. He never returned. Waiting for her beau, Lizzie used the ring to etch her name in the window, a signature still visible. Said to have died of a broken heart, Lizzie was buried in the shadow of a pink marble tombstone. Her ghost makes random returns. A woman, there to book an event, recently saw Lizzie on the staircase, wearing a blue-gray dress. A photographer believes he caught her image gazing out a window. $$$–$$$$

Linden House

P.O. Box 23; Route 17 South; Champlain, VA 22438; tel: 800-622-1202 or 804-443-1170.

This planter's house, built around 1750, sat vacant for 30 years. During restoration in the early 1990s, a mysterious light often appeared, even penetrating through keyholes. A contractor, staying in the Robert E. Lee room, watched his hat lift from the back of a chair and move across the room. Worse, an invisible hand proceeded to unwrap candies in a dish. The light has also been known to assume a flesh-colored form. Strange footsteps and a voice that sounds like a recorded message are regular house oddities. Six guest rooms have private baths, three have fireplaces, one a Jacuzzi and steam room. Rooms are furnished with antiques. Amenities include a gazebo, five porches, and 200 acres of private land. $$–$$$

Williamsburg Inn

136 East Francis Street; Williamsburg, VA 23187; tel: 800-447-8679 or 804-229-1000.

Past guests in this elegant inn include Queen Elizabeth II, Emperor Hirohito, and Franklin D. Roosevelt. Built in 1937, the inn is decorated in Regency style, reflecting the ambiance of a 19th-century English country house. The inn's 235 handsome rooms have private baths. Tennis courts, swimming pools, lawn bowling, croquet, a fitness center, and a gift shop are available. $$$–$$$$

TOURS

Haunted Williamsburg Walking Tour

203 1/2 B Harrison Avenue; Williamsburg, VA 23185; tel: 757-565-0171.

In addition to sharing ghostly tales about Colonial Williamsburg, guides show actual photos of the spirits discussed.

Original Ghosts of Williamsburg

Maximum Guided Tours, 1310 Jamestown Road, 2nd Floor; Williamsburg, VA 23185; tel: 757-253-2094.

Guides lead year-round tours by lantern light through historic Williamsburg, sharing eerie tales and history.

Excursions

Moore House

Yorktown Battlefield; Yorktown, VA 23690; tel: 757-898-3400.

Fresh sheets in the master bedroom have, through the years, been discovered with a deep impression, as if someone slept on them. Legend says that it could be the spirit of Augustine Moore, Jr., who was shot while working the family fields during the American Revolution. He perished several days later in the house. The museum, part of Yorktown Battlefield, is open from April to August.

Scotchtown

Route 2, P.O. Box 168; Beaverdam, VA 23015; tel: 804-227-3500.

Patrick Henry, of "Give me liberty or give me death" renown, moved into this house in 1771. His wife, Sarah Shelton Henry, grew mentally ill shortly thereafter. Kept under lock and key in two basement rooms, she had nothing of the liberty her husband so cherished, but soon gained his rhetorical alternative: death. Her spirit has not, some say, left the basement. Scotchtown, built by Charles Chiswell in 1719, is haunted by another ghost. John Chiswell, son of Charles, reputedly took his life in the house after killing a man in a tavern tussle in 1766. John's body is buried on the premises, and his spirit is said to wander the house.

Sherwood Forest Plantation

Route 5; Charles City, VA 23030; tel: 804-829-5377.

Long before Sherwood Forest was the home of John Tyler, the nation's 10th president, the Greek Revival building housed the Gray Lady. It is thought that this spirit was the governess of a child who died here. Her footsteps have been heard on a hidden stairway, as has the sound of rocking in a second-floor nursery and in what was a first-floor bedroom. For generations, guests and employees have attributed odd happenings to the Gray Lady. The original house, built in 1720 and expanded a number of times, is bordered by many original plantation outbuildings.

Civil War Ghosts

CHAPTER **12**

History's pages are full of rivalries and conflicts of such dimensions that they unleash hateful impulses for generations. They also can spawn a legion of brooding ghosts destined to revisit the violent episodes they suffered in life. This was the case on a grand scale in the American Civil War. ◆ Perhaps the most celebrated spirit to rise from the war is that of John Brown, the wild-eyed extremist intent on causing an insurrection that would bring down the "peculiar institution" of slavery. Already notorious for the murder of five pro-slavery partisans in Kansas, Brown and a handful of followers turned up in October 1859 at Harpers Ferry, Virginia. There they captured a federal armory, issued a call for rebellion, and planned to sweep south at the head of an army of slaves. ◆ It was a quixotic adventure, promptly quashed by a company of U.S. Marines under Col. Robert E. Lee. A marine and a few civilians were killed, and for **Some old soldiers fade** that and other offenses, John Brown was **away only to reappear** hanged. He is, it seems, dead but not gone. Walking **again and again.** the streets of what is now **Harpers Ferry, West Virginia**, these days is a remarkable likeness – tall, gaunt, fierce-looking. Tourists have gone up to the man, remarked on his resemblance to the historical figure, and asked him to pose for a snapshot. Sometimes he obliges, but when the film is developed, there's nothing to be seen. ◆ Brown set off the powder keg, and in 1861 general hostilities commenced. The fighting swiftly took on an intensity little known in modern times. At **Antietam, Maryland**, on September 17, 1862, the bloodiest single day of the war saw 23,000 men killed, wounded, or missing. Of that number, 540 belonged to the thousand-member Irish Brigade from New York. Fighting under a green banner emblazoned with the

Harpers Ferry, West Virginia, is visited by the spirit of militant abolitionist John Brown, whose failed uprising helped move the nation toward civil war.

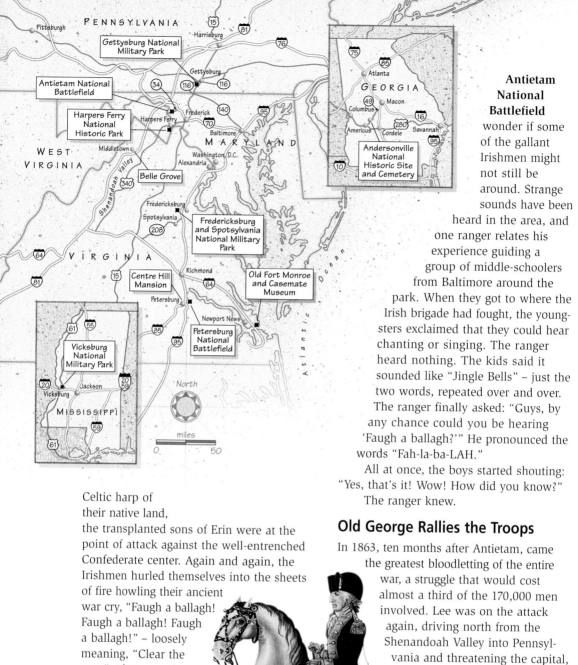

The map shows various Civil War sites:
- Gettysburg National Military Park
- Antietam National Battlefield
- Harpers Ferry National Historic Park
- Belle Grove
- Fredericksburg and Spotsylvania National Military Park
- Centre Hill Mansion
- Old Fort Monroe and Casemate Museum
- Petersburg National Battlefield
- Vicksburg National Military Park
- Andersonville National Historic Site and Cemetery

PENNSYLVANIA — Pittsburgh, Harrisburg, Gettysburg
WEST VIRGINIA — Middletown, Harpers Ferry, Shenandoah Valley
MARYLAND — Frederick, Baltimore, Washington, D.C., Alexandria
VIRGINIA — Fredericksburg, Spotsylvania, Richmond, Petersburg, Newport News
GEORGIA — Atlanta, Macon, Columbus, Americus, Cordele, Savannah
MISSISSIPPI — Vicksburg, Jackson

North

miles
0   50

Celtic harp of
their native land,
the transplanted sons of Erin were at the
point of attack against the well-entrenched
Confederate center. Again and again, the
Irishmen hurled themselves into the sheets
of fire howling their ancient
war cry, "Faugh a ballagh!
Faugh a ballagh! Faugh
a ballagh!" – loosely
meaning, "Clear the
way." After some hours
and frightful casualties, the
Irish Brigade was instrumen-
tal in clearing the way. The
Confederates under Robert
E. Lee retreated across
the Potomac River
to Virginia whence
they had come.
    But the rangers
who manage

Antietam National Battlefield

wonder if some
of the gallant
Irishmen might
not still be
around. Strange
sounds have been
heard in the area, and
one ranger relates his
experience guiding a
group of middle-schoolers
from Baltimore around the
park. When they got to where the
Irish brigade had fought, the youngsters exclaimed that they could hear
chanting or singing. The ranger
heard nothing. The kids said it
sounded like "Jingle Bells" – just the
two words, repeated over and over.
The ranger finally asked: "Guys, by
any chance could you be hearing
'Faugh a ballagh?'" He pronounced the
words "Fah-la-ba-LAH."
    All at once, the boys started shouting:
"Yes, that's it! Wow! How did you know?"
The ranger knew.

Old George Rallies the Troops

In 1863, ten months after Antietam, came
the greatest bloodletting of the entire
war, a struggle that would cost
almost a third of the 170,000 men
involved. Lee was on the attack
again, driving north from the
Shenandoah Valley into Pennsylvania and threatening the capital,

General George Washington (left)
appeared to Union troops
more than 65 years after
his death.

General Warren's statue
(opposite, right) surveys
the ghost-ridden terrain
of Little Round Top at the
Gettysburg Battlefield.

Harrisburg. Union forces met him 40 miles south of the city, outside the small town of **Gettysburg**. The combat raged back and forth for three days. At a critical juncture, the soldiers of the 20th Maine were defending a strategic hill known as Little Round Top. They sensed that to lose **Little Round Top** might just be to lose the battle itself. After two hours, the situation became desperate. As the determined southerners of the 4th Alabama worked their way up the hill, the 20th Maine expended the last of its powder and ball, and the cry went up, "Ammunition! For God's sake, ammunition!"

Then a figure materialized before the men from Maine: an officer on a shining white stallion with his upraised sword aflame. He was garbed in the uniform of the American Revolution, a tricorn on his head. The men, including their general, recognized his face. George Washington had come to lead them. With his sword, the Father of His Country commanded an advance. "Fix bayonets! Charge!" rang out the order. The 20th Maine

John Brown (right) was regarded as a martyr by abolitionists and an insurrectionist by slaveholders.

charged down from Little Round Top to rout the astonished Alabamians. Fortune now favored the Union, and after another day of savage battle, Lee decreed a Confederate retreat and never again invaded the northern states.

Lee's Ongoing Retreat

Those who live in and around Gettysburg maintain that on certain hot summer nights a rider on a splendid white steed, both man and beast enveloped in a luminous haze, can be seen galloping across the battlefield, the stallion's hooves striking sparks wherever they touch.

There is a postscript to Gettysburg. It comes from a number of residents on **Route 116** near the Maryland border. The

event occurs only on the nights of July 4 and 5 and begins with a faint moaning sound, almost like wind in a wall. The moans gradually grow louder. After a few minutes, voices, cries, and creaking noises are heard. The source comes into view: a long, ghostly string of wagons escorted by mounted men in Confederate gray. Here and there, an agonized head or an arm rises above the wagon boards. Then it's gone, as if the last wagon had turned a corner. The sounds continue for another minute or two, until suddenly they cease. The shaken witnesses do not doubt what they have seen: a phantom segment of Lee's army retreating from Gettysburg, carrying the wounded in a convoy of wagons that stretched for 17 miles.

Foes Reconciled in Death

Just as Robert E. Lee had been a U.S. Marine, so hundreds, even thousands of officers facing each other across the battle lines had once been friends and fellow cadets at West Point. In the spring of 1860, George Armstrong Custer, an Ohioan, had organized a grand gala for a chum named Stephen Dodson Ramseur, a North Carolinian graduating in the class ahead of him. Now, in October 1864, Custer was a 24-year-old Union cavalry brigadier zealously laying waste to Virginia's Shenandoah Valley, and Ramseur was a 27-

year-old Confederate major general determined to stop him. Their reunion was bleak and sorrowful.

Leading his troops against the Yankees, Ramseur had two horses shot out from under him and was mounting a third when a bullet smashed into his chest. His division cracked and broke. Ramseur was captured and taken to Union headquarters at **Belle Grove** mansion in **Middletown**, where doctors pronounced his wound mortal; the shot had penetrated both lungs. As word spread, blue-clad classmates hurried to his side: Custer, of course, and Henry du Pont, a captain of artillery, and Wesley Merritt, a cavalry general. They could do nothing but grieve.

A few years ago, a visitor knowing nothing of Belle Grove's history happened into the room where Ramseur had died. The visitor was surprised to see a number of men in blue Civil War uniforms around a bed on which lay a figure in gray. No one said anything, but a palpable sadness pervaded the room. The visitor thought he'd come upon a Method Acting session, but the mansion's manager knew of no such class. A month or so later, the man was in a bookstore idly flipping through a book on the war in the Valley when he turned pale as he looked at photographs of Ramseur and Custer. They were among the men in the room at Belle Grove, the one on the bed and the other sitting beside it. He had witnessed Ramseur's reconciliation and death 130 years after the fact.

The Sound of Music

By March 1865, the long, terrible war was coming to a close. The Shenandoah Valley had been lost, the Union had been victorious in the West, and Lee himself had been stalemated for nine months in the trenches around **Petersburg**, **Virginia**. Yet Lee had one gamble left: If he could break out of Petersburg with his Army of Northern Virginia and join other Confederate forces to the south, he might yet regain the initiative. The focus of the desperate attack was **Fort Stedman** in the center of the Union line.

War Eagle

Were there ever a pecking order among military mascots, Old Abe would stand – or rather perch – at the very top. Abe was a bald eagle, a real one, the living symbol of the United States of America.

Abe started out in life as the nestling pet of a Chippewa chieftain, then went to a trader, and finally found his vocation in April 1861, when he was sold for $5 to Capt. John E. Perkins, commanding Company C of the 8th Wisconsin Infantry Regiment. Perkins immediately named the young bird in honor of President Abraham Lincoln, and the men built a fine red, white, and blue perch for their hefty good-luck charm. That October, when the regiment marched off to war, Old Abe went with it.

The 8th Wisconsin experienced its first real baptism of fire the following May at Farmington, Mississippi. As the shells started exploding, some of the men failed to take cover and remained standing in confusion. Not Abe; he hopped down from his perch and flattened himself on the ground – spread-eagled, you might say. Several times his handler put him back on the perch, but to no avail, so the handler joined him on the ground. A few weeks later, during an assault on Vicksburg, the 8th Wisconsin came under withering canister fire. Old Abe's handler slipped and fell. Undaunted, the powerful bird dragged both him and the perch to safety in a nearby ravine.

The men never regarded Old Abe as gun-shy; it was simply that he had a sense of when discretion becomes the better part of valor. In his 42 battles and skirmishes, he sometimes remained on his perch, beak thrust forward, shrieking defiance at the enemy. On parade, Abe learned to spread his seven-foot wings and salute the national colors with a special scream. He offered the same greeting to high-ranking officers, for which he might be rewarded with a tot of whiskey or brandy.

Not surprisingly, the state of Wisconsin raised a memorial to Old Abe at Vicksburg National Military Park. The six-foot bronze statue is imposing enough by day. But at night under a full moon, especially in late fall and early winter, tourists driving through the park occasionally insist that they have seen Old Abe – or his spirit – rise from the memorial and go swooping and calling through the silvery sky.

The war cry of the Union's Irish Brigade still echoes across Antietam National Battlefield (opposite).

A monument to Old Abe (above) in Vicksburg National Military Park honors the mascot that won the hearts of Wisconsin infantrymen. A bald eagle believed to be the spirit of Old Abe has been seen soaring over his memorial.

But the assault ultimately failed – at a cost of between 4,300 and 5,500 men, some of whose spirits may remain.

Battlefield rangers report that one recent visitor, who had heretofore scoffed at ghost stories, was dumbstruck at the sight of Union troops drawn up for battle on the hills where a vital counterattack had gone in against the Rebels. One moment they were there, he said, and the next they had vanished. Moreover, a former park supervisor who'd lived near the fort frequently had been awak-ened at 5:30 in the morning by the sound of regimental band music coming from the fort. It happened often enough for the supervisor to call the music his "spiritual alarm clock."

Phantom Feet

Petersburg itself was evacuated on April 2, as the weary, ragged, half-starved regiments slipped out of the city under cover of dark-ness. As might be expected, the victorious Union generals had commandeered **Centre Hill**, one of the town's most magnificent

Andersonville

Union soldiers sent to Andersonville, Georgia's infamous Confederate prison, escaped little of the war's misery. In a conflict marked by squalid prison camps, none was so wretched as Andersonville. Indeed, the best that one can say about the prison is that it seems only to have produced seven ghosts.

Andersonville Prison (right), now a national historic site dedicated to all American prisoners of war, was notorious for its horrific conditions. More than 13,000 Union sol-diers are buried at the prison cemetery (below).

The camp's commandant, Capt. Henry Wirz, the only Confederate officer tried for war crimes, was hanged in Washington, D.C., on November 10, 1865. Notwithstanding the fierce hatred of his prisoners, scholars generally regard Wirz's fate as politically motivated, not deserved. The captain had, in fact, attempted to improve conditions in the camp. Fully dishonored by contemporaries, feebly vindicated by posterity, Wirz returns to the place where everything went wrong. His apparition has been seen traversing the camp and lingering over graves in the cemetery.

The prisoners' contempt for their commandant is understandable, if misguided. Nearly 13,000 Yanks, 30 percent of those imprisoned in the camp, died at Andersonville. This grim statistic represents an even grimmer irony: the camp was established in 1864 to provide a better food supply for the prisoners. Starvation and disease, however, seized inmates from the start. The Confederacy, weakened by an ebbing economy, was unable to feed many of its own soldiers, let alone prisoners.

A phantom locomotive spotted outside Albany, New York, is believed to be Lincoln's funeral train (opposite), seen here in an 1865 photograph.

As many as 33,000 inmates were crowded into the 27-acre camp. Makeshift tents offered scant protection from the elements. Human waste mixed with the sole water supply and caused dysentery. Thirsting prisoners, searching for uncontaminated water, ventured over the "dead line" into the forbidden zone and were shot.

Worse yet, prisoners preyed upon one another, stealing clothes, tents, firewood. Groups called "Raiders" not only robbed fellow soldiers but sometimes killed them. Eventually, other inmates fought the Raiders and won. Thereafter, six of the greatest offenders were hanged. Their ghosts return each July 11, the anniversary of their execution. Their eyes pop out in agony, their necks drag ropes pun-gent with rot. – *Michael Castagna*

homes, for their headquarters. But they would not enjoy it – nobody would – on one day of each year. At 7:30 in the evening that January 24, a Union officer was alone in the house when he heard the front door hurled open with a terrific bang. Next came the tramp-tramp-tramp of hundreds of marching feet accompanied by the rattle of weapons. The officer rushed into the hall. It was empty. Still the marching sounds grew until they were loudest right beside him. Tramp-tramp-tramp went the phantom feet, down the stairs, across the vestibule and out the door, which at last slammed shut. The officer ran to a window. Nothing. The street was deserted.

So regular was the procession of Centre Hill's Ghost Brigade that in subsequent years the mansion's owners invited friends and neighbors to behold the phenomenon. But why at precisely 7:30 on January 24? No one knows. The marching feet have quieted now that Centre Hill is city property and open to the public. Perhaps they will resume, and a visitor will come upon the secret one of these days.

Lincoln's Ghostly Train

Neither the date nor the hour are precise, and the happening may not occur every year. But railroad men along a right of way near **Albany**, **New York**, have learned to start looking late at night during the last week in April. When it comes, the train is moving slowly, not more than 20 miles an hour. It is a fine new 1860s Union locomotive emitting puffs of white smoke and pulling nine Pullman cars.

From the cowcatcher all the way to the rear, the locomotive is draped in black; the cars, too, are shrouded in black, with little flags here and there and brightwork gleaming like ribbons of silver. Groups of men, some of them in blue Civil War uniforms, are riding the Pullmans, and in the next to last car they are gathered about a long, narrow object. It is a raised casket, the bier of President Lincoln, who was felled by an assassin's bullet on April 15, 1865. The funeral train is carrying the president and 300 mourners 1,700 miles from Washington, D.C., to Springfield, Illinois.

Abraham Lincoln's phantom funeral train makes no noise, say the witnesses, except for the occasional tolling of the Union's bell. Should it meet a real train, the sound of the real train is suddenly muted. And along the right-of-way, clocks and watches stop as the train passes.

TRAVEL TIPS

DETAILS

When to Go

Winter in the mid-Atlantic region is cold, with average daytime temperatures in the 30s. Summer is hot and humid, with temperatures often rising into the 90s. Spring and fall are pleasant; temperatures are fickle, ranging anywhere from the 40s to the 70s.

How to Get There

Major airports in the region include Dulles International, 26 miles west of Washington, D.C.; Baltimore-Washington International, 32 miles northeast of Washington, D.C.; and Philadelphia International.

Getting Around

Cars are necessary for travel between battlefields and may be rented at the airports. Gettysburg National Military Park, 717-334-1124, offers ranger-led walking tours June through September. Private companies offer a number of walking and bus tours in the park. Petersburg National Battlefield, 804-732-3531, also offers summer walking tours, as well as some bus tours.

INFORMATION

The Gettysburg-Adams County Area Chamber of Commerce

33 York Street; Gettysburg, PA 17325; tel: 717-334-8151.

Gettysburg Travel Council, Inc.

35 Carlisle Street; Gettysburg, PA 17325; tel: 717-334-6274.

Hagerstown/Washington Convention and Visitors Bureau

16 Public Square; Hagerstown, MD 21740; tel: 800-228-7829 or 301-791-3130.

Jefferson County Convention and Visitors Bureau

P.O. Box A; Harpers Ferry, WV 25425; tel: 800-848-8687.

HAUNTED PLACES

Antietam National Battlefield

P.O. Box 158; Sharpsburg, MD 21782; tel: 301-432-5124.

The gallant Irish Brigade from New York lost over 500 men on this battlefield during the bloodiest day of the Civil War. Now their ghosts are said to haunt the park.

Belle Grove Plantation

P.O. Box 137; Middletown, VA 22645; tel: 540-869-2028.

Confederate officer Stephen Dodson Ramseur, fatally wounded by a bullet, reportedly haunts the room where he died. Surrounding the major general are Union officers, his West Point classmates. Also haunting the mansion is the ghost of Hetty Cooley, murdered by a black servant.

Gettysburg National Military Park

97 Taneytown Road; Gettysburg, PA 17325; tel: 717-334-1124.

The ghost of George Washington, who appeared on his white stallion to rally the troops of the 20th Maine during the Gettysburg campaign, still gallops across this battlefield in summer.

Harpers Ferry National Historical Park

P.O. Box 65; Harpers Ferry, WV 25425; tel: 304-535-6298.

This is the site of John Brown's famous raid. The fiery abolitionist sometimes returns, moving gently among pedestrians on the streets of Harpers Ferry.

Petersburg National Battlefield

P.O. Route 36 East, Box 549; Petersburg, VA 23804; tel: 804-732-3531.

Spirits of Union soldiers may haunt the site of a crucial counterattack against Confederate forces. Ghost troops have been seen, regimental band music heard.

LODGING

PRICE GUIDE – double occupancy

$ = up to $49 $$ = $50–$99
$$$ = $100–$149 $$$$ = $150+

Cashtown Inn

1325 Old Route 30; P.O. Box 103; Cashtown, PA 17310; tel: 800-367-1797 or 717-334-9722.

Generals Robert E. Lee and A. P. Hill conferred here on July 1, 1863, when the inn served as the latter's headquarters. Built in 1797, the inn was the first stagecoach stop west of Gettysburg, eight miles away. Fittingly, the house is haunted by the ghost of a Confederate soldier whose footfalls are heard in the attic. The ghost also enjoys knocking on the door of Room 4 after nightfall. The inn's seven guest rooms offer private baths and either four-poster or canopy beds. A tavern and garden are on the premises. $$–$$$.

Farnsworth House Inn

401 Baltimore Street; Gettysburg, PA 17325; tel: 717-334-8838.

Union soldiers riddled this brick house with more than 100 bullets; Confederate sharpshooters occupied its garret. Today, the house is riddled with ghosts. Female guests have long experienced labor pains and overwhelming sadness in the Sweeney Room, where the ghost of a woman has been seen beside the fireplace. The ghost, it turns out, is that of a midwife who delivered a still-born baby. Many oddities hail from the garret – the sound of a jew's-harp, pacing steps, heavy objects being moved around. Other ghosts include a soldier with a red beard and a grieving father holding a child trampled to death by horses. Decor in the nine guest rooms reflects the style of the Civil War period – wood floors, canopy beds, Victorian antiques. $$

Spring Bank Bed and Breakfast

7945 Worman's Mill Road; Frederick, MD 21701; tel: 800-400-4667 or 301-694-0440.

Situated within 30 miles of Gettysburg and Antietam battle-fields, this Mediterranean-style villa went from lavish private residence to untenanted animal shelter to lovingly restored bed and breakfast. One thing never changed: Tilly, the wife of the home's first owner, George Houck. Tilly died of unknown causes at the age of thirty-three. The ghost, her hair in a bun, wears a burgundy gown and a corsage. She is most often encountered near the paintings recently restored to the house by Houck's great-granddaughter – two of which are signed "Tilly." Exquisitely decorated, the house contains original friezes and stenciled ceilings. Four of the inn's five guest rooms have shared baths. $$

TOURS

Ghost Tours of Harpers Ferry

Tel: 304-725-8019

Walking tours stop at haunted sites, putting them into the con-text of the town's rich history.

Historic Farnsworth House Candlelight Ghost Walks

401 Baltimore Street; Gettysburg, PA 17325; tel: 717-334-8838.

A guide in period dress candle-light walks through historic Gettysburg, telling "first-hand" ghost stories.

Excursions

Boyhood Home of Robert E. Lee

607 Oronoco Street; Alexandria, VA 22314; tel: 703-548-8454.

The famed Virginian lived in this elegant brick house until the age of 18. His ghost, it seems, has regressed to those uncomplicated years, appearing as a prankish four-year-old who enjoys ringing the doorbell, rearranging objects, and giggling in the halls. Also spotted have been a phantom black dog, seen playing in the yard with the boy, and the ghost of two girls, possibly Lee's sisters.

Fredericksburg Battlefield

1013 Lafayette Boulevard; Fredericksburg, VA 22405; tel: 540-373-6122.

Called the "bloodiest ground in the North American continent," Fredericksburg and its environs witnessed four major battles – Fredericksburg, Chancellorsville, Wilderness, and Spotsylvania Court House – resulting in about 110,000 casualties. The Battle of Fredericksburg, fought on December 13, 1862, ended with over 12,000 Union losses, more than twice that of the Confederates. During the engagement, Gen. Ambrose

Burnside ordered futile charges on Confederate-controlled heights, and his troops suffered extrava-gant losses. One soldier, Sergeant Richard Kirkland, repeatedly imperiled himself to fill canteens for dying Union soldiers. His ghost is sometimes spotted tending to the casualties, whose phantom moans will not be silenced.

Old Fort Monroe and Casemate Museum

Casement Museum; Box 51341; Fort Monroe, VA 23651; tel: 757-727-3885.

The country's largest stone fort was built between 1819 and 1834. Surrounded by a moat, the heptagonal installation is now headquarters of the U.S. Army Training and Doctrine Command. Jefferson Davis, president of the Confederate States, was imprisoned here on false charges that he participated in the assassination of President Lincoln. His prison, a focal point of the museum, is haunted by his wife, Varina Lee, whose portly ghost sometimes peers from the casemate. Edgar Allan Poe, stationed here in 1828, haunts Building No. 5, his former barracks. The ghosts of both Lincoln and Ulysses S. Grant haunt Old Quarters No. 1.

Charleston
South Carolina

CHAPTER **13**

O ne supposes that before the late 17th century the only spirits haunting the Low Country of what are now the American Carolinas were aboriginal ones, with a sprinkling of ghostly conquistadores up from the Spanish toehold in Florida and the usual freebooters who seem to have rated haunting a close second to rape and pillage. Since that time, however, the spectral demographics of Charleston have undergone great change, so that today the city is, by some accounts, among America's most haunted communities. This rumored ghostliness, like the immutable city itself, is rooted in the region's violent past. ◆ Indeed, from the time that England's King Charles II rewarded eight loyal followers with the coastal lands between the 29th and 35th parallels of latitude, this estuarine tangle of salt marsh, islands, meandering rivers, **The turbulent, romantic** and brooding forests draped in Spanish moss has **past of Charleston has** been a cauldron of conflict. Charleston, **left behind a wealth** installed in 1680 on a thumb of ground jutting southward **of spectral debris.** between the mouths of the rivers **Ashley and Cooper**, has somehow remained more or less intact as one war after another swept past it: the 18th-century Queen Anne's War, a running skirmish with the Yamasee Indians, a virulent infestation of pirates, the American Revolution, and a brutal British occupation. Charleston's Fort Sumter is where the Civil War began. How could one not perceive the agonized murmurings of so many lost souls? ◆ Modern Charleston has expanded in every direction, sending municipal tendrils over to **Johns Island, James Island, Folly Beach** and northeastward. But that jut of land between the Cooper and the Ashley where old Charleston still lies has been altered only a little. It still

Graceful mansions and antebellum costumes are staples of tradition-proud Charleston.

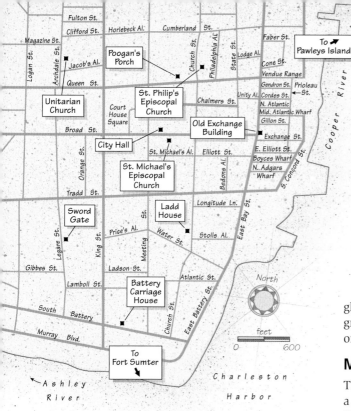

overlain by the same veil of changeless etiquette and culture. Now, as then, the visitor would note its abundance of old churches and dub Charleston the Holy City, as it is called today in the **Low Country**. Of course, churches mean cemeteries, and cemeteries mean ghosts; every patinated stone in every graveyard in those close-walled repositories of the dead has some ghostly story to tell.

Manifold Hauntings

The fact is that the Holy City has also been a magnet for the unholy – spirits who can find no rest on the far side of the grave. Few venues could be more attractive to ghosts, who abhor change, flee modernity and bustle, avoid the light, make their nests in the buildings and things of the past. Perhaps this antique core of Charleston was designed with these spectral residents in mind. And perhaps there are so many reported sightings and hearings and other spectral encounters that the more discriminating residents have to do a good deal of winnowing. After all, you just can't believe everything you hear.

has cobbled, narrow streets, bounded by scores of buildings erected before the Revolutionary War and hundreds before the War Between the States. The great homes peer across the **Battery** at **Charleston Harbor** today much as they did a century ago. A clipper captain landing there at the turn of the 21st century would find it much as it was at the opening of the 20th and

Poogan's Porch

Poogan's Porch in downtown Charleston is a restaurant with a certain reputation. Poogan was a Yorkshire terrier who spent much of his life dognapping on the building's porch. The little fellow passed from one owner of the place to another until he died. The beloved Yorkie may haunt the premises to this day – he has a gravestone there, after all – but he isn't the top ghost at the establishment that bears his name.

The historic Battery district (opposite) has the sort of unchanging atmosphere that ghosts find appealing.

Here lies Poogan (above), namesake of a popular and supposedly haunted restaurant (right).

Before the building was transformed into a restaurant, it was a private apartment building. Zoe St. Amand, a Charleston schoolteacher, lived there, very much alone. Now, long after her death, she apparently still inhabits the building. She doesn't appear as a transparent wraith but as a very old woman (some put her age at 95) who shyly takes a seat at one of the less conspicuous booths. Evidently, she hopes that no one will notice her, but restaurant staffers often see her, as do diners and guests at Mills House Hotel next door. Indeed, some employees have gone elsewhere after meeting Zoe.

This timid visitor from the Other Side is, however, too diffident to be dangerous. She vanishes at the slightest hint of contact with the living. Most people believe that she haunts Poogan's Porch in the same way she lived – as a loner who yearns for the warmth of human company.

"We get calls all the time about different ghosts all over the place," explains Julian Buxton, co-author with Ed Macey of *The Ghosts of Charleston and Other Macabre Ventures* and owner of **Tour Charleston**, the city's preeminent purveyor of nocturnal ghost walks. "Our criteria are that people have similar experiences over and over again. Otherwise we'd have all kinds of stuff." Buxton's ghost tours follow a different route every night, steering visitors from headstone to headstone, haunt to haunt. But the experts have their favorites, shades they like to call the *real* ghosts of Charleston.

The Headless Soldier

Down on South Battery, where large, big-windowed mansions erected a century ago stare across the seawall at the confluent rivers, a former carriage house has been converted into the **Battery Carriage House Inn**, with a set of rooms decorated to take

the visitor back 150 years in time. From here, looking out over the estuary at the ghostly silhouette of the USS *Yorktown*, it's not difficult to imagine the harbor crossed by Yankee men-of-war, standing the blockade that the fictional Rhett Butler ran with such apparent ease in *Gone With the Wind*. But spooky intimations of lost ships are not the only ghosts here. In fact, the Battery Carriage House Inn claims two.

One is known as the Headless Torso, who appears now and then, groaning miserably. In life, he was one of a Confederate Army detail sent to blow up all the munitions stored along the Charleston seafront and to spike the cannon so they would not fall into the hands of Gen. William Tecumseh Sherman, then not many miles away. Something went seriously wrong, however, and the young soldier's head was ripped away in the explosion – along with his chance of eternal rest.

The other Carriage House Inn specter is an amiable young fellow who died on the premises long ago and may be seen strolling the grounds by night and, rarely, by day. He is best known for his penchant for crawling into bed with female guests. Of course, he immediately takes his leave if they protest, hence his ghost-name: The Gentleman.

Doomed Doctor

Only a block or two away, the premises at **59 Church Street** are haunted by Dr. Joseph Brown Ladd, a pensive young physician from Providence, Rhode Island. Defending the honor of a Charleston woman in 1786,

Ladd was wounded in a duel with a drunken associate named Ralph Isaacs and died of complications and fever. Few believe Isaacs intended to kill the popular doctor, and Ladd's ghost seems to bear the living no ill will. Generations of families occupying the Church Street house, built in 1730, have reported seeing and hearing the doctor, who appears on the staircase as a protective spirit in times of crisis and stress. Reports that he also whistles have been impossible to verify.

A Colonel's Revenge

A contemporary of Dr. Ladd haunts the Old Exchange Building, where Charleston was

The Gray Man

Most of Charleston's ghosts, concentrated by all of the place's psychic and emotional energies, gather in the heart of the Holy City. But South Carolina's best-known specter prefers the tidal marshes and beaches of **Pawleys Island** about 50 miles to the north. Known as the Gray Man, this ghost appears on the beach as an anthropomorphic cloud of sea mist wearing a military cap. In life, according to legend, the Gray Man was a young British officer who was overtaken and killed by a terrible tempest from the sea as he hurried to warn his fiancée's family of the approaching storm.

This restless spirit is believed still to warn the living when a deadly storm is on the way. People begin looking for him when the Atlantic hurricane season starts in late spring. To those who see the Gray Man, his message is succinct: A major storm is coming; flee while you can. One Carolinian who claims to have seen the Gray

Man just before hurricane Hugo smashed into the South Carolina coast in 1989 took the spectral warning to heart and spirited his family off the island. After Hugo had passed, the man returned to find that the hurricane – or, as some believe, the Gray Man – had miraculously spared his vulnerable coastal home.

Not far from the Gray Man's haunt wanders a ghost who might easily have been dubbed the Blue Girl had not history passed down the spirit's real name. Alice Belin Flagg belonged to an aristocratic family during the mid-18th century. When the 16-year-old received a diamond ring from her beau, a turpentine dealer, the family not only ended the affair but threw away the ring. Alice soon died of typhoid fever. The ghost of her suitor is said to be responsible for the red roses and camellias sometimes laid on Alice's grave, located in **All Saints Waccamaw Episcopal Cemetery**, three miles west of Pawleys Island. Alice, meanwhile, wanders the island searching for her ring.

Pawleys Island (above) is the haunt of the Gray Man, a phantom who warns residents of coming storms.

Alice Belin Flagg's grave (left) is sometimes strewn with flowers – gifts, perhaps, from her suitor's ghost.

St. Philip's (opposite) is one of several Charleston churches whose cemetery harbors ghostly occupants.

once centered; the building even has a dungeon, pervaded, as dungeons invariably are, by the emotional imprints of prisoners who died there. But a Revolutionary patriot is the principal ghost in the Old Exchange Building, and Col. Isaac Hayne attained that ethereal position with his life. After British forces occupied Charleston in 1780, the Redcoats were at pains to discourage further resistance by the rebels. The city was secure, but guerrillas like the wily "Swamp Fox," Col. Francis Marion, nibbled at supply lines and harassed British forces pretty much at will. The British captured Hayne and used him as a lever to crack the American spirit.

Given a choice between swearing allegiance to the Crown and death, Hayne opted for the latter. His captors let him contemplate his own coffin for 48 hours in his prison cell, then hanged him for all to see. This only served to infuriate his fellow rebels and prompt them to fight even more determinedly. And Hayne himself was not quite finished, either. The tread of his oak-heeled cavalry boots is still heard in the building's **Great Hall**, and he's believed to be responsible for a host of other unexplained phenomena in and around the Old Exchange Building.

Women in the Graveyards

Charleston's many church cemeteries are veritable hives of ghostliness. Sue Howard, who died in 1888 of complications from a pregnancy that produced a stillborn child, haunts the graveyard of **St. Philip's Protestant Episcopal Church** on Church Street near Queen. On the anniversary of the child's death, she appears as a cloaked figure leaning over her lost baby's grave, which is adjacent to her own. One summer night in 1987, a Charleston photographer accidentally captured her on film, producing what many regard as one of the finest paranormal photographs ever taken.

Mary Bloomfield haunts the cemetery of the **Unitarian Church** off Archdale Street. Known as the Woman in White, she takes the shape of an angel or a luminous, white form. Mary died suddenly in 1907 in Charleston. On the same day – perhaps at

that very moment – her husband died at sea of yellow fever. His body was buried in Boston, but his spectral widow looks for him in the Unitarian graveyard.

The Duelist

A young man was wounded in a 19th-century duel in **St. Michael's Alley**, in the heart of the old city. His friends carried him into a house on the corner of the alley, up the stairs, and placed him on a bed, where he soon expired. Ever since, people have reported hearing his final moments replayed: the sounds of a body being dragged up the stairs, then dropped on a bed.

St. Michael's Protestant Episcopal Church later bought the corner house for a rectory, and the ghostly duelist is said by some to have wandered off, perhaps uncomfortable with clergy. But Julian Buxton, the expert on Charleston's ghosts, is not so sure the spirit has gone away. It may be that the clergy are just reluctant to acknowledge that their rectory is haunted. "I think," Buxton said, "he's still there."

TRAVEL TIPS

DETAILS

When to Go

The average temperature year-round is 66°F but usually feels about 10 degrees warmer due to the humidity. Winter is mild, with an average January temperature of 50°. Summer is hot, with an average temperature in July of 80°. The most popular times to visit are spring and fall.

How to Get There

Charleston International Airport is 12 miles northwest of the city. Car rentals are available at the airport.

Getting Around

The Downtown Area Shuttle (DASH) provides service throughout the central city. Day shuttle passes can be purchased at any visitor center. There's also a city bus system. For information, call 843-724-7420.

INFORMATION

Charleston Area Convention and Visitors Bureau

P.O. Box 975; Charleston, SC 29402; tel: 800-868-8118 or 843-853-8000.

Historic Charleston Foundation

51 Meeting Street; Charleston, SC 29401; tel: 843-722-3405.

South Carolina Division of Tourism

1205 Pendleton Street, Suite 104; Columbia, SC 29201; tel: 800-346-3634 or 843-734-0122.

HAUNTED PLACES

Ladd House

59 Church Street; Charleston, SC.

Just as Dr. Joseph Brown Ladd died protecting a lady's honor, so is his spirit said to protect residents of his former home. The doctor, who was fatally wounded in a duel in 1786, is sometimes heard walking near the house's entrance and whistling an English ballad. Another ghost, that of a girl who died in the 1830s, also haunts the premises. The Ladd House is a private residence; please do not disturb the occupants.

Old Exchange Building

122 East Bay Street; Charleston, SC 29401; tel: 843-727-2165.

Col. Isaac Hayne, an American patriot, haunts this building, situated in the historic heart of Charleston. Captured by the British, Hayne refused to vow allegiance to King George. Hayne's captors left his coffin before him to contemplate in the dungeon, where he awaited the gallows.

Poogan's Porch

72 Queen Street; Charleston, SC 29401; tel: 843-577-2337.

The ghost of a 95-year-old woman passes among diners at this restaurant. Zoe St. Amand, a schoolteacher, lived alone in this building, once an apartment facility. The word is that the spirit just wants to escape loneliness, though some patrons are eager to remove themselves from her strange presence.

St. Michael's Protestant Episcopal Church

14 Saint Michael's Alley; Charleston, SC.

The rectory of this church is haunted by the ghost of yet another fallen duelist. Taken to the house after his gentlemanly clash, the young man promptly died. The sound of a body being dragged on the stairs and dropped on a bed still can be heard.

St. Philip's Protestant Episcopal Church Graveyard

146 Church Street; Charleston, SC.

A female spirit visits this graveyard on the anniversary of her stillborn infant's death. The ghost of Sue Howard, who died in 1888 of complications resulting from pregnancy, appeared in a brilliant photograph taken in 1987. Also haunting the graveyard is the spirit of a man reputed to be Boney, a slave who won his freedom in 1796 after extinguishing a fire on the roof of St. Philip's.

Unitarian Church Graveyard

8 Archdale Street; Charleston, SC.

The Woman in White, the spirit of Mary Bloomfield, searches this graveyard for her husband, who died at sea on the same day that she died in 1907. Some people liken Bloomfield's resplendent spirit to an angel.

LODGING

PRICE GUIDE – double occupancy

$ = up to $49 $$ = $50–$99
$$$ = $100–$149 $$$$ = $150+

Battery Carriage House Inn

20 South Battery; Charleston, SC 29401; tel: 800-775-5575 or 843-727-3100.

Built in 1843, this mansion and carriage house, situated in Charleston's historic district, were featured in the TV series "North and South." One of the inn's ghosts, the spirit of a young man, leaves guests with "happy, secure feelings." Another ghost, the Headless Torso, is more threatening. The inn has 11 cozy rooms with private baths, four with steam baths, two with whirlpool tubs. $$–$$$$

1837 Bed and Breakfast

126 Wentworth Street; Charleston, SC 29401; tel: 843-723-7166.

Wide porches grace this former cotton planter's home. There are six rooms in the main building and three in the carriage house, all of which have queen-sized canopy beds, private entrances, and baths. The inn's ghost is a young boy named George, a former slave who lived on the property. He's said to be mischievous but gentle, shaking beds, locking doors, and quietly moving around objects. Amenities include a full gourmet breakfast and afternoon tea in the parlor. $$–$$$

Planters Inn

112 North Market Street; Charleston, SC 29401; tel: 800-845-7082 or 843-722-2345.

The inn dates to 1844 and is set in the heart of downtown Charleston, overlooking the historic city market. The two buildings have 41 rooms, most with large windows, canopy beds, and dramatic high ceilings. The ghosts in rooms 214 and 215 are generally friendly, but not always. In one incident, a large mirror crashed to the floor near a bride on her wedding day. Other guests have encountered a woman in 19th-century attire at the foot of their beds who abruptly disappears. Amenities include a four-star restaurant and in-room breakfast. $$$$

TOURS

Ghosts of Charleston

Tour Charleston, 18 Broad Street, Suite 709; Charleston, SC 29401; tel: 800-854-1670 or 843-723-1670.

Tours and stories of the city's legendary ghosts, haunted inns, Gullah superstitions, and recent encounters with specters.

Low Country Ghost Walk

Original Charleston Walks, 334 East Bay Street, Suite 186; Charleston, SC 29401; tel: 800-729-3420 or 843-577-3800.

A walking tour of the city's best-known ghost haunts.

Excursions

Sword Gate

39 Legare Street; Charleston, SC.

An impressive wrought-iron gate marked the entrance to a girls' boarding school. These days, the gate is said to be haunted by the ghost of Madame Talvande, former school mistress, who kept the gate locked to keep her charges from nighttime rendezvous with neighborhood boys. The gate didn't stop one resourceful girl. She filched the key and was married to an undesirable young man in a midnight ceremony at St. Michael's Church. Enraged parents withdrew their daughters, and the chagrined mistress took her own life. Her ghost, however, nightly patrols the gate and the second-floor dormitory to see that her students are safely abed.

Zion Cemetery

Corner of Highway 278 and Folley Field Road; Hilton Head, SC.

A planter named William Baynard was laid to rest here in 1849, but Yankee marauders vandalized his colossal tomb and removed his body. Since then, a ghostly funeral procession has been seen passing the ruins of Baynard Plantation en route to his empty mausoleum. The carriage and servants stop at each house along the way; Baynard emerges, shields his face with his hands, approaches the entrance, and returns to his cortege. Meanwhile, his mistress' ghost haunts the nearby Eliza Tree, where she was hanged after poisoning Baynard's wife.

City Hall

80 Broad Street; Charleston, SC 29401; tel: 843-724-3799.

Confederate Gen. P. G. T. Beauregard parried a number of Union attacks on Charleston, where he remains a hero. An art gallery in City Hall displays two portraits of Beauregard and his sword, which he willed to the city. The general was reputedly a man of high principles who would think nothing of embarrassing those who had the audacity to break the law. It's believed that he still roams the corridors of City Hall in search of lawbreakers or people engaged in shady dealings. Or perhaps he just wants to keep his saber untarnished.

Savannah
Georgia

Over the years Savannah has seen more than its share of tragedy and sorrow. Somehow it survived the Revolutionary War, when more than a thousand residents died in a siege. It went on to experience all the horrors of slavery, the Civil War, and an epidemic of yellow fever that took hundreds of lives. With such a traumatic past, it is not surprising that this historic seaport brims with specters. ◆ One of Savannah's dubious distinctions that dates back to colonial times involved Alice Riley, a servant indentured to a vain and cold-blooded man with long, white hair. Every morning, Alice had to wash that hair in a bucket. It got to be too much, and one morning, abetted by her husband, she washed her master out of her hair forever: She drowned him. The couple fled but were captured and sentenced to hang from one of the graceful oaks in the city's Wright Square known as the hanging tree.

A bizarre bevy of phantoms inhabits Savannah's old squares and buildings.

◆ Alice's husband was hanged first. When her turn came, it was discovered that she was pregnant. Since it was against the law to execute a woman with child, things were delayed until the child was born and put up for adoption. And then Alice had the unhappy distinction of being one of the first women hanged in the American colonies. ◆ Her executioners, however, were so embarrassed to be hanging a woman that they strung her body high in the top limbs of the oak, so that passersby wouldn't be able to see it. Since then it has been said that it isn't the wind rushing back and forth that stirs the tops of the trees but the trembling ghost of Alice searching for her lost baby. And this is why Spanish moss, so common in this southern port, does not drape the high, dark branches in **Wright Square**.

Bonaventure Cemetery on the banks of St. Augustine Creek is a beautiful haven for both the living and the dead – and perhaps for denizens who are neither.

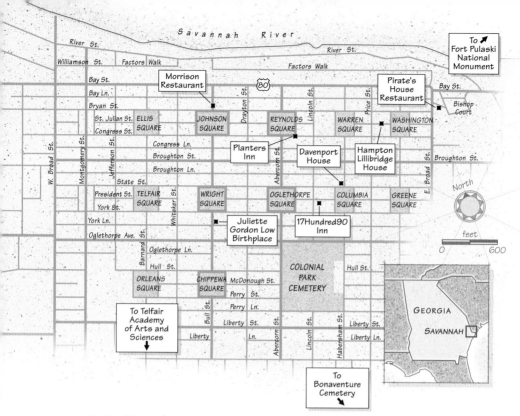

Savannah River

River St.

To ↗
Fort Pulaski
National
Monument

Williamson St.   Factors Walk

Bay St.

Bay Ln.

Bryan St.

St. Julian St.   ELLIS
Congress St.   SQUARE

Congress Ln.

Broughton St.

Broughton Ln.

State St.

President St.   TELFAIR
York St.   SQUARE

York Ln.

Oglethorpe Ave.

Oglethorpe Ln.

Hull St.

ORLEANS
SQUARE

To Telfair
Academy
of Arts and
Sciences
↓

River St.

Factors Walk

Morrison
Restaurant

80

JOHNSON
SQUARE

Planters
Inn

WRIGHT
SQUARE

Juliette
Gordon Low
Birthplace

CHIPPEWA
SQUARE   McDonough St.

Perry St.

Perry Ln.

Liberty St.

Liberty
Ln.

REYNOLDS
SQUARE

Davenport
House

OGLETHORPE
SQUARE

17Hundred90
Inn

COLONIAL
PARK
CEMETERY

Liberty St.

Pirate's
House
Restaurant

Bay St.

Bishop
Court

WARREN
SQUARE

WASHINGTON
SQUARE

Hampton
Lillibridge
House

Broughton St.

COLUMBIA
SQUARE

GREENE
SQUARE

North

Hull St.

Liberty St.

Liberty Ln.

feet

0   600

GEORGIA

SAVANNAH

To
Bonaventure
Cemetery

Unlocking the Past

Savannah was founded by an Englishman of vision, Edward Oglethorpe, a member of the British Parliament who wanted to deliver debtors from the cruelty of his nation's prisons. Oglethorpe sailed his shipload of poor to America in the utopian hope that they would find new, productive lives in this virgin land, and he set about drawing up plans for a spacious, lovely city to be built around commons. Today 17 squares serve as cool, shaded oases amid all the historic buildings crowding narrow streets in the heart of Savannah.

One of the oldest is shrub-lined **Johnson Square**, where the **Pulaski House** once stood. It was here that Gen. William Tecumseh Sherman stayed his first night in town. After the Civil War, the house was demolished; the locals probably were not fond of this reminder of the man known for destroying a wide swath of Georgia in his scorched-earth march to the sea.

Few buildings in this low country have basements, but workers tearing down the Pulaski House found one. Or was it a dungeon? They uncovered shackles, manacles, and instruments of torture, and they heard sounds of rattling chains, shuffling feet, and groaning. Then they unearthed a human skull.

Psychics and historians determined that slaves had been imprisoned in the basement of the Pulaski House, a basement that now contains the men's and women's restrooms of the **Morrison Restaurant**. Patrons have been locked in the bathrooms, stalls have unlocked by themselves, and so much weirdness has transpired that the locks have been removed from stalls and doors.

On the Most Haunted List

The Pulaski House was a grim relic, somewhat at odds with a city known for its somnolent, southern charm. Savannah's architecture is a sight to behold – intricately

The Davenport House (left) is the abode of a ghostly child in search of a playmate.

carved clerestories, ornate wrought-iron fences, patterned brickwork. Percherons pull carriages full of sightseers sitting beneath swaying fringes. Ghosts, supposedly, are afraid of the dancing threads, so the tourists are safe as long as they keep all parts of their bodies inside the carriages.

But tourists who want to meet ghosts might visit a place that Duke University parapsychologists have called "one of the most haunted houses in America." This is the **Hampton Lillibridge House**, a boxy, four-story, 200-year-old structure with a gambrel roof and a widow's walk at 507 East Julian Street. This is not its original location. In 1963 a Savannah refurbisher bought two houses located side by side. In moving them, one collapsed and killed a worker. When movers picked up the second house, they discovered an old crypt beneath its foundation. It was empty.

After restoration began on the vacant house at its present location, the new owner stopped by one evening with friends to view the progress. They heard footsteps. It was late for the crew to be there, so they climbed the stairs to investigate. They ascended to the second floor, then to the third, and even to the widow's

walk. They found no one – and the phantom footsteps began echoing below them.

On another occasion, a friend of the owner went to check out sudden noises overhead. He didn't return. He was found minutes later, fully conscious but lying face down on the floor. He said he felt as if he'd stepped into a cool body of water and been overpowered by a frightening force, pushing him toward the gaping 30-foot unfinished chimney shaft. He dropped to the floor to avoid being killed.

Witnesses said objects in the house levitated. Tools disappeared, and padlocks mysteriously unlatched. Even after the owner moved in, crashing noises were heard in locked rooms, and distinguished-looking men in suits were seen at windows. At night neighbors reported a female contralto singing in the house; they glanced across to see figures dancing and a party in full swing on the upper floor. Later they found out that both of the house's occupants were out of town and knew nothing of a party.

The Hampton Lillibridge House is the only one in Savannah to undergo a rite of exorcism. It was performed by an Episcopal priest because the Catholic bishop refused

Edward Oglethorpe (left) established Savannah to improve the lot of those who would otherwise suffer the horrors of British debtor prisons.

Spanish moss (right) adds gloom as well as grace to Savannah's green spaces, although, mysteriously, it doesn't grow at the top of the "hanging tree" in Wright Square.

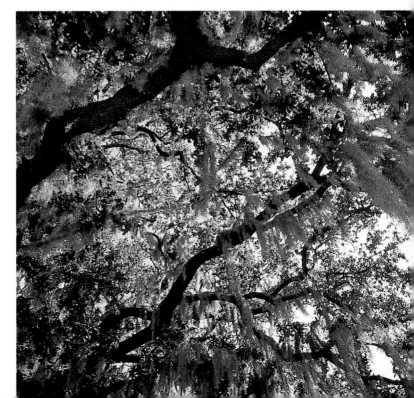

Graveyard of Good Fortune

Nobody with any taste buried in Bonaventure Cemetery would remain underground forever, since the place is such a pleasure to the senses. Set on the banks of tidal St. Augustine Creek, it's wild yet kempt, a native garden of live oaks, Spanish moss, and ancient shrubbery, and it's as artful as a French palace with decorative ironwork and statuary.

Bonaventure, which means "good fortune," is situated on land granted to John Mullryne, a Georgia colonist, in 1760. Here Mullryne and his son-in-law Josiah Tattnall became planters. Because the Mullrynes and the Tattnalls declared loyalty to the king in the Revolutionary War, Bonaventure Plantation was confiscated, but it was later repurchased by Josiah Tattnall, Jr.

With guests arriving regularly by boat and by carriage, the plantation soon became known for the elegant hospitality of young Tattnall. In the fall of 1780, a dinner party was in progress when a servant drew his master aside and informed him that the house was on fire – possibly ignited by the very candles and blazing hearth fires that made it look so welcoming.

A host of peerless grace, Tattnall saw no reason to let this catastrophe discommode his guests any more than absolutely necessary, so he asked his servants to transfer their chairs and the laden tables to the wide front lawn. The guests retired outside and resumed their party as the roaring fire destroyed the house. During the meal, one Savannah gentleman gave a toast: "May the joy of this occasion never end, and may we always be as we are tonight." At that Tattnall rose and slung his goblet against an oak, and his guests merrily followed suit.

The gentleman got his wish, some say. On warm autumn nights in the environs of Bonaventure Cemetery some people hear the muffled clatter of china and silver, faint laughter, and shattering crystal. Apparently, the party continues.

Four of Josiah Tattnall's children died young and were buried in a family plot on the plantation. They were joined in 1802 by their mother, Harriet Fenwick, and a year later by Josiah himself. The Tattnalls were the first people to be buried at Bonaventure. During subsequent land trades, a portion of Bonaventure Plantation became a public cemetery, and in 1907, the city of Savannah purchased 160 additional acres.

Group burials include veterans of the Civil War, the Spanish-American War, and the two world wars. The ghost of a Confederate soldier is said to guard the burial ground at night against any who might vandalize the graves of his comrades.

Bonaventure gained national fame when Jack Leigh's photograph of one of its burial statues, "The Bird Girl," was used on the cover of John Berendt's bestseller, *Midnight in the Garden of Good and Evil*. But locals found the great numbers of tourists visiting the statue unseemly, and it was removed.

Sorrowful statuary (left) accents the eerie loveliness of Bonaventure Cemetery.

The "Bird Girl" statue (below) featured on the cover of *Midnight in the Garden of Good and Evil* caused an unwelcome rush of tourists to the cemetery; the statue is now housed in the Telfair Museum.

A statue of John Wesley (opposite) in Reynolds Square may have banished the parson's shadowy ghost.

to enter. The ritual seemed to keep the ghosts at bay, but only temporarily; within 10 days, some of the weird auditory phenomena resumed.

Researchers representing the American Psychical Research Foundation visited the house, according to the *Savannah Morning News*, and reported that mysterious incidents indeed happened there, events that were "not caused by natural phenomena or human fakery." Psychics sense a feminine presence in the mansion, and its present owners say that occasionally they hear sounds of furniture being moved, doors closing, and warped strains of Dixieland jazz.

From Toys to Tears

The **Davenport House** at East State Street and Columbia Square dates from about 1820 and is noted for its fine woodwork and plasterwork. It was the first home restored by the Historic Savannah Foundation and is now a museum. Some early visitors reported seeing on the fourth floor the ghost of a beautiful little girl dressed in Victorian-era clothes playing with toys. Some investigators believe that the child doesn't know she is dead; she's just looking for a playmate, and she doesn't mean to spook the tourists. Nevertheless, the fourth floor of the Davenport House is now off-limits.

The haunted restaurant at the corner of President and Lincoln Streets, near Colonial Park Cemetery, is said to be built "on foundations of sorrow and sadness" because the bricks used in its 1790 construction were hand-pressed by slaves. Room 204 of the **17Hundred90 Inn and Restaurant** is believed to be occupied by an unlikely visitor – not the specter of a slave but the lonely and sad spirit of young Anna Powers, a woman caught in an unhappy marriage to an Englishman in the 1820s.

Anna took a merchant sailor as her lover, and they were happy together until he had to leave her to go to sea. Voyages to Europe in those days could take many weeks, but her sailor was gone for 18 months, so the heartbroken Anna leaped from her balcony. Visitors now see her in a rocking chair in

her room, where telephones ring without reason, and guests sometimes find their clothes unaccountably laid out for them. One honeymoon couple staying in Room 204 testified that they were awakened by drops of water falling on them. These droplets were thought to be the tears of Anna, still mourning her lost love.

Another ghost, possibly of an indentured servant, is said to be stationed in the inn's kitchen, where she announces herself via the jangle of invisible bracelets on nonexistent arms. Pots drop from pot racks, silverware tumbles from tables.

Seaman's Revenge

The **Pirate's House Restaurant** on the banks of the **Savannah River** also hosts some spectral guests. It used to be an inn for seamen; pirates and sailors came here to drink and be merry as they bragged about their adventures on the high seas. Some of them drank themselves into oblivion and woke up the next morning on strange ships bound for distant ports. Shorthanded crew-masters used the inn as a hunting ground to shanghai unwary men. They dragged the victims – unconscious with drink or drugs – through a tunnel that ran below the inn to the waterfront, where ships waited. Legend has it that one Savannah police officer, who stopped for a drink and woke aboard a schooner sailing to China, did not return home for two years.

Today the tunnel is sealed, but the restaurant conveys an atmosphere of spirited adventure on the Seven Seas. And some sort of spirit roams the upper storage room and makes mysterious noises. Employees refuse to go there. Some think the ghost is Captain Flint, the swashbuckling pirate of Robert

Louis Stevenson's *Treasure Island*. Savannah, after all, is mentioned in the book. On the other hand, the spirit may have been a seaman who is taking revenge on the place where he was shanghaied.

Shadow in the Square

Savannah seems populated by many such anonymous ghosts, but there are also specters of some renown. One of these is thought to be the shade of John Wesley, the founder of Methodism, who ministered to the colonists in 1734 and 1735. His parsonage was located on **Reynolds Square**, where a motel called the **Planters Inn** now stands. When the inn was being built, workers would see a shadow pass in the square at twilight. Every evening it appeared, moving about on a predictable course. One evening a worker bravely volunteered to examine the shadow up close. He followed it, only to come running back to his friends with a frightening story: The shadow was big and dense, and when he approached it, he felt himself surrounded by a clammy mist.

In 1969 a statue of John Wesley was erected in the square. Since then, there have been no further reports of the shadow in the square.

Even so, the Planters Inn may not be free of ghosts. Originally built for twin sisters as a "mirror house" – matching structures hooked together – it's had a checkered history. It reputedly was used as a hospital during an outbreak of yellow fever in the 19th century and later served as Savannah's premier brothel. Employees and guests at the inn have reported seeing a woman in a long gown move about the floors rearranging pictures on the walls. She's also been seen wandering the lobby late at night. Sightings were so frequent on the seventh floor that that level is now used only for serving breakfast. Rumors are that the specter is one of the twins who inhabited the house.

Lady in Blue

And then there's the case of Willie and Nellie Gordon. One of their six children was Juliette Gordon Low, founder of the Girl

Fort Pulaski

On claw-shaped Cockspur Island east of Savannah, occupying a point that reaches toward Tybee Island, Fort Pulaski guards the mouth of the Savannah River. In April 1862, Union forces on Tybee Island, a mile away, bombarded the fort with experimental rifled cannon for 30 hours. Projectiles were penetrating the thick brick walls, and tons of gunpowder stored against the north wall were in danger of exploding under the unremitting fusillade, so Confederate Col. Charles H. Olmstead, only 25 years old, decided to surrender rather than lose all his men. "I yield my sword. I trust I have not disgraced it," he said, but his decision haunted him for decades.

During the terrible winter of 1864-65, the Union held 500 Confederate prisoners in Fort Pulaski's unheated casemates on a starvation diet in retribution for cruelty to Federal prisoners. Later, Confederate officers, cabinet leaders, and governors were held as prisoners of war in the same iron cages.

In light of the suffering and death that occurred at Fort Pulaski, it's no wonder that ghosts are reported there. On full-moon nights, uniformed men have been seen walking atop its ramparts. Late one balmy night not many years ago, for example, two friends decided it would be fun to slip across the river from Tybee and visit the fort. They landed on Cockspur and were walking outside the moat when they heard footsteps. As the men rounded a patch of bushes, they expected to find another late-night trespasser. There was nothing, yet the swish-swish of footsteps continued. As they watched, the marsh grass flattened, then lifted

again as if it were bearing the intermittent weight of a human body.

Fort Pulaski was restored in the 1930s and is open to the public. Its reenactments and artillery demonstrations, surrounded by the haunting silence of the marsh, make only too real the spirit of misery, despair, and death that lingers in the salt air.

Fort Pulaski (above and below) was captured by Union forces and later used to hold Confederate prisoners.

Artistic treasures like this fountain in Forsyth Park (opposite) enhance the city's haunting beauty.

Scouts, but they are known as well for their legendary love for each other. They lived in an elegant townhouse at the corner of Bull and Oglethorpe that is now a museum – the **Juliette Gordon Low Birthplace** – filled with antiques and memorabilia. The night Nellie joined her husband in death, two people in the house saw the ghost of Willie come back to escort her.

These days, when the museum is closed, objects are sometimes moved from their places, and the faint sound of a pianoforte can be heard. When museum personnel stay late or come in early, they sometimes glimpse the figure of a woman in a long, blue robe and recognize her as Mrs. Gordon.

Centuries fade together in this old and haunted city, where yesterday could be a hundred years ago and tomorrow never. Ghosts seem perfectly at home here and add their own dimension to the enchantment of Savannah.

TRAVEL TIPS

DETAILS

When to Go

Savannah is green year-round, with average temperatures ranging from 81°F in July and August down to 52° in December and January. Summer is hot and sticky. Spring is rainy but popular for its flowering plants, especially azaleas. Fall is pleasant, winter mild.

How to Get There

Savannah International Airport is eight miles northwest of downtown. Taxis, limousines, and shuttles offer transportation from the airport to the city.

Getting Around

Car rental is available at the airport. Chatham Area Transit (CAT) provides bus service throughout Savannah and the surrounding area. CAT offers shuttle service from downtown hotels, inns, and the visitors center to the historic district and other attractions.

INFORMATION

The Savannah Area Convention and Visitors Bureau

P.O. Box 1628; Savannah, GA 31402; tel: 800-444-2427 or 912-944-0456.

Savannah Visitors Center

301 Martin Luther King, Jr. Boulevard; Savannah, GA 31402; tel: 912-944-0455.

Georgia Tourism

285 Peachtree Center Avenue; Suite 1000; Atlanta, GA 30303; tel: 800-847-4842 or 404-656-3590.

HAUNTED PLACES

Bonaventure Cemetery

330 Bonaventure Road; Savannah, GA; tel: 912-651-6843.

Few cemeteries are as lovely or as haunted as this popular tourist stop.

Davenport House

324 East State Street; Savannah, GA 31401; tel: 912-236-8097.

Visitors at this attractive historic house, now a museum, have seen the ghost of a girl wearing Victorian-era dress.

Fort Pulaski

U.S. Highway 80 East, P.O. Box 30757; Savannah, GA 31410-0757; tel: 912-786-5787.

Spectral soldiers reside here; some may have been prisoners during the Civil War.

Hampton Lillibridge House

507 East Julian Street; Savannah, GA 31401.

The old house is a fountainhead of things phantasmal: strange footfalls, levitating objects, a bow-tied ghost. This is a private residence. Do not disturb the occupants.

Juliette Gordon Low Birthplace

142 Bull Street; Savannah, GA 31405; tel: 912-233-4501.

The ghost of Nellie Gordon dressed in a blue robe is said to haunt this building.

Morrison Restaurant

15 Bull Street; Savannah, GA; tel: 912-232-5264.

A series of inexplicable mishaps in the restrooms have been blamed on the ghosts of slaves who were tortured in a house that once stood on this site.

Pirate's House Restaurant

20 East Broad Street; Savannah, GA 31401; tel: 912-233-5757.

The spirit of Capt. Flint, a notorious pirate, may still reside in his former house, now a restaurant.

Planters Inn

29 Abercorn Street; Savannah, GA 31401; tel: 912-232-5678.

This building served as a hospital and a brothel before becoming an inn. The most recent ghostly event involved a woman wearing a long gown who rearranged pictures on the seventh floor.

17Hundred90 Inn and Restaurant

307 East President Street; Savannah, GA 31401; tel: 800-487-1790 or 912-236-7122.

Some things should not be discussed at the table. For instance, patrons at this restaurant may wish to avoid talk of Anna Powers, who leaped to her death from the building's balcony in the 1820s. Guests in the 14-room inn have reported ghostly incidents relating to Anna and, possibly, an indentured servant.

LODGING

PRICE GUIDE – double occupancy

$ = up to $49 $$ = $50–$99

$$$ = $100–$149 $$$$ = $150+

The Gastonian

220 East Gaston Street; Savannah, GA 31401; tel: 800-322-6603.

Two ghosts are occasionally heard but not seen in this 1868 Regency Italianate inn. In the main house, mischievous behavior is attributed to the spirit of a child. The inn encompasses two houses and a carriage house, all furnished with antiques and reproductions. Its 17 rooms and three suites have private baths and fireplaces. $$$$

Kehoe House

123 Habersham Street; Savannah, GA 31401; tel: 800-820-1020.

Two rooms are haunted here: the Shannon Suite and Room 301. A mysterious woman appears in the former, but only when the room is occupied by two people of the same sex. In Room 301, a female figure has been seen, accompanied by the scent of rose water. Staff members report feeling an unseen presence as they work. The four-story mansion, built in 1892, was a funeral home in the 1950s. Each of the fifteen guest rooms has a private bath and antiques. Amenities include afternoon tea and evening hors d'oeuvres. $$$$

Magnolia Place Inn

503 Whitaker Street; Savannah, GA 31401; tel: 800-238-7674.

This 19th-century building is the site of strange and perhaps ghostly happenings: Water flows mysteriously from a faucet in an empty bathroom, odd noises awake the innkeeper, a guest is unaccountably pinned to a bed in which an old man died 50 years earlier. The neo-Gothic inn has 15 guest rooms, including two suites furnished with English antiques. Most rooms have working fireplaces; half have Jacuzzis. $$$–$$$$

TOURS

Ghost Story Tour

Carriage Tours of Savannah, 10 Warner Street; P.O. Box 2402; Savannah, GA 31402; tel: 912-236-6756.

Passengers on these evening ghost tours ride in horse-drawn carriages.

Ghost Talk, Ghost Walk

127 East Congress Street, P.O. Box 8672; Savannah, GA 31412; tel: 912-233-3896.

Two popular year-round tours – one of Historic Savannah, the other of the Victorian district – recount the city's rich history and ghostly lore. Reservations required.

Old Savannah Tours

250 Martin Luther King Drive; Savannah, GA 31401; tel: 800-517-9007.

Visitors board open trolleys for a narrated trip past homes with a spectral history, then disembark at Colonial Cemetery to finish the tour on foot. Reservations required.

Excursions

Fort McAllister State Park

3894 Fort McAllister Road; Richmond Hill, GA 31324; tel: 912-727-2339.
Workers restoring the fort refused to spend the night because of the strange sounds that some people attribute to the ghosts of about 40 soldiers who were killed here during the Civil War. Legend has it that another ghost strolls the grounds with a picnic basket, but only under a full moon in late summer.

St. Simons Island

St. Simons does nothing to dim our belief in the romance of islands. On the contrary, this island teems with ghosts. Should you hear mysterious African chants around Dunbar Creek, don't be alarmed: this is the sound of Ibo tribesmen captives who, when they arrived on American soil, drowned themselves in the creek in order to escape a life of slavery. If, on the other hand, you should glimpse a candle flickering over a grave in Christ Church Cemetery, know that its fuel is supernatural and that the grave belongs to a woman morbidly afraid of the dark. Meanwhile, the ruins of Fort St. Simons are haunted by the ghost of the learned Dr. Christian Priber, who can be heard speaking Cherokee, German, and a number of Romance languages.

Telfair Academy of Arts and Sciences

121 Barnard Street; Savannah, GA 31401; tel: 912-232-1177.
When spinster Mary Telfair died in 1875, she left her family mansion, built 57 years earlier, to the public. It formally opened in 1886 and has undergone extensive changes since, but still has a number of original furnishings that, some say, Mary still watches over. Bizarre occurrences attributed to Mary's ghost include footsteps, opening and slamming doors, and harp music. Some note that the ghost is most likely to appear when her portrait is moved from its customary spot in the dining room.

New Orleans
Louisiana

Colorful and cosmopolitan, sultry and sophisticated, garish and ghoulish. New Orleans is a veritable mélange, and its history contains more than a few skeletons in the attic. ◆ This was almost literally true in the case of one house, at 1140 Royal Street, that is notorious even by the bizarre traditions of the French Quarter. Built in 1831, the three-story edifice was the home of Dr. Louis Lalaurie and his fashionable wife Delphine, esteemed for her elegant balls as well as for her charitable work among the sick and the poor. ◆ From time to time, it was true, guests of the Lalauries remarked among themselves about the haggard appearance of their hosts' slaves. And Madame Lalaurie was once fined by the authorities after a slave girl she was beating leaped to her death from the roof. But many people in the antebellum South tended not to worry about such matters. ◆ Attitudes shifted one day in 1834, however, when a fire broke out in the Lalaurie residence. Firemen smashed open a locked interior

Earthbound souls are everywhere in old and exotic New Orleans, said by many to be the most haunted city in the United States.

door and came upon a scene surpassing horror: There, chained and suffocating in the heat and smoke, were seven starved and severely beaten slaves. Upstairs, in a sort of macabre laboratory, the fire patrol found more slaves, some dead, others barely alive with limbs amputated or purposefully deformed. Preserved organs and other body parts completed the picture. ◆ When word spread that the elite Lalauries were ghouls and monsters, a mob of outraged citizens surrounded the house. But the Lalauries escaped, some said to France, and were seen no more in New Orleans. The abandoned building became known far and wide as the **Haunted House**. Neighbors were

St. Louis Cathedral towers over a statue of Andrew Jackson in Jackson Square; the church is visited by the spirit of the courageous Father Dagobert.

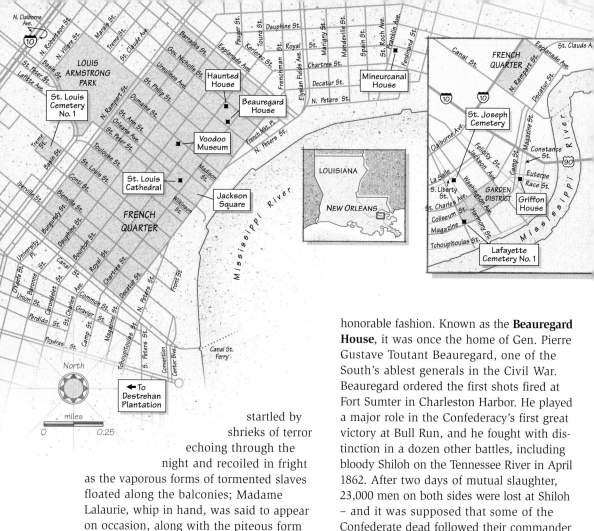

North

miles
0   0.25

←To
Destrehan
Plantation

startled by shrieks of terror echoing through the night and recoiled in fright as the vaporous forms of tormented slaves floated along the balconies; Madame Lalaurie, whip in hand, was said to appear on occasion, along with the piteous form of a little slave girl she had been savaging.

In time, the abandoned house was restored. It first became a school for girls, then a music conservatory, finally a private domicile again. Residents there today do not complain of ghosts; perhaps after all these years the specters have faded to nothingness. But tour guides still point out The Haunted House to visitors in the Vieux Carré.

The Grieving General

A stone's throw away, at 1113 Chartres Street, another building in the Quarter came by its haunts in a no less grim but far more honorable fashion. Known as the **Beauregard House**, it was once the home of Gen. Pierre Gustave Toutant Beauregard, one of the South's ablest generals in the Civil War. Beauregard ordered the first shots fired at Fort Sumter in Charleston Harbor. He played a major role in the Confederacy's first great victory at Bull Run, and he fought with distinction in a dozen other battles, including bloody Shiloh on the Tennessee River in April 1862. After two days of mutual slaughter, 23,000 men on both sides were lost at Shiloh – and it was supposed that some of the Confederate dead followed their commander home to New Orleans.

Visitors have reported the ghosts of soldiers roaming the halls of Beauregard House, and at times ethereal panoramas are said to take shape with men bayoneting and slashing each other. The ground is strewn with moaning wounded, and the whole scene is punctuated by the sound of cannon and rifle fire. As with Madame Lalaurie, Gen. Beauregard himself is said to appear from time to time, a gaunt figure in Rebel gray sorrowfully whispering the words "Shiloh. Shiloh."

Battling the Mafia

Now open to visitors, the Beauregard House is remembered for yet another haunting. In 1909, a wealthy Sicilian family named Giacona found itself under intense pressure from the local branch of the Mafia: Pay up or perish. But the Giaconas were made of stern stuff, and when four mafiosi came calling, family members shot three of them to death. This event precipitated what witnesses have described as a recurring phantom tableau of courageous householders overwhelming their oppressors.

Scary doings, but not scary enough to have deterred the distinguished lady novelist who owned Beauregard House for more than 20 years. Frances Parkinson Keyes bought the Giacona home in the 1940s and lived there contentedly until her death in 1970. She used the former slave quarters out back as a studio and wrote about New Orleans eccentricities in such best-sellers as *Dinner at Antoine's* and *Steamboat Gothic*.

The Brave Priest

The wealth of anecdotes makes it seem as if scarcely a block of the mile-square Quarter lacks ghosts, or "haints," as Orleanians like to call them. Visitors to the great, triple-spired **St. Louis Cathedral** on **Jackson Square** will learn that it was on this sacred ground that the sainted Father Dagobert defied the Spaniards in 1769 to secure a Christian burial for six insurgent parishioners.

A short-lived revolt by the French-speak-ing colonists had been put down with partic-ular vindictiveness, its leaders executed and left to rot under the guard of troops. But Pere Dagobert could not abide such sacrilege. Somehow he retrieved the bodies and took them into the nearby cathedral; perhaps the soldiers turned a blind eye to the man of God, or perhaps they even helped him. Dagobert then gathered the martyrs' families, sang a proper mass for the dead, and led the cortege through a pounding rain to St. Louis Cemetery No. 1, not far from the Quarter, where the fallen were properly laid to rest.

Even now, on rainy nights, the disem-bodied voice of the beloved Capuchin priest is said to sing hymns that can be heard along the streets between the cathedral and

A French Quarter balcony (above) decorated for Halloween.

Gen. P. G. T. Beauregard (opposite) haunts his home on Chartres Street, mourning the loss of his soldiers.

The Haunted House (below) on Royal Street was the scene of tortures whose ghostly presence lingers.

Queen of Voodoo

She might have been nothing more than a minor priestess in Haiti, where voodoo was the ultimate religion and competition for followers fiercely intense. But in New Orleans during the mid-19th century, Marie Laveau reigned as undisputed queen of the cult.

Much about Laveau is cloaked in mystery. She seems to have been a freeborn mulatto, with possibly a drop or two of Indian blood. She was beautiful: tall, lithe, with fine features and commanding black eyes. Her fame commenced in the 1830s as the all-wise, all-knowing hairdresser to the wives of New Orleans' white masters; she became the ladies' boudoir confessor, their fortune-teller, their well-paid instrument in love and fury.

Marie Laveau (right), the Queen of Voodoo, was revered and feared in old New Orleans. Her tomb (below) is covered with Xs left by those in need of her supernatural influence.

Marie Laveau's House of Voodoo (opposite, top) is a commercial establishment that trades on the Voodoo Queen's notoriety.

The Beauregard House (opposite, bottom) has been visited by phantom soldiers sometimes engaged in spectral scenes of battle.

Servants of the whites and of the mixed-blood mistresses kept by Creole gentlemen were only too willing to spy for her, and so adept was Laveau at manipulating the secrets she learned that she seemed omnipotent. As she willed, marriages and affairs were consummated or torn apart, good or evil luck summoned, concubines procured, crimes absolved. A person's enemies, it was whispered, could even be made to die for the payment of $1,000.

By the 1850s, Laveau had turned voodoo into a sort of happening with a particular New Orleans twist. The rituals by Lake Pontchartrain included all the essentials: the giant snake, or Zombi, with which she danced; the boiling cauldron; the black cat and crowing cock; the thudding drums; the blood-quaffing; the naked, screaming, wildly cavorting, increasingly drunken participants; and at climax, the frenzied fornication. To this Laveau solemnly added statues of Roman Catholic saints, prayers, incense, and holy water, as if in resolutely Catholic New Orleans, noted one observer, she were "offering voodoo to God." Nor was there any semblance of secrecy in her rites: Press, politicians, and police were cordially invited. It was said that on occasion white women would fling off their clothes to join in.

There were also private gatherings in Laveau's backyard on St. Ann Street. At these orgies, it was said, babies were offered to Zombi in sacrifice – or smoked like hams and mummified into rock-hard little gris-gris icons. But no one really knew, or was telling. And when Marie Laveau promenaded down the street, holding her head high as if she owned New Orleans, the fear and the idolatry she inspired were palpable.

Tales abounded of hellish voices and rattling chains when the Voodoo Queen died in June 1881 at the age of about 85. Others said that she passed away quietly in her sleep, having renounced Zombi and all his works. Yet old beliefs die hard. What is thought to be **Marie Laveau's crypt** in **St. Louis Cemetery No. 1** is covered with hundreds of rust-colored Xs inscribed by supplicants seeking favors. People take away spoonfuls of earth as charms, and sometimes they leave presents: beans, Mardi Gras beads, candles. And stories are told of wraiths dancing nude among the tombs, led by a tall woman with a huge snake coiled around her body.

the cemetery. And people say that they've seen his spectral form floating along the aisles of St. Louis Cathedral itself.

A Slave to Love

Amour as well as courage plays a role in the ghostly chronicles. Indeed, the French Quarter could scarcely be the French Quarter without it. A melancholy tale from antebellum days revolves around a beautiful slave girl who yearned to marry her master, a handsome Creole aristocrat. This could not be, but the man, in a mean jest, made the girl a proposition: He would set her free and marry her if she would spend a cold December night naked on the roof of his house on Royal Street. On just such a night, while he and a friend spent the evening companionably playing chess and drinking brandy, the young girl stepped stark naked out on the roof above them. And there she remained through the bitter cold night.

When she failed to appear at the usual time the next morning, the master went in search. He found her on the roof, dead from the cold.

The house is now home to two ghosts. On cold December nights, passersby tell of seeing the nude form of the slave girl standing on the roof. Just below in a lighted window sits the ghost of a man playing chess.

The Jilted Witch

Royal Street is said to be among the haunts of yet another female phantom, who at times also frequents **St. Ann, Toulouse,** and **Bourbon Streets**. She is called the **Witch of the French Opera House**, for it's from that building, since destroyed by fire, at the

corner of Bourbon and Toulouse Streets, that she first emerged. Anyone who encounters her will understand the appellation "witch." Her hair and face are a chalky, deathly white, but her eyes are as red and burning as those of a goshawk, renowned among predatory birds for its implacable nature.

The Witch of the French Opera House is avowed to be the ghost of a sensuous but aging woman whose younger lover rejected her in favor of a new mistress. The distraught older woman committed suicide. But then she returned from the dead and in a spectral fury killed her faithless lover and his new favorite. Even murder could not slake her thirst for vengeance, however, so she roams the Quarter still, held earthbound by hatred.

The Haunted Jail

Some visitors, ghost hunters, and casual tourists alike find the French Quarter so fascinating that they never venture beyond its boundaries. But New Orleans is a metropolis of many parts. Downriver from the Quarter lies the **Garden District**, with

Succor from the Grave

Cities of the Dead figure in New Orleans' rich ghostly traditions as they do in most communities. But New Orleans' cemeteries rest on terrain remarkably accommodating to haunts.

On dredged swampland between Lake Pontchartrain and the Mississippi River, the city is an average six feet below sea level. The water table was so high that early citizens despaired of burying their dead. Seeping water floated the coffins right out of the graves, so mourners filled the caskets with rocks or drilled holes in them and hoped that the water itself might weigh down their loved ones. That did not work. The answer was to inter New Orleans' departed in marble and concrete tombs and crypts high, dry, and secure above the oozy ground – Cities of the Dead where spirits could come and go at ease.

Tales are legion of encounters in **St. Louis No. 1** and **Lafayette No. 1**, the city's two oldest cemeteries, as well as in the various St. Josephs, St. Patricks, St. Vincents, and St. Rochs. One story relates how a grieving widow fell asleep by the tomb of her husband in St. Louis No. 1 late one afternoon. When she woke in the night, her wondering eyes beheld a veritable convocation of ghosts: young, old, male, female, white, black, rich, poor – hundreds upon hundreds of them. Every tomb seemed to release a spirit. They were smiling, she saw, relaxed and happy, quite different from dwellers in the angry, hurly-burly world of the living. Her husband came to her. He was at perfect peace. She sorrowed no longer, knowing that one day she would be with him.

Most other accounts are of single encounters, sometimes terrifying, but often gentle, comforting, even illuminating. Shortly after World War I, a young woman whose fiancé had perished was being hotly pursued by a suitor bent on marriage. Alone and confused, she went to the grave of her fiancé and remained there all night. As the hours passed, an owl materialized on silent wings and began dropping roses into her lap: a red rose, then a white rose, one after another until there were 14 red roses and 15 white ones. The young woman was puzzled at first, then the significance of the roses dawned on her: Fourteen red roses stood for the 14th letter of the alphabet; 15 white roses meant the 15th letter. Together they spelled "NO."

The wise old owl, or perhaps the spirit of her beloved fiancé, was urging her not to marry the new suitor. She took the advice, and sometime later she learned that the man was a scoundrel, that he made a practice of courting gullible young women and abandoning them once he had his hands on their dowries.

A bright cherub (opposite, top) sits atop a makeshift altar at St. Louis Cemetery No. 1, one of the city's oldest graveyards.

A French Quarter gift shop (opposite, bottom) hawks souvenirs to tourists with a taste for the macabre.

The owl (below), a harbinger of death in some cultures, conveyed a grave message to an imperiled woman in St. Louis Cemetery No. 1.

its stately mansions. Here also is **Lafayette Cemetery No. 1**, last resting place for the legions of Irish and German immigrants carried away by yellow fever in the mid-1800s, and, many believe, home to a multitude of ghosts.

Visitors who want to see the cemetery find it an easy walk from the streetcar line that borders the Garden District and other uptown neighborhoods, as it runs along St. Charles Avenue from Canal Street to Carrollton Avenue. Traveling by trolley south of the Garden District, they pass the site of the **Old Carrollton Jail**, once home to a haunting of consequence.

Legend allows that in the late 1890s a man accused of murdering his wife was beaten to death by the jailhouse guards. The man's final words as he lay dying against a wall were that he would return from the grave.

The eerie happenings started in 1899 when a woman standing near the jailhouse wall was rudely and forcefully propelled out into the room. Three times she returned to lean against the wall – with identical results. Later the same week, a policeman lay down for a nap on a couch next to the wall. Suddenly, both he and the couch were hurled across the room. Next, paintings on the wall started spinning and

crashing to the floor, heavy paperweights flew through the air, and the tramp of heavy footsteps reverberated around the room. One officer claimed that powerful hands tried to strangle him as he dozed in his chair, and prisoners in their cells complained of being beaten by ghosts. In time, the old jail was torn down. And it surprised no one when members of the demolition crew swore that they saw ghosts laughing amid the rubble.

Mysterious Madame

Other ghostly encounters have commonly occurred all through the city. Around 1900 in a fine house at **2606 Royal Street** in the **Fauborg Marigny**, just north of the French Quarter, a grand Creole lady named Madame Mineurcanal unaccountably killed her cherished little white dog and then hanged herself from a beam in the third-floor stairwell. The house remained unoccupied for many years.

But after World War II, a family known only by the names of two grandchildren, Ramon and Theresa, moved in and immediately began seeing the misty figure of a woman in a white dress descending the stairs, accompanied by a little white dog.

For no reason at all, the children started calling the apparition "mini-canal," a fair approximation of the name Mineurcanal. No harm came to them, but when a visiting cousin took up the chant, he was heard screaming in the night and was found to have a scarlet cheek, as if someone had slapped him hard.

On another night, the father turned in bed to embrace his wife only to clasp the figure of a phantom. And the pregnant wife had such a terrifying encounter with the lady in white that she almost lost her baby. After the child was born, a ghostly figure was seen bending over the crib doing what or attempting to do what no one could tell. Moaning sounds and the barking of a dog came from the attic, but investigation turned up nothing.

Rebel Revenants

That same sense of intermittent harassment long afflicted the **Griffon House** at 1447 Constance Street in the **Irish Channel**, a neighborhood that lies between the Garden District and the Mississippi River. Built in 1852 by one Adam Griffon, the place became a barracks and prison when Union troops occupied the city during the Civil War.

The Federals were under strict orders to shoot anyone among their number caught looting. Shortly after these orders were issued, two supposed Union officers were arrested and jailed in the Griffon House. They made a point of loudly singing northern songs until they learned their fate; then they changed their tune, for they were actually Confederates masquerading in Yankee uniforms. Knowing that they were to be executed, the two Rebels bribed a guard for his pistols and shot each other in the heart.

Subsequent occupants of Griffon House heard the sound of marching boots and the singing of "John Brown's Body." A woman noticed blood dripping from the ceiling and rushed upstairs – to find nothing. Later, when the place was a factory, its two owners were startled to see a huge chunk of concrete come hurtling down the stairs. When they charged upstairs, they found nothing, not even footprints on the newly painted floor.

The neighborhood disintegrated after a devastating hurricane in 1951, and drug addicts took over many of the abandoned buildings. But they did not inhabit 1447

Constance Street, where two figures described as "white men in police uniforms" were seen walking through walls singing.

Restless Dead of Destrehan

No excursion through the spirit world of New Orleans should end without notice of the **Destrehan Plantation** mansion, widely reputed to be the most haunted house on the Mississippi.

This magnificent home at 9999 River Road, only 30 minutes by car from the French Quarter, was built in the late 1780s in the two-story West Indies style with a dozen rooms facing out on wide, cooling galleries. About 1,000 of the plantation's 6,000 acres were originally given over to indigo, then to sugar cane cultivated by an army of overworked slaves.

Maltreatment of slaves on sugar plantations was so general and of such brutality that one of the greatest slave uprisings in American history erupted upriver in 1811 and spread to Destrehan; in all, perhaps 200 slaves were involved, and when the Louisiana militia crushed the revolt, 21 ringleaders were tried at Destrehan and sentenced to die, their heads to be stuck on pikes along River Road as a warning to others. And it was at Destrehan Plantation that a series of family tragedies gave rise to the ghosts that still seem to haunt the place.

One early Destrehan resident, Nicholas Noel, suffered several losses. His 15-year-old bride died soon after their marriage, and a second wife died young in an epidemic of yellow fever. Nicholas Noel lost his right arm when the cape he was wearing became enmeshed in some plantation machinery. His sister Zelia died mysteriously at 30 in New York City, and a brother, Rene Noel, died at 28, also in curious circumstances, and also in New York. Neither death certificate listed a cause.

Despite all this ill luck, the Destrehan family held on to the plantation until 1910, when it was sold to a sugar corporation. Later it passed to an oil company, which eventually turned it over to the historic trust

that manages Destrehan today.

Its phantoms appear in various forms in every section of the house but most often in the back hall. One employee told of a cold and formless miasma that dogged her footsteps as she checked the upstairs rooms just before closing. Tourists have exchanged greetings with a tall, courtly, French-accented man, whom they later identified from pictures as the original owner, Jean Noel Destrehan. Others have encountered a strikingly handsome but forbidding specter with no right hand; that description would fit the star-crossed Nicholas. And two ghostly little girls of unknown parentage have been seen playing in the rooms.

A fallen angel (above) strikes an ironic pose during the city's annual Mardi Gras celebration.

Destrehan Plantation (left), site of a 17th-century slave uprising, houses a multitude of ghosts.

TRAVEL TIPS

DETAILS

When to Go

The city's subtropical climate makes for uncomfortably hot and sticky summers. Winter is pleasantly mild, with temperatures in the 50s and 60s, as is autumn, when temperatures are usually above 68°F. Expect frequent rain showers from March to September.

How to Get There

New Orleans International Airport is 12 miles northwest of the city. Car rentals are available at the airport. Amtrak trains, 800-872-7245, service Union Station. Airport Shuttle, 504-522-3500, makes frequent runs between the airport and city.

Getting Around

For information about bus and streetcar transportation, call Regional Transit Authority, 504-569-2700.

INFORMATION

Greater New Orleans Tourist and Convention Commission

1520 Sugar Bowl Drive; New Orleans, LA 70112; tel: 504-566-5011.

HAUNTED PLACES

Beauregard House

1113 Chartres Street; New Orleans, LA 70116; tel: 504-523-7257.

Gen. P.G.T. Beauregard, who led Confederate troops in the battle of Shiloh, lived here until 1869. Now, his spirit unites with many others for the most authentic Civil War re-enactment east or west of the Mississippi.

Destrehan Plantation

9999 River Road, P.O. Box 5; Destrehan, LA 70047; tel: 504-764-9315.

Spirits and hovering ghost faces have appeared in this manor house since its restoration in the 1980s. The Destrehan family suffered many tragedies and left as many ghosts, including a specter with only one hand. Year-round tours of the plantation are available.

Griffon House

1447 Constance Street; New Orleans, LA.

This house has surrendered many oddities over the years, not least of which is blood dripping from a ceiling. Two Confederates, disguised as Union officers and arrested for looting, allegedly committed suicide here to avoid execution. Please do not disturb the occupants of this private residence.

Haunted House

1140 Royal Street; New Orleans, LA.

For many years, this three-story house in the French Quarter, built in 1831, could not hide its terrible secret. Slaves, tortured here in unmentionable ways, returned as agonized ghosts. Delphine Lalaurie, their tormenter, also appeared, her trusty whip in hand. The Lalaurie House is a private residence; please do not disturb its occupants.

Lafayette Cemetery No. 1

1400 Washington Avenue; New Orleans, LA.

Many wraiths are believed to frequent this cemetery, where scores of Irish and German immigrants, victims of yellow fever, are buried.

Mineurcanal House

2606 Royal Street; New Orleans, LA.

It is virtually axiomatic that those who kill their pet and hang themselves will be doomed to haunt this world. So it was with Madame Mineurcanal, whose spirit has been seen here

with that of a white dog. Please do not disturb the residents of this private house.

St. Louis Cathedral

615 Pere Antoine Alley; New Orleans, LA 70116; tel: 504-525-9585.

The ghost of a Capuchin priest has been heard singing hymns here and, according to some reports, seen hovering down the aisle.

St. Louis Cemetery No. 1

400 Basin Street; New Orleans, LA 70116; tel: 504-482-5065.

The Voodoo Queen, Marie Laveau, is purportedly buried here. Around her crypt, covered with X-shaped graffiti, have been seen capering naked specters led by a woman with the decency to wear at least something: a snake.

LODGING

PRICE GUIDE – double occupancy

$ = up to $49 $$ = $50–$99
$$$ = $100–$149 $$$$ = $150+

Delta Queen

Robin Street Wharf; New Orleans, LA 70130; tel: 800-543-1949 or 504-585-0630.

This floating paddleboat hotel navigates the inland waterways. Its 87 rooms range from cozy to mid-sized, all with private baths and views of the river. The grand staircase of this 1926 boat, lit by crystal chandeliers, bespeaks a more glamorous era. Adding to the ambience are Tiffany-style stained-glass windows, teak handrails, and brass fittings. Captain Mary Green, one of the few female pilots of the 1940s, is said never to have left the vessel. A strict teetotaler, she's been spotted around the bars, wearing a green housecoat. $$$$

Hotel de la Poste

316 Chartres Street; New Orleans, LA 70130; tel: 800-448-4927 or 504-581-1200.

This five-story French Quarter hotel has a European-style

courtyard and 100 rooms, all with private baths. Haunting the premises are several ghosts, including Gerald, a former carriage servant who hangs out in the garage. Diane sometimes makes appearances in the kitchen and sometimes on the second floor, where the fleeting vision of a chic, slim redhead creates quite a stir. $$–$$$$

Oak Alley

3645 Louisiana Highway 18; Vacherie, LA 70090; tel: 225-262-2151.

The main house at Oak Alley is a spectacular 1839 Greek Revival mansion. Four sharecropper cottages serve as guest quarters. All have private baths, and some include more than one bedroom. Oak Alley offers daily tours. Ghost talk centers on the one-legged daughter of the original owners. She resents the able-bodied and has pinched the legs of some tour guides, who wind up with nasty bruises. $$–$$$

TOURS

Haunted History Tour

Tel: 888-644-6787 or 504-861-2727.

Walking tours explore the grim and ghastly deeds committed in the French Quarter.

Hauntings Today Ghost Expeditions

Tel: 504-522-0045.

Paranormal investigators conduct tours of the French Quarter.

Tour of the Undead

Voodoo Museum; 724 Rue Dumaine; New Orleans, LA; tel: 504-523-7685.

Guides lead patrons on walking tours past eight haunted sites – but not until they've handed out gris-gris bags for protection.

Excursions

Myrtles Plantation

P.O. Box 1100; St. Francisville, LA 70775; tel: 504-635-6277.

Built in 1796 by General David Bradford, Myrtles Plantation allegedly witnessed ten murders and one suicide before becoming a bed-and-breakfast. The most ghastly story involves Chloe, a slave nanny caught eavesdropping on an important business meeting. Bradford's son-in-law Clarke Woodruff cut off the slave's ear. To show her worth, Chloe designed to make her owner's family sick and then heal them. Her choice of oleander leaves, however, made the mother and two children more than sick: the leaves, which contain a residue of arsenic, killed them. Chloe was hanged for her perverse program, but her ghost remains at the plantation.

Natchez

Natchez Convention and Visitors Bureau; 311 Liberty Road, Natchez, MS; tel: 601-446-6345.

Natchez is something of a ghost commune. One of the city's many haunted sites, Longwood, is a 32-room, unfinished octagonal mansion. Dr. Haller Nutt and his wife Julia ceased construction of the house at the outbreak of the Civil War. The home's interior was never finished, prompting a local wag to dub the mansion "Nutt's Folly." The Nutts, however, have gotten their money's worth out of the house, which their spirits still proudly occupy. Any number of ghosts are apt to be seen by visitors to the Natchez-Under-the-Hill section of the city. Located near the river, this area is haunted by a Union spy, decapitated criminals, and an odious slaver.

Oak Alley

3645 Louisiana Highway 18; Vacherie, LA 70090; 225-262-2151.

Built in 1839 for French sugar planter Jacques Telesphore Roman, the mansion stands at the end of a quarter-mile lane lined with 28 sheltering oaks. Now a bed-and-breakfast and tour site, the house is haunted by the Lady in Black, thought to be the ghost of Roman's daughter, Louise. Fleeing the advances of a drunken suitor, Louise fell and gashed her leg on the wire hoop of her dress. Soon gangrenous, the leg was amputated and stored for burial with the rest of her body. Louise returned to her home following years in a convent. The Lady in Black remains active, riding a horse, combing her long hair, and pacing the widow's walk.

Chicago
Illinois

CHAPTER **16**

The place has always been known as a tough town, a kind of latter-day urban Dodge City, and even the ghosts have that hard edge. Chicago revels in its reputation for toughness, not just in the brutality of its celebrated gangland past but also in the indomitable, working-class spirit immortalized by poet Carl Sandburg. It's a true melting pot, the most American of cities, inhabited by ghosts with shady reputations, blue-collar ghosts, ghosts with dirty faces. ◆ Even some of its victims weren't particularly admirable, as for example the men huddled in the garage at 2122 North Clark on the snowy morning of February 14, 1929. One of them, Johnny May, was an ex-safecracker turned mechanic. Brothers Frank and Pete Gusenberg were bootleggers. James Clark, Adam Heyer, and Al Weinshank were low-level hoodlums. And Dr. Reinhardt Schwimmer, an optometrist by trade, was a man who liked to hang out with Chicago's seamier element – a sort of gangster groupie. ◆ What all seven had in common was a connection to George "Bugs" Moran, one of Chicago's most famous mobsters. It was Moran's garage, his headquarters, and the men inside were waiting for a shipment of bootleg booze they'd been told was heading their way from Detroit. ◆ But the shipment story was phony, a setup. As the men waited for the whiskey, a police car pulled up and several uniformed officers, along with a few men in plain clothes, got out and walked toward the garage. The Moran men probably expected a bust, but they were in far more trouble than they knew. After ordering the seven to line up against a wall, the "police" pulled shotguns and

Chicago's shady past may not be so past after all. For some nefarious spirits, this is still their kind of town.

The gangster as a sort of lowbrow folk hero is an American icon born in Chicago, where tommy guns made ghosts of a good many mobsters.

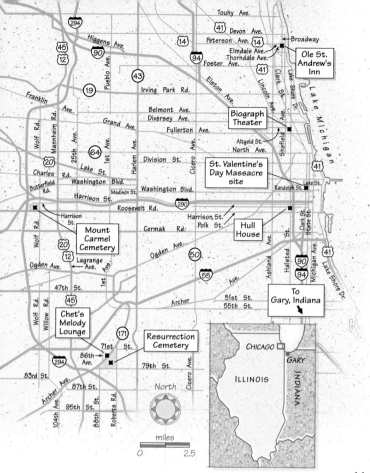

Scarface – Al Capone, who was battling Moran for control of North Side vice profits.

Moran was right. Capone was taking the sun in Florida at the time of the murders, but he'd set up the hit – an execution that would become legendary in American criminal history as the St. Valentine's Day Massacre.

Moran's garage is gone now, but the ghosts of the massacre seem to remain. Pedestrians walking past **2122 North Clark**, now a nursing home, have claimed to hear screams and moans ricocheting off the chain-link fence that surrounds the front yard of the building, sounds that may be the spectral echoes of gangland's most notorious killing. Sometimes, dogs passing the yard whimper or growl as though suddenly aware of ghostly presences.

Moreover, some say that the garage engendered not only ghosts but also a curse. When it was torn down in the late 1960s, its grisly reputation prompted a Canadian businessman named George Patey to cash in on its history by selling off its bricks as souvenirs. Rumors circulated that those who bought them invariably suffered bad luck: illness, financial ruin, family problems.

Capone's rise to the top of the Chicago mob was predicated on his will-ingness to kill anyone who got in his way. But perhaps he wasn't entirely without conscience. In later years, Capone was said to have been convinced that the ghost of James Clark, Bugs Moran's brother-in-law and one of the men gunned down in the 1929 massacre, was stalking him. Today, at his grave in **Mount Carmel Cemetery**, along Roosevelt Road in the suburb of **Hillside**, the crime king's headstone bears a brief inscription to a man who died

machine guns from their coats and began blasting away. Witnesses to the aftermath of the killings would remember blood splattered everywhere, smearing the wall and pooling on the cold cement floor. "Only Capone kills like that," Moran reportedly said when told of the carnage. He was referring, of course, to the notorious

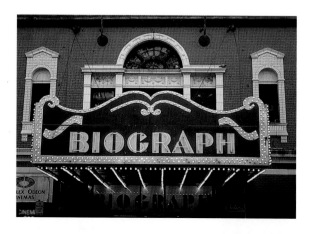

with a haunted soul:
"Alphonse Capone: 1899-1947.
My Jesus Mercy."

Public Enemy

John Dillinger was another
criminal with Chicago ties,
although he had no links to
Capone or the mob. Dillinger
was an independent, though
just as bloodthirsty as most
mobsters. Beginning in the
summer of 1933, he and his
gang had racked up an impressive 12-month tally of six major
bank robberies and at least five
murders, four of the victims being law
officers. In July 1934, Dillinger was resting
in Chicago after his labors – and trying to
elude the federal agents who'd been
hunting him for a year. Twice he had
escaped capture in that stretch, and he'd
helped his gang sneak or shoot its way out
of about half a dozen other police traps.

On July 22, Dillinger went to the
Biograph Theater on North Lincoln
Avenue accompanied by his girlfriend and
another woman, Ann Sage, who would go
down in crime lore as "the woman in red."

Al Capone (left) was
haunted by the ghost of
a rival mobster he had
slain.

The Biograph Theater
(opposite) beckoned
John Dillinger to his
death: The gangster was
gunned down by G-men
while exiting the build-
ing.

**The St. Valentine's Day
Massacre** (below) is
reenacted in the 1967
film of the same name.

FBI agents, alerted to the outing through a
message from Sage, had staked out the
Biograph. They cut down the country's
Public Enemy No. 1 in the theater's back
alley after Dillinger had sniffed out the trap
and gone for his gun.

But the drama behind the Biograph
didn't end with Dillinger's death. In the
late 1970s, stories began to surface of a
ghostly figure running down the alley
behind the theater, a figure that would
suddenly trip, fall, and then disappear.
People also reported feeling cold spots in

the alley, or experiencing inexplicable fears on entering it, as though they sensed a spectral presence. John Dillinger may not have been so easy to catch after all.

Mount Carmel Miracle

Not all Chicago shades, of course, are linked to crimes. While many curiosity seekers visit Al Capone's final resting place, not far away in **Mount Carmel** lies the grave of another Italian-American, one who inspires a different sort of pilgrimage.

Young Julia Buccola Petta died in childbirth in 1921. In 1927 her mother, who saw her daughter in a dream, demanded that the body be exhumed. The mother's request was honored, and an astonishing discovery was made. After six years in the ground, the young woman's body was almost completely intact, hardly touched by decay. People who believe a miracle was involved still visit the grave and wonder at the photograph placed on top of it, a picture of a very lifelike Julia taken at the time of the exhumation. Some say that her ghost walks the cemetery dressed in the wedding gown that was Julia's burial dress.

Resurrection Mary

Perhaps Chicago's most famous specter is associated with another graveyard, this one in the small suburb of **Justice** on the far south end of the

city. She's called Resurrection Mary.

The first stories about her began around 1939, when drivers heading past **Resurrection Cemetery** on Archer Avenue reported that a young blond in a white dress had tried to jump from the side of the road onto their cars' running boards. Later witnesses would claim to have met Mary at a dance – usually one held at the O. Henry Ballroom just south of the cemetery – and then to have offered her a ride home. The stories usually ended the same way, with Mary jumping out of the car, running into the cemetery, and disappearing into the mist.

Mary is also said to haunt a neighborhood bar, **Chet's Melody Lounge**, across the street from the cemetery. Pub patrons claim to see Mary walking past the bar's doors every now and then; a few even say they've danced with her. In 1973, a cabdriver rushed into Chet's and demanded to know where his fare, a young blond woman, had gone. The bar manager informed him that no such person had come into the bar. Thirteen years later, the owner of Chet's was approached early one morning by a frantic man who said he'd just run over a woman on Archer Avenue but couldn't find her body. A truck driver who'd seen the incident testified that the story was true. No body was ever found.

No one is quite sure who Mary was in life, or why she haunts the cemetery and its environs, but sightings of the pale and willowy spectral blond have been so numerous over the years that quite a few Chicagoans, at least in her part of town,

High Spirits

It's said that there are two sorts of drunks: mean ones and happy ones. Frank Giff was a happy drunk – and perhaps still is.

Giff owned a bar at 5938 North Broadway in the Edgewater neighborhood of Chicago. He liked to drink, and he depleted his own stock with regularity and cheerful abandon. Those who knew him said he'd often continue to imbibe well after he'd closed the bar for the evening; he was sometimes found in a booth the next morning after having passed out.

As might be expected, it was a surfeit of vodka, his favorite, that killed Giff, although not in so ordinary a way as liver damage. The story goes that one evening he ended up dead drunk as usual and fell off his bar stool, slamming his head onto the floor with fatal force.

Death would have ended the drinking days of lesser men, but not Frank Giff. Subsequent owners of the bar, now known as **Ole St. Andrews Inn**, surmised that the former proprietor was still around when their patrons began complaining that someone, or something, was finishing off their drinks. The ghostly freeloader was said to be especially partial to vodka. Occasionally a young woman would feel a ghostly hand giving her knee an affectionate squeeze. Like Giff's wife, most of these ladies were redheads.

Other evidence for the bar's spirit include tales of disembodied voices and of drinking glasses mysteriously flying through the air. Given Giff's love of life, liquor, and this particular bar, he's widely believed to be responsible.

Visitors to Ole St. Andrews Inn need fear no harm from the bibulous shade; Giff is far too amiable a ghost to do damage. But they would be well advised to keep close watch on their Bloody Marys.

Ole St. Andrews Inn (left) is home to a phantom tippler who steals drinks.

John Dillinger (opposite, bottom), just months before his death, holds a real submachine gun along with the wooden pistol he used in a jailbreak.

A simple grave (opposite, top) in Mount Carmel Cemetery marks the final resting place of Al Capone.

believe the ghost is real. Today, a Bloody Mary rests on the end of the bar at Chet's. It's on the house for Mary, just in case she turns up.

Devil Baby

A link between ghosts and cemeteries has a certain logic, but a connection between specters and a monument to good works is less explicable. Nevertheless, a demonic spirit supposedly haunts **Hull House**, site of the most famous settlement house in America.

In 1889, Jane Addams and another social worker took over the Hull mansion at 800 South Halsted and turned it into a community center. The house, now part of the Chicago campus of the University of Illinois, is currently a museum dedicated to Addams and her work.

Addams was a hard-headed, progressive

reformer, a proud and determined do-good-er in an age sorely in need of one. She and her colleagues turned Hull House into a community center, supplying shelter, food, and practical advice to the huge numbers of bewildered young immigrant women in the late 1800s and early 1900s.

In the winter of 1913, Addams could have used some advice herself to deal with what must have seemed to her no-nonsense mind a case of mass hysteria. Women were streaming into Hull House with a very peculiar request: They wanted to see the Devil Baby. Stories were circulating throughout the city about a child born with scaly skin, horns, hooves, and a tail. Some of the rumors included accounts of the young demon flying about the rooms of Hull House while social workers tried desperately to catch him. "He looks just like Satan himself," a witness told newspaper reporters.

Depending on who told the story, the infant's origins varied. Jewish women

The Sobbing Woman

Not far from Chicago and the home of Resurrection Mary, another ghostly hitch-hiker haunts the streets, this one in the working-class industrial town of **Gary, Indiana**. Known as the Woman in White, the ghost will occasionally stop a taxi or a passing vehicle near the intersection of Cline Avenue and Fifth Avenue and request a ride to Calumet Harbor. She always disappears before getting there.

According to local legend, the Woman in White is looking for the children that she drowned in the Calumet River. That interpretation suggests that Gary's Woman in White may be a version of the famed specter La Llorona – the Sobbing Woman – the protagonist of a Mexican folk tale.

Long ago, the story goes, a beautiful Indian princess, Dona Luisa de Loveros, fell in love with a handsome Mexican nobleman named Don Nuna de Montesclaros. The princess loved the nobleman deeply and had two children by him, but Montesclaros refused to marry her. When he finally deserted her and married another woman, Dona Luisa went mad with rage and stabbed her two children. Authorities found her wandering in the street, sobbing, her clothes covered in blood. They charged her with infanticide and sent her to the gallows.

Ever since, it is said, the ghost of La Llorona walks the country at night in her bloody dress, crying out for her murdered children. If she finds any child, she's likely to carry it away with her to the nether regions, where her own spirit dwells.

Gary is the northernmost site of possible visitations by La Llorona, but not the only one outside Mexico. The pitiful shade of Dona Luisa has also been reported in the western United States and in Florida.

Hull House (above), the famous community center founded by Jane Addams, is said to have sheltered the mysterious Devil Baby.

The Woman in White (below) walks the streets of Gary, Indiana, searching for the children she's believed to have drowned.

The statue of a bride (right) marks Julia Buccola Petta's grave – as does the photograph taken of the young woman six years after her death.

claimed he was the offspring of an unfeeling father with a large family of daughters who declared that he'd rather his wife give birth to a demon than to another baby girl. Italians said the Devil Baby's mother was a God-fearing woman who had had the misfortune to marry an atheist. When the woman put a picture of Jesus on her wall, the husband angrily tore it down, saying that he'd rather have the devil himself in the house. And, according to this version, he got his wish. These and other variations ended with a desperate family taking the baby to Hull House and pleading for help.

In the beginning, Addams was furious at the rumors, which she tried to combat with appeals to common sense. Eventually, however, she worked out a sociological explanation that, to her way of thinking, explained the phenomenon. She noted that many purveyors of the Devil Baby story were older immigrant women, isolated in their new country, deprived of whatever domestic power and authority their age might have afforded them in their native villages. "The old women who came to visit the Devil Baby believed the story would secure them a hearing back home," Addams reported, "and as they prepared themselves with every detail of it, their faces shone with timid satisfaction."

But despite Addams' sensible, secular debunking of the Devil Baby as the outcome of a pitiable bid for attention, many Chicagoans still believe that a strange creature of some sort really existed. Some suggest that the Devil Baby may simply have been a horribly deformed child, kept

by the Hull House workers to shelter it from an unforgiving world. Other believers still claim to see a devilish little face peering out of one of the House's second-floor windows.

Addams would doubtless have scoffed at such superstitious claptrap – or maybe not. In her diaries, she reported hearing strange noises coming from the upper rooms of Hull House. She didn't know what made the racket, but she habitually put large buckets of water at the top of the stairs to keep it – whatever it was – at bay.

TRAVEL TIPS

DETAILS

When to Go

Summer, sometimes very hot but always breezy, is the best time to visit. The average summer temperature is 78°F. Winters are justly notorious, with biting gales, lots of snow, and temperatures plummeting well below freezing. Spring and fall are moderate but brief.

How to Get There

O'Hare International Airport is 18 miles northwest of the city, Midway Airport 11 miles southwest. Amtrak trains, 800-872-7245, service Union Station. Continental Air Transport, 312-454-7800, offers bus transportation to the downtown area every 5 to 10 minutes.

Getting Around

The city has a very efficient bus and subway system, operated by the Chicago Transit Authority. For information, call 312-836-7000. Taxi cabs are plentiful. Car rentals are available at the airport.

INFORMATION

Chicago Office of Tourism

78 East Washington Street; Chicago, IL 60602; tel: 800-487-2446 or 312-744-2400.

HAUNTED PLACES

Biograph Theater

2433 North Lincoln Avenue; Chicago, IL 60614; tel: 773-348-4123.

Critics have long decried movies as a danger to society. The ghost of John Dillinger would agree. Eager to take in a motion picture, the gangster risked exposure to attend a film at the

Biograph Theater. But FBI agents gunned him down in the theater's back alley. Dillinger's ghost is said to flee down the alley and may be responsible for the chilling sensation experienced by some people who pass through the area.

Hull House

800 Halsted Street; Chicago, IL 60607; tel: 312-413-5353.

Jane Addams turned this mansion into a community center in 1889. Some people believed that Ms. Addams' spirit of community was large enough to shelter a "devil baby." Whether or not the social worker took in such a child – rumored to have had horns and a long tail – stories persist of a beastly child seen in a second-floor window of the Hull House Museum.

Mount Carmel Cemetery

1400 South Wolf Road; Hillside, IL 60162; tel: 708-449-8300.

Most of us will not appear quite ourselves after six years in the grave. Not so with Julia Buccola Petta in 1921. The body of this young woman was exhumed at the request of her mother. Remarkably, six years had done little to mar Julia's looks. Nor does her ghost appear the worse for frequent visits to the grave, dressed in a wedding gown. The Petta grave is marked by a life-size statue of Julia and a photograph of her in a wedding dress.

Ole St. Andrews Inn

5938 North Broadway; Edgewater, IL 60660; tel: 773-784-5540.

Former bar owner Frank Giff may be behind reports of mysteriously emptied drinking glasses at this neighborhood watering hole. If so, old Giff hasn't lost his quest for "a drop too many." A drunken fall off a bar stool allegedly claimed his life.

Resurrection Cemetery

7200 Archer Avenue; Justice, IL 60458; tel: 312-767-4644.

Mary Bregavy, who died in a 1934 automobile accident, haunts this cemetery, surrounding roads, the

Willowbrook Ballroom (formerly the O. Henry Ballroom), and Chet's Melody Lounge (across the street from the cemetery). Resurrection Mary, as she is called, likes to dance with men at the ballroom or lounge and to hitchhike, often vanishing before reaching her destination.

St. Valentine's Day Massacre Site

2122 North Clark; Chicago, IL.

The actual building is long gone, but it was here that seven men were savagely killed by a crew of Al Capone's hit men. In what became known as the St. Valentine's Day Massacre, Capone's men set up rival gangsters, who expected to receive a shipment of booze at Moran's Garage, headquarters of mob leader George "Bugs" Moran. Instead, the doomed men were approached by machine-gun-toting hoodlums disguised as police officers. Some people report hearing tortured sounds and moans when passing the site.

LODGING

PRICE GUIDE – double occupancy

$ = up to $49 $$ = $50–$99
$$$ = $100–$149 $$$$ = $150+

Blackstone Hotel

636 South Michigan Avenue; Chicago, IL 60605; tel: 800-548-3311 or 407-740-6442.

Built in 1910, the Blackstone is fragrant with history. Every U.S. president has stayed here since the hotel's opening. Magnificent crystal chandeliers, marble statues, Oriental rugs, and French walnut paneling set the tone in the lobby. Guests have a choice of 250 large and comfortable rooms, with private baths and double or king-sized beds; some have views of Grant Park and Lake Michigan. Amenities include a restaurant and lounge. $$

The Gold Coast Guest House

113 West Elm Street; Chicago, IL 60610; tel: 312-337-0361.

This 1871 row house is located on Elm Street. Sound familiar? The present owner claims the real nightmare here involved not ghosts but "frightening colors" – orange, lime green, and navy blue – and wrap-around smoke mirrors. The necessary alterations being made, the brick three-story now sports smart neutral colors and a blend of both contemporary and antique furniture. An 18-foot atrium has a view of the garden. $$$–$$$$

The Palmer House Hilton

17 East Monroe Street; Chicago, IL 60603; tel: 800-445-8667 or 312-726-7500.

This turn-of-the-century hotel, a Chicago landmark, contains some of the most ornate public rooms in the city, including a main lobby with ceiling murals by Louis Rigal. Situated in the Loop, not far from the Art Institute, the hotel's 1,639 rooms offer modern conveniences without loss of traditional elegance. Amenities include a shopping arcade and five restaurants. $$$

TOURS

Chicago Supernatural Tours

Richard T. Crowe; P.O. Box 557544; Chicago, IL 60655-7544; tel: 708-499-0300.

Motor coach tours are hosted by ghost hunter Richard T. Crowe and visit cemeteries, murder sites, haunted buildings, and Indian burial grounds.

Ghost Bus Tours

P.O. Box 528124; Chicago, IL 60652; tel: 773-776-6591.

Bus and walking tours of Chicago are led by paranormal investigators Howard and Karen Heim and involve actual ghost hunting.

Excursions

Dunes State Park

1600 North 25th East; Chesterton, IN 46304; tel: 219-926-1952.

Modest ghost enthusiasts may want to avoid Dunes State Park. Diana of the Dunes, the ghost of Alice Mable Gray, often appears here in purest nature (i.e., naked). Ms. Gray is dying proof of the old saw that too much education corrupts. Before she took to haunting naked, this daughter of a prominent physician graduated from the University of Chicago with honors. Soon, however, both her eyesight and her family life ebbed. She retreated to the rugged shores of Lake Michigan, where she lived from 1915 to 1926. Her death, the result of blows to the abdomen, was imputed to the drifter who occupied a shack with her beginning in 1920.

Graceland Cemetery

4001 North Clark Street; Chicago, IL 60613; tel: 312-525-1105.

In this old cemetery, a statue above the grave of seven-year-old Inez Clarke is sometimes seen crying before vanishing, only to return the next day. Meanwhile, a howling, green-eyed ghoul, loudest when the moon is full, visits the oversized tomb of Ludwig Wolff. The cemetery is also home to the Getty Tomb, listed on the National Register of Historic Places, and the grave of famed architect Mies Van der Rohe, but so far their graves are not reported to be haunted.

Greenwood Cemetery

606 S. Church Street; Decatur, IL 62522; tel: 217-422-6563.

The many apparitions here include the Greenwood Bride, whose fiancé was killed just before they were set to elope;

swirling white lights that may represent wandering spirits whose caskets were uprooted during a 19th-century flood; and a semitransparent woman with her head bowed, who weeps almost nightly at the steps near the Barrackman family graves. Ghosts have also appeared in the Civil War Memorial section, where Confederate soldiers are buried in unmarked graves.

Ghosts of the Old West

The ghosts of the Old West still stir, whether walking the meadows of the High Sierra or the shimmering sagebrush plains of Nevada, hiding in Gold Rush shantytowns or soaring as ravens through the red rock canyons of the Southwest. Here no Salems beckon with widely known tales of witchcraft and ghostly mayhem. You have to know where to look. You have to get out of the car, ask questions, make your interest known. When you do, the tales tumble forth like a closet full of old luggage bearing tags and stickers from many countries – the tales of immigrants who went west to work the mines or scratch crops from dry soil. ◆ Remote areas – where the wind-kicked, rain-stripped boardwalks of forgotten mines and settlements moan and clatter – have spawned a thousand stories. Elsewhere the lights and bustle of advancing cities have swallowed some of the West's pioneer flavor, but a mysterious world still finds shelter in historic houses and hotels, as if the ghosts are confused by the millions

Strangers in a strange land, some early pioneers who journeyed to the West never seemed to set down roots, even after death.

of newcomers who have arrived since they themselves left for the Other Side. ◆ The term "ghost town" usually refers to a settlement so quickly abandoned that residents simply walked away, leaving many of their possessions behind – and sometimes their spirits. Preserved by dry, high-desert air, the old structures can defy everything except fire, flash floods, and the voracious appetites of souvenir hunters. Most towns were products of the West's great mining period between 1849 and the early 1900s. For many men, the mine work was like death itself: Tens of thousands found themselves as deep as 3,200 feet in the earth under a million tons of rock that

The Bird Cage Theater in Tombstone, Arizona, once the wickedest saloon in the West, is a suitable lair for phantom cowboys.

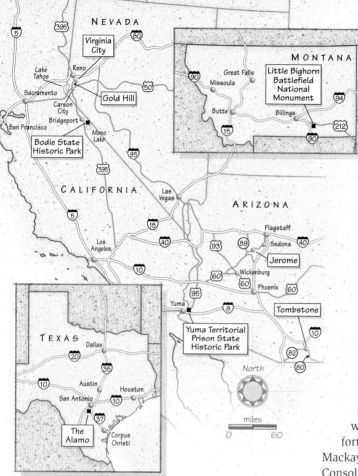

boardwalks today is an exercise in anything but ghostly presences. The smell of hot dogs mingles with the visual chaos of thousands of T-shirts and souvenirs. But Virginia City is rich with ghosts and paranormal occurrences.

Just one block off the main avenue, John Mackay's mansion seems as quiet as an abandoned mine in the famed Comstock Silver Lode. Hundreds of shafts crisscross the mountainside beneath Virginia City, and a good deal of refined gold and silver brought up from their grim maws passed through **Mackay Mansion**. First built by George Hearst in 1859 with a borrowed sum of $400, the mansion served as assay office and living quarters. Hearst made millions in Virginia City, and went on to seed the Hearst family fortune. He sold the house to James Mackay, who had even better luck. His Consolidated Virginia Mine struck the largest silver deposit in North America and made more than $133 million.

Nothing in the Mackay Mansion's printed tour guide hints at its hauntings, but several generations of caretakers will swear the ghosts are there.

"Shhh! Mamie's comin'!" says the little girl in the pink party dress at the top of the stairs, then vanishes. But no one has lived in the house for decades. In the parlor, a lady in a maroon dress occasionally appears near the sofa. Recently, during a wedding reception at the house, a similarly dressed "guest" that no one knew circulated among the revelers. She's also alleged to have appeared mistily in a group photograph of a tourist family posing on the front porch.

And then there's the doll room. Sometimes the rocking chair there moves by itself. Once, after caretakers thoroughly vacuumed and carefully repositioned all the dolls, they returned to find the small rocker turned completely around and a doll flat on

might give way at any moment. Clinking pickaxes found seams of gold- or silver-rich ore – or poisonous gases and gushing water that filled the shafts until the life was squeezed out of miners as they floated face up against the rock ceilings, sucking the last oxygen from trapped air pockets.

Knowing the shafts were filled with spirits, miners watched for signs and nurtured superstitions, hoping to anticipate the next cave-in. Cornishmen believed in buccas, hobgoblins who first arrived in the West by hitchhiking in a miner's knapsack from the coal mines of England to the Comstock Lode of **Virginia City, Nevada**. Miners carefully left a bite from every meal for the little imps, and in return the buccas would tap on the walls and timbers, warning them of danger.

Spirits of the Comstock Lode

By the 1950s, ghost towns like Virginia City began attracting tourists. Walking its the floor even though a wire gate, designed to protect the dolls from theft, remained securely locked.

In winter, when the entire town rests from the tourist onslaught, the true desolation of this mountain outpost hits home. Sometimes, if passersby look hard enough through the fog or snow, they see the outline of a little girl standing in a side street where was run down and killed by a team of horses many years ago.

Sea of Sin

Potable spirits have vanished from **Bodie, California**, the best-preserved ghost town in America and former site of 65 saloons, but paranormal spirits remain untapped.

About a half-day's drive from Virginia City, Bodie is now a state park inhabited solely by rangers. In the 1870s, however, the town had some 10,000 residents. Preachers decried Bodie as a "sea of sin, lashed by the tempests of lust and passion."

Today, Bodie is not so much lashed by sin as by dust and decay. The town itself is a ghost, an ethereal, creaking apparition barely clinging to the sagebrush of a lonely high range, then lost each winter beneath snow.

A cobweb (left) bespeaks abandonment and decay in the forlorn town of Bodie, California.

Bodie (below), once home to 65 boisterous saloons, is one of the best-preserved ghost towns in the West.

The town's ghosts include one wasteful of electricity in the **J.S. Cain House**. Built in the late 1870s, the house now accommodates rangers' families. The presumed ghost of Cain's mistress is either afraid of the dark or bored enough to play pranks. One of the ranger's daughters flipped off the light in her bedroom and crawled under the bedcovers. The light went back on. She turned it off again. Back in bed, she watched the switch flip on again. "You turn that light off, right now!" the girl yelled. The light went out.

In another incident, a professional photographer was shooting the **Standard**

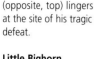

Yuma Territorial Prison (below) may hold the spirits of long-dead inmates.

Lt. Col. George Armstrong Custer (opposite, top) lingers at the site of his tragic defeat.

Little Bighorn Battlefield (opposite, bottom), now a national monument, is the resting place of more than 270 fallen cavalrymen.

The Dark Cell

The first seven prisoners escorted into cells at the new **Yuma Territorial Prison** on July 1, 1876, would have longed for the relative comforts of a Devil's Island. An ungodly heat funneled down the Colorado River's course along the border between California and Arizona Territory. The "Yuma Seven" were dehydrated, exhausted. They'd built their cells themselves, raising the walls and sealing their fate, block by block. As more prisoners arrived, they, too, were set to work. The prison grew as they gouged deeper into the baked rock layers of the Mojave Desert, seeming to burrow toward relative coolness – or perhaps hell itself – like a tormented reptile.

Until its closure in 1909, the prison housed a total of 3,069 prisoners. All of them knew about the Dark Cell. Most prisons have a Solitary, a Hell Hole, but Yuma had a particularly tortuous destination for recalcitrants. Set deep in the hillside, the Dark Cell saw no light except from an air shaft's pinpoint beam. At high noon the ray briefly found its way to the floor, narrow and ephemeral as the hopes of the incarcerated. Prisoners sometimes went mad there or had their madness confirmed by the unremitting isolation.

Today the Dark Cell, now part of a state historic park, seems unwilling to release a few of its old residents. Visitors often feel extremely uncomfortable in the cave-like confines and refuse to go back in. Some rangers avoid the Dark Cell for reasons they can't, or won't, explain. But it's the pinching that scares them the most. One female ranger, dressed in a turn-of-the-century-style red dress during a living-history tour, stepped into the Dark Cell and felt someone pinching her. Others have felt the same exploratory fingers. Apparently the lonely soul in the Dark Cell enjoys visitors – if they wear red.

Mill's reflection in a window of **Boone Store**. A man dressed in Confederate gray was walking down **Main Street**. The photographer turned from his viewfinder to see how long the pedestrian would take to pass. The street was empty, just as it has been since the 1950s.

Remember the Alamo

Violence inevitably spawns ghosts, and such was the case at two of the bloodiest conflicts in the frontier West.

On February 23, 1836, 5,000 Mexican troops arrived in **San Antonio** bent on destroying a band of rebellious Texans. The rebels had secured the four-acre compound of Mission San Antonio de Valero, better

known as the **Alamo**. Although the Franciscan mission had been transformed into an arsenal, the compound had yet to hear its most fervid prayers.

Fortifying the Alamo, along with 185 others, were Col. William B. Travis and frontiersmen James Bowie and Davy Crockett, who arrived with his fiddle. Outnumbered 10 to one, and sneering at the words surrender and escape, the rebels inflicted 600 casualties.

The battle ended in a manner as gruesome as it was abrupt. Answering a pre-dawn bugle call on March 6, the Mexicans made it over the walls and into the raging holdout. The invaders, furious at their high losses, were encouraged to mutilate bodies. Bowie was tossed into the air and skewered on bayonets. His corpse, along with those of his fallen comrades, was burned on a pyre.

Today, both locals and tourists have no problem remembering the Alamo. When they are not catching the faint sound of a mysterious bugle or Crockett's fiddle, they sometimes inhale the odor of an equally mysterious smoke. Occasionally, hideous apparitions are spotted emerging from the mission's walls.

Little Bighorn

Another lopsided 19th-century clash holds enduring interest for ghost-hunters: the Battle of Little Bighorn, better known as Custer's Last Stand. The clash took place on June 25, 1876, when the Seventh Cavalry, commanded by Lt. Col. George Armstrong Custer, encountered a large camp of Sioux and Cheyenne Indians on the plains of eastern Montana.

The brash young officer made three errors that fateful day: He underestimated the number and ability of the Indian warriors; he failed to wait for reinforcements; and he divided his regiment into three battalions. It was a classic, and fatal, blunder. All 272 members of the Seventh Cavalry were killed.

If Davy Crockett's ghost plays the fiddle, Custer's ghost enjoys a ritual no less serene. More than a century of contemplation has softened the egotistical Indian-fighter,

transforming the soldier into, well, a security guard. At his haunt, the museum and visitor center at **Little Bighorn Battlefield National Monument**, Custer's apparition is said to pass through late at night, checking the place before retiring.

Don't worry, the general's not alone. A soldier's ghost, wearing a black cartridge belt slung across a brown shirt, has also been seen roaming the museum. As for the battlefield, park personnel have spotted what some people believe to be the ghost

of 2d Lt. Benjamin Hodgson, who was killed by an arrow while dragging his bullet-shattered leg up a hill.

Spooks in the Bird Cage

Ghosts of a more subtle nature prowl the **Bird Cage Theatre** in Arizona's famous shoot-em-up town, **Tombstone**. Closed in 1885 but reopened in the 1930s, the Bird Cage sometimes smells of phantom cigar smoke, and faint piano music comes from some unseen source. Most unusual are the "cribs" hanging from the ceiling: tiny rooms that once hosted men and their favorite saloon girls. When the Bird Cage reopened as a tourist attraction, the new owners made the mistake of putting a mannequin of Wyatt Earp into the Clanton family's favorite crib. Day after day Wyatt's hat sailed mysteriously to the floor, knocked off by some unseen force, until he finally was moved to a crib of his own.

The Haunted Hospital

A building that spooked more teenagers than any other in the West still stands on a hillside in

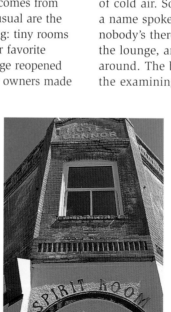

Jerome, **Arizona**, about a day's drive from Tombstone. Once a busy hospital serving the **Verde Valley,** it languished after closure for 44 years until it was renovated and reopened as a hotel. Break-ins and late-night beer busts had been common there as Verde Valley teens drove up the hill to the vacant structure and participated in a James Dean-like rite of passage. Many thought the hospital had been an insane asylum, a legend fueled by ornate iron bars on an upstairs balcony. In fact, though, it was a place where miners and ranch families went for healing. Many died there of natural causes, but some died mysteriously, including a caretaker who was found in the basement with his head crushed by the elevator.

Perhaps death is what bothers the Lady in White most as she wanders the halls. Was she a nurse? No one knows for sure, not even Nancy Smith, a Jerome historian who attends the hotel front desk at night.

"We hear voices," she says. "Feelings of cold air. Sometimes people have heard a name spoken, turned around, and nobody's there. Bartenders hear music in the lounge, and things have moved around. The bar, by the way, used to be the examining rooms."

Smith also points out that the sounds may be only water in the pipes or noisy woodpeckers who used to hammer on metal and wood in the attic and sent many trespassers hurrying into the night with tales of ghostly clanging.

Whatever it is, Smith is waiting. "Time is real to me, but not to them," she says. "Of course, you have to be careful what you're looking for. You just might see it."

Ghost Dance

Jack Wilson's vision came to him on January 1, 1889, by some accounts during a solar eclipse; by others, as he lay near death from scarlet fever. The Great Spirit showed him the future – a paradise in which his people would live with the happy, eternally youthful ghosts of their ancestors. There would be no strife, no misery, no famine, no death. The spirits would replenish their culture and religion, restore their lands, and give them victory over an enemy that seemed unstoppable. The key to this miraculous outcome was the summoning of those ancestral souls, which could be hastened, Wilson believed, by an excruciating, exhausting ritual – the Ghost Dance.

Wilson had come to this revelation along two very different paths. A Northern Paiute Indian by birth, he'd spent years with a Presbyterian family, from whom he took his surname and the Christian notion of paradise to come. But as the Indian Wovoka, he was reviving a short-lived spectral choreography developed by Wodziwob, a Northern Paiute prophet whose cult had spread across the Pacific Northwest 20 years earlier. Wovoka's father, Tavibo, had assisted Wodziwob and had no doubt planted the seed of revelation in his own son.

Wovoka hoped to become the Indian messiah and even inflicted nail wounds on his hands and feet. His message of a great, peaceful miracle to come spread through the tribes as swiftly as a pox, for it came at a time when the futility of further warfare was clear. To a desperate people facing cultural extinction, the idea of ancestors riding to the rescue looked like victory.

His Ghost Dance swept the western tribes, each of which had its own view of paradise. To the Sioux, for example, it would be a world restocked with herds of buffalo, and it would not necessarily be tranquil. The ghosts were summoned by a shuffling circle of dancers whose melancholy, trance-inducing steps could last for several nights and continue until morning on the last night. Most dancers chose the costumes of an earlier time and shunned such things as metal buckles and ornaments. But many wore consecrated buckskin shirts bearing designs of animals and stars – "ghost shirts," they thought, that no bullet could penetrate.

Late in 1890, as relations between Ghost Dancing Sioux and government agents deteriorated, troops were called in, and the dominos of tragedy began to fall. On December 15, the great chief Sitting Bull was killed when Indian police arrived to arrest him. A fortnight later, a band of exhausted Sioux Indians surrendered at Wounded Knee Creek. The next morning, a disturbance erupted between captors and captives. The Indians were fearless, believing their charmed garments would protect them, but they did not. Hundreds of Sioux were run to earth and killed, adding Wounded Knee to the ledger of famous atrocities. It also marked the beginning of the end of the Ghost Dance. The spectral ancestors, whom the dancers had called and called again, never came. – *Carl A. Posey*

Ghost Dancers (above) photographed in 1890; the ritual could last for several nights.

Wovoka (below), a.k.a. Jack Wilson, aspired to be an Indian messiah.

Ghost town scenes: a mortuary in Bodie, California (opposite, top), and an aptly named bar in Jerome, Arizona (opposite, bottom).

TRAVEL TIPS

DETAILS

When to Go

Summer temperatures in desert areas routinely exceed 100°F. Climate in the western states varies dramatically by region, season, and elevation. Bad weather – violent rain, snow, lightning, dust storms – can strike unexpectedly. Exceedingly hot days do not preclude equally frigid nights.

How to Get There

Air service is available throughout the region. Airports closest to those areas covered in this chapter are: Tucson International, San Francisco International, McCarran International (Las Vegas), and San Antonio International.

Getting Around

Car rentals are available at the airports. An automobile is essential for reaching remote ghost towns. A four-wheel-drive vehicle may be necessary for travel on unpaved roads. Amtrak, 800-872-7245, offers rail connections between many towns.

INFORMATION

Arizona Office of Tourism

1100 West Washington Street; Phoenix, AZ 85007; tel: 800-842-8257 or 602-542-8687.

California State Division of Tourism

801 K Street, Suite 1600; Sacramento, CA 95814; tel: 800-462-2543 or 916-322-2881.

San Antonio Convention and Visitors Bureau

121 Alamo Plaza; P.O. Box 2277; San Antonio, TX 78298; tel: 210-270-8700.

HAUNTED PLACES

Alamo

300 Alamo Plaza; San Antonio, TX 78205; tel: 210-281-0710.

The faint strains of a phantom violin and the smell of smoke are but two of the spectral phenomena associated with the "cradle of Texas liberty."

Bird Cage Theatre

P.O. Box 248; Tombstone, AZ 85638; tel: 520-457-3421.

The presence of ghosts merely adds to the bizarre character of this old burlesque hall, which the *New York Times* in 1882 dubbed the "wildest, wickedest night spot between Basin Street and the Barbary Coast."

Bodie State Historic Park

P.O. Box 515; Bridgeport, CA 93517; tel: 760-647-6445.

This once-humming town averaged seven shoot-outs a week during the 1880s. The crime rate has vanished in Bodie, along with just about everyone and everything except ghosts. More than 160 buildings remain here. How many phantoms move through these structures is anyone's guess.

Little Bighorn Battlefield National Monument

P.O. Box 39; Crow Agency, MT 59022; tel: 406-638-2622.

Custer's Last Stand has proved a long one. Since his premature demise, the ill-fated young officer apparently has taken to protecting the battlefield's museum, checking up on things at night.

Mackay Mansion

129 South D Street; Virginia City, NV 89440; tel: 702-847-0173.

Any house that saw hundreds of millions of dollars breeze through its drawing room is bound to prove dizzying. The Mackay Mansion is that and more: it's chilling. A number of spirits have been seen in the mansion.

United Verde Hospital

Jerome Grand Hotel, 200 Hill Street; Jerome, AZ 86331; tel: 520-634-8200.

Check into this 1917 hospital, now a hotel and restaurant, and you're apt to experience a ghost's bedside manner.

Yuma Territorial Prison State Historic Park

1 Prison Hill Road; Yuma, AZ 85364; tel: 520-783-4771.

Don't wear red in the "Dark Cell" of this horrid prison: an unidentified ghost tends to pinch those clad in this color.

LODGING

PRICE GUIDE – double occupancy

$ = up to $49 $$ = $50–$99
$$$ = $100–$149 $$$$ = $150+

Baldpate Inn

4900 South Highway 7; Estes Park, CO 80517; tel: 970-586-6151.

Adjacent to Rocky Mountain National Park, this inn was named after a mystery novel, *Seven Keys to Baldpate*. The innkeepers have a collection of about 20,000 keys; among them are some from Buckingham Palace, Westminster Abbey, Edgar Allan Poe, Clarence Darrow, and Stephen King, who surrendered the key to the room where he wrote *The Shining*. The inn's 12 rooms and three cabins are small and rather European in feel; 10 have shared baths. The ghostly figures of Ethel and Gordon Mace, who built the inn, have been seen in the hallway or in front of the fireplace, reading the Bible. Guests have also reported hearing footsteps and having their drinks stolen or their cigarettes snubbed out. A restaurant is on the premises. Open Memorial Day weekend to September 30. $$–$$$$

Driskill Hotel

Sixth and Brazos Streets; Austin, TX 78701; tel: 800-252-9367 or 512-474-5911.

A "frontier palace" built in 1886 and located in Austin's downtown entertainment district, the Driskill seems to have everything: Victorian elegance, modern conveniences, the industrious ghost of an old caretaker. Peter J. Lawless lived in Room 537 during the 30 years he worked here. Though he died in 1920, his transparent form is often seen supervising workers or sitting on a couch, reading a newspaper. The hotel's main lobby has a marble floor and towering columns. Guest rooms – there are 170 – have private baths and period furniture. A restaurant, bar, and 24-hour room service are available. $$$–$$$$

Gold Hill Hotel

Box 710; Virginia City, Nev. 89440; tel: 702-847-0011.

Built in 1800, the Gold Hotel is the oldest operating hotel in Nevada. The stone-and-brick building has 12 cozy rooms, two of which share baths. Gold Hill has two guest cottages and operates a bookstore with Western titles, as well as a restaurant and saloon. The hotel's ghost is a redhead known as Rosie, who's accompanied by the scent of roses and might originally have been a lady of the night. There's also William, a violin-carrying spirit who enjoys moving things from one part of the hotel to the other. $–$$$

TOURS

Ghost Hunts of San Antonio

Tel: 210-436-5417.

Walking tours of San Antonio's most haunted sites – including the Alamo, and the Menger and Gunther Hotels.

Excursions

Fort Concho National Historic Landmark

630 South Oaks; St. Angelo, TX 76903; tel: 915-657-4444.

Built in the 1860s, this isolated outpost was abandoned in 1889 and is now a museum. One Christmas, tour guide Conrad McClure was tending to the fireplace. Suddenly, he says, a shadowy form in soldier's garb brushed past him. Examining the fort's records soon thereafter, McClure discovered that only one soldier died at the fort: Second Sergeant Cunningham.

An alcoholic, Cunningham was hospitalized for liver disease and released for the holidays. He died in his barracks on Christmas Day. McClure has also seen the spirit of the camp's surgeon. Several drifters were murdered in one of the buildings in the 1890s; their phosphorescent ghosts haunt the museum's library, once Officers' Quarters No. 7.

Taos

Taos County Chamber of Commerce, P.O. Drawer I; Taos, NM 87571; tel: 800-732-8267 or 505-758-3873.

Several ghosts hang around this scenic mountain town. The spirits of New York socialite and patron of the arts Mabel Dodge Luhan and her Indian husband Tony are said to inhabit their former home, Las Palomas de Taos Adobe, where they once entertained such illustrious guests as D. H. Lawrence and Georgia O'Keeffe. Just north of the Plaza, the Governor Bent Museum is haunted by a less savory crew. On January 18, 1847, Governor Charles Bent found himself confronted by a mob protesting American rule in this former Mexican province. Attempting to address the crowd from his terrace, he was shot with bullets and arrows and scalped. His family managed to escape by digging through an adobe wall. His murderers were hanged, and their ghosts still linger at the site of their grisly deed. The spirit of legendary mountain man and Indian fighter Kit Carson lingers in Taos, too, haunting his house, now a museum.

San Francisco
California

CHAPTER **18**

ention San Francisco and earthquakes come to mind – especially the devastating shock in 1906 or the one that shook up the place during the 1989 World Series. Less known are the milder tremors that visit not the terra firma but the firmly terrified. Hauntings, as these tremors are termed, are plentiful in this town of old edifices and new eccentricities, as if the place were built on a supernatural fault line. Let the facts be known, and ghost hunters will rush here much as the gold seekers of another era.　◆　One of San Francisco's best ghost stories was spawned just as the city's raucous boomtown days were coming to a close. It involved a duel fought in 1857 between a senator and a judge. The senator was a California Democrat and ardent abolitionist named David Broderick. His critical comment about an antagonist, David Terry, who wanted California to join the ranks of the slave states, cost Broderick his life. Neither was a choir boy. Broderick had made his

Some people leave their hearts in San Francisco. Do others leave their spirits?

fortune during the Gold Rush by turning gold dust into slugs and selling them for more than they were worth. Terry had recently been released from jail for stabbing a man in the neck.　◆　Using ornate French pistols, they settled their feud on a dueling field outside town. (The pistols are on display at the city's Museum of Money.) Broderick was wounded and carried to the home of fellow abolitionist Leonidas Haskell on property that is now part of **Golden Gate National Recreation Area**. The senator lingered for three days before expiring in a second-floor bedroom overlooking the sea.　◆　Haskell's house, now known as **Quarters Three**, became a residence for army officers after the property was acquired in

Spirits in Alcatraz may not be free of their earthly shackles. Tormented sounds have been heard reverberating in the old prison's cells and corridors.

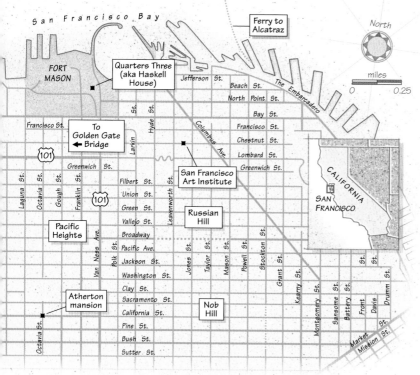

And it's typical that Broderick's fate hinged on an affair of honor, since honor was a matter of such importance to Victorian types, including their ghosts. Honor figures as well in the tale of the Atherton mansion.

After her husband died and left her a good-sized fortune, Dominga de Goni Atherton left suburban San Francisco and moved into the city proper. She built the **Atherton Mansion** at Octavia and California Streets in the exclusive Pacific Heights district in 1881. Dominga lived there with her son George, an aimless bumbler, and his wife Gertrude. George was somewhat of an embarrassment to the socially prominent Athertons, and the two strong-willed women with whom he lived constantly called his manhood into question. That is probably why, in 1887, he accepted an invitation to sail to Chile. Ostensibly he was going to visit friends, but in actuality he sought to prove his mettle and earn a place of honor in his family.

The trip proved to be his undoing. George Atherton developed kidney problems during the voyage and died. The ship's captain preserved George's remains by storing the body in a barrel of rum, which was shipped back to the Atherton household several weeks later.

George was duly dried out and buried, but shortly thereafter, his spirit apparently decided to avenge itself on the women who'd tormented him in life. Dominga and Gertrude reported being awakened at night by knocks at their bedroom doors and by a cold and disturbing presence. The phenomenon grew

1863 and turned into Fort Mason. Soldiers who have lodged there have reported seeing a man in a long, black coat and top hat walking pensively through the rooms. A colonel said he sensed that "something or someone follows me about the house at times."

An Affair of Honor

The spirits of San Francisco seem to be associated largely with the Victorian era.

Deadly Waters

The Golden Gate Bridge connects more than San Francisco and Marin County; it connects the world of the living and the dead. Since its opening in 1937, the 4,200-foot suspension bridge that spans San Francisco Bay has played dispassionate host to more than 1,000 suicides.

The bay's deadly saga, however, predates the bridge. In the 1800s, the clipper ship *Tennessee* disappeared into the dense fog of Golden Gate Strait and went down with a full crew. The phantom ship has been sighted by credible witnesses over the years, often passing below the bridge, its deck unpeopled, its sails untroubled. In 60 seconds, the ship fades.

Occasionally, the clipper passes alongside more substantial vessels. Such was the case in November 1942, when crew members of the USS *Kennison* fixed their gaze on the outmoded *Tennessee*. Curiosity became amazement, amazement became bafflement: The strange ship left a wake, but nothing registered on the destroyer's radar.

The bay's choppy waters have swallowed more than sailors and suicides. On February 17, 1937, 10 construction workers rode a falling scaffold through a safety net. On misty nights when the wind howls through the cables, one can almost hear the ghastly cries of men plummeting to their deaths.

Be assured that this venerable bridge conveys more traffic than meets the eye. Some para-psychologists speculate that for every reported ghost sighting, dozens remain undisclosed. What one sees on this imposing structure and what one chooses to report are two different things, separated by no lack of goose bumps and perplexity.

A phantom ship (left) thought to be the ill-fated *Tennessee* sails the waters of San Francisco Bay.

The Golden Gate Bridge (below), scene of hundreds of suicides, teems with uncanny presences.

A tilted camera makes houses look queasily out of kilter in Russian Hill (opposite), where removing graves for new construction unleashed a bevy of disgruntled ghosts.

so troublesome that Dominga sold the mansion and moved out. Subsequent tenants also have been unsettled by phantom knockings and roaming cold spots. A séance conducted by a local psychic identified several spirits active in the house, including those of George and Dominga.

The Rebellious Daughter

Eight blocks east of the Atherton mansion down California Street, the ghost of a teenage girl in a white Victorian dress may be encountered. She's said to wander aimlessly along the sidewalks of **Nob Hill**. Legend identifies the shade as that of Flora Sommerton, a girl who disappeared from the home of her distinguished family in 1876.

Sommerton's father had arranged a marriage for Flora to a much older man. Being rather independent-minded, and not crazy about the prospect, Flora ran off. The family offered a huge reward for information as to her whereabouts, but in vain. Nothing was heard of her until 1926, when her body was found in a flophouse in Butte, Montana. Some say she haunts the area near her former home in penance for her failure to uphold the family honor.

Ghosts are also identified with the **Russian Hill** area several blocks north of Nob Hill. Some of these ghosts, however, seem anchored to earth not by honor but by anger, a fury engendered by the violation of their resting place. A cemetery once occupied the land here, but the graves were moved to make room for new homes and office buildings. Some of the displaced spirits appear to have attached themselves to the tower at the **San Francisco Art Institute** on Chestnut Street.

The Institute was built in the 1920s, and its red-tiled roofs and ochre-colored walls distinguish it as a fine example of Spanish Revival architecture. Its tower, styled like the bell towers of the California missions, has been the site of several strange encounters. Early in its history, a night watchman with a room on the top

floor was surprised to hear the street-level doors he had locked open and close. Waiting fearfully, he listened to footsteps slowly ascend three sets of stairs. The door to his room opened and closed, but he saw no one enter.

Some years later, students partying in a room at the top of the tower had a similar experience. Eerie lights are said to flicker in the tower at night, and power tools used by sculptors have inexplicably turned on by themselves. When the Institute was renovated in the 1960s, some construction workers quit because the site scared them, and a series of near-fatal accidents delayed work for months.

Shades in the Cell Block

The Institute's frightening spectral inmates pale in comparison with the ghosts of **Alcatraz**, who, after all, were pretty scary when they were physically alive.

The prison on Alcatraz Island, a lonely outcropping in the middle of San Francisco Bay, was opened in 1933 as a maximum-security facility for America's most dangerous criminals. Among its most celebrated internees were Chicago crime boss Al Capone and Robert "Birdman" Stroud. Life on Alcatraz was hard: Inmates were lucky to spend one hour a day outside their cells, and those so favored usually spent the time breaking rocks. Violating prison rules could mean months of solitary confinement, sometimes in the Hole, a tiny cell with no light.

The prison was shut down in 1963, and Alcatraz Island became a national park site.

But the building still stands, and some of the poor souls that served time and died there seem to be locked forever behind its dank walls. Several visitors have reported hearing moans, agonized cries, and chains rattling in cell blocks A, B, and particularly C. A psychic who visited the site claimed to identify the unruly spirit of a man named Butcher inhabiting the place.

Prison records confirm that Abie Maldowitz, a mob hitman nicknamed Butcher, was killed by a fellow inmate in the laundry area of cell block C.

The D cell block is supposedly haunted as well, with visitors reporting cold spots and the sound of phantom banjo music coming from rooms that once housed Al Capone.

Winchester House

In the center of San Jose, California, stands the sprawling **Winchester Mystery House**, one of the most bizarre Victorian-era houses ever built. It has 160 rooms, 10,000 windows, 2,000 doors, 47 fireplaces. A decorative spider web motif appears in lamps and stained-glass windows.

Another peculiar feature involves the number 13. There are 13 bathrooms, 13 windows in several rooms, 13 hooks in closets, and a chandelier with 13 lights. Stranger still is the haphazard design of the place. Stairways lead to ceilings. Doors open to walls or sheer drop-offs, and rooms are so out of proportion that an average-size person can't stand upright in them.

All this weird construction was directed by the mansion's owner, Sarah Winchester, heir to the Winchester rifle fortune. She lived an idyllic life in Connecticut with her husband, William Worth Winchester, until he died from tuberculosis in 1881. The family's millions did nothing to appease her grief, so she sought comfort in Spiritualism, a new and wildly popular quasireligion that offered believers the hope of communing with the dead through spirit mediums.

During a séance with a Boston medium named Adam Coons, Sarah did indeed make contact with her late husband – or at least she believed she did – and he issued a strange command: She was to build a house to appease the spirits of people killed by Winchester rifles. And the construction must never stop; if it did, she'd be haunted by the gunshot dead. Convinced that the message was genuine, she moved west to California in 1884 to do the spirit's bidding.

Sarah wound up in San Jose, then a small backwater about 50 miles south of San Francisco, and bought an eight-room farmhouse. Inside it she held daily séances, getting instructions from her spirit guides, who apparently had a bottomless appetite for remodeling. Construction crews worked 24 hours a day, seven days a week, for 38 years, constantly adding to the house. The nonstop work ended only with Sarah's death in 1922.

The house was always an oddity, of course, but when it was turned into a museum, its peculiarities seemed to exceed mere matters of design. Caretakers reported hearing chains rattling and mysterious footsteps and seeing doors and windows opening of their own accord. Psychics who spent a night in the house didn't feel the presence of Sarah Winchester, but it seemed to them that the spirits she summoned for advice still inhabit the place, apparently feeling much at home at a site tailor-made for lost souls.

The Winchester Mystery House (above) was built by heiress Sarah Winchester at the behest of her late husband's spirit.

Strange incidents at the San Francisco Art Institute (opposite, bottom) have been attributed to an infestation of angry spirits.

Al Capone and other former inmates may still be imprisoned on Alcatraz Island (opposite, top).

TRAVEL TIPS

DETAILS

When to Go

Keep in mind Mark Twain's famous quip: "The coldest winter I ever spent was a summer in San Francisco." Sunny but cool weather is the norm from late spring to mid-fall. Blustery days are common. As always, dressing in layers is the best bet, so remember a jacket or sweater. Temperatures from June to October average 61°F. Micro-climates abound, with hot spots in the East Bay and San Jose. Winters are mild (58°F) but gloomy and wet.

How to Get There

Commercial airlines serve San Francisco and Oakland International Airports, each about 15 miles from downtown San Francisco. Shuttles run between the city and airports.

Getting Around

Car rentals are available at the airports. Public bus and streetcar transportation is provided by MUNI, 415-673-6864. Rail service is provided by BART, 650-992-2278.

INFORMATION

San Francisco Convention and Visitors Bureau

201 Third Street; Suite 900; San Francisco, CA 94103; tel: 415-391-2000.

California State Division of Tourism

801 K Street; Suite 1600; Sacramento, CA 95814; tel: 800-462-2543 or 916-322-2881.

HAUNTED PLACES

Alcatraz

Golden Gate National Recreation Area, Building 201, Fort Mason; San Francisco, CA 94123; tel: 415-556-0560.

The specters of many public enemies remain at Alcatraz more than 35 years after the prison closed. This house of detention intrigues and spooks in equal measure. Revenants here include a ghost named Butcher and another who strums a phantom banjo.

Atherton Mansion

1900 California Street; San Francisco, CA.

When a sherry-sipping aristocrat ends up pickled in a barrel of rum, one needn't imagine the mood of his ghost. George Atherton's spirit returned to vex his family, who had repeatedly questioned his manhood. Later, after the family had moved, he troubled other occupants of this mansion. Please do not disturb the residents of this house.

The Haskell House (Quarters Three)

Golden Gate National Recreation Area, Building 201, Fort Mason; San Francisco, CA 94123; tel: 415-556-0560.

The ghost of Sen. David Broderick, who died following an 1857 duel, haunts Quarters Three, his former house and site of his death.

San Francisco Art Institute

800 Chestnut Street; San Francisco, CA 94132; tel: 415-771-7020.

Ghostly footsteps and unearthly lights have been known to chill students and workers alike in the institute's campanile.

Winchester Mystery House

525 South Winchester Boulevard; San Jose, CA 95128; tel. 408-247-2000.

Spirits haunt this bizarre mansion built by Sarah Winchester to placate the ghosts of those killed by Winchester firearms.

LODGING

Mansions Hotel

2220 Sacramento Street; San Francisco, CA 94115; tel: 415-929-9444.

Owner Bob Pritikin makes no bones about his unseen resident – her presence has been verified by psychics and demonologists. Claudia Chambers, niece of the original owner, was killed in a freak accident after inheriting the buildings in 1901. Guests have witnessed apparitions, a door coming unhinged, an exploding crystal wine glass, and a toilet seat lid ripping loose and flying across the room. Renowned for their celebrity guest list as well as their splendor, the Mansions' two connected Victorians offer 21 spacious rooms and suites, each with private bath. Amenities include a restaurant, sculpture garden, billiard room, and cabaret. $$$–$$$$

San Remo Hotel

2237 Mason Street; San Francisco, CA 94133; tel: 800-352-7366 or 415-776-8688.

The San Remo is said to be haunted by the ghost of a madame who died in the southern section of the hotel in the late 1960s. Her body was not recovered for a number of days. Front-desk staff, especially those who work at night, report odd happenings, such as lights that come on after being switched off. Built by A. P. Giannini soon after the 1906 earthquake, the San Remo is one of San Francisco's finest value-priced hotels. The 62-room Victorian is within walking distance of the Powell and Taylor Cable Car route. Rooms are small yet charming; most have shared baths. $$.

Sir Francis Drake

450 Powell Street; San Francisco,

CA 94102; tel: 800-795-7129 or 415-392-7755.

This grand San Francisco landmark opened in 1928. Rumor has it that a honeymooning couple suffered a double tragedy here. As the bride watched from her window, her husband was hit and killed by a cable car while trying to cross Powell Street below. She is said to have jumped to her death, and her ghost is believed to haunt the hotel. It's just off Union Square. All 417 spacious rooms and suites have private baths, cable TV, and feature California Colonial decor. $$$$

York Hotel

940 Sutter Street; San Francisco, CA 94109; tel: 800-808-9675 or 415-885-6800.

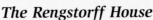

Formerly known as the Empire Hotel, the York has a colorful history. In the late 1920s, a tuxedo-clad piano player named Lester died during a performance in the Plush Room, the hotel's cabaret. His ghost haunts the card room upstairs. Housekeeping staff have experienced "weird stuff," including doors shutting and an invisible presence. Site of a forbidden speakeasy during Prohibition, the York served as the film location for Alfred Hitchcock's *Vertigo*. Built in 1925, the York's 96 spacious rooms and suites include private baths, walk-in closets, and mini-bars. Breakfast is served in the Corinthian-columned lobby. $$$-$$$$

TOURS

San Francisco Ghost Hunt Walking Tours

764 North Point #12; San Francisco, CA 94109; tel: 415-922-5590.

Follow the trail of documented ghost sightings in the stylish Pacific Heights neighborhood.

Excursions

Moss Beach Distillery
140 Beach Way; Moss Beach, CA 94038; tel: 800-675-6677 or 650-728-5595.

Located on the coast about 30 minutes south of San Francisco, the Distillery is visited by at least three very disturbed spirits. Back in the 1920s, a beautiful young wife and mother fell in love with a dashing musician, meeting him for secret trysts at the hotel next to her home. On her way to meet her lover during a terrible storm, she was killed in a violent auto accident. She now haunts the Distillery dressed in her favorite color: blue. When the musician's other girlfriend discovered his betrayal, she flung herself off the cliff into the ocean. Today her spirit wanders the beach, searching for her lover, her body covered with slime and seaweed. The musician's ghost is said to haunt the ladies' room.

Red, White, and Blue Beach
Six miles north of Santa Cruz on Highway 1.

Ambrose Bierce, the famed American cynic, found in the alleged appearances of clothed ghosts proof against the spectral world. How, he reasoned, could people who believed in the human soul account for something comparable in textiles? Well, you'd think a ghost at a nude beach would at least disrobe. Not at Red, White, and Blue Beach, however, where the ghost of a sea captain haunts a wood house and campground. The old tar elects to wear a raincoat and cap. Plenty of nudists have encountered his specter; one had to dodge a mysteriously tossed flowerpot.

The Rengstorff House
Shoreline Park; Mountain View, CA 94040; tel: 650 903-6073

Once a trough for socialites, then a dilapidated beacon for tramps, now an open house for tourists, this mansion has welcomed just about every social stratum. It also harbors ghosts. The builder, Henry Rengstorff, a German immigrant who made his fortune farming and shipping grain, enjoyed entertaining. He died in 1906. His grandson, Broadway star Perry Askam, transformed the house back into a social hot spot in the 1940s. But after his death in 1961, new tenants detected quirks in the home – flashing lights, the sound of a child crying, a young woman with long hair gazing through an upstairs window. A séance revealed both an embittered man being pushed about in a wheelchair and another man strangled by a bell cord in one of the bedrooms.

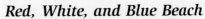

Los Angeles

California

CHAPTER **19**

Many of Hollywood's ghosts behave alike. The spirit clings to a certain area, seemingly oblivious to viewers, acting out the same scenes again and again. Seeing them is rather like watching a movie in an endless loop – a particularly apt simile in Los Angeles, moviemaking's company town, where cinematic hauntings are played out in a number of public and private places. If reports are true, the city has a smattering of celebrated "reel" ghosts, as well as shades of despondent would-be stars who never made it and are fated even in death to hover around the elusive spotlight. ◆ In its heyday, the venerable **Hollywood Roosevelt Hotel** was a monument to movie glamour. It was built in 1927 by a partnership that included actor Douglas Fairbanks and his equally celebrated movie-star wife, Mary Pickford, and a year after it opened, its ballroom, the Blossom Room, was the site of the first Academy Awards presentations. The 12-story Spanish Revival building was one of Los Angeles' premier hotels for four decades. It began declining in the 1960s and '70s, but its location at the commercial heart of **Hollywood Boulevard** and its historical value were such that in 1984 new owners decided to make extensive renovations. If reports are true, the new plaster and paint revived more than the hotel's former grandeur. ◆ Almost from the day of the Hollywood Roosevelt's reopening, staff and guests have encountered inexplicable phenomena: Phone calls came to the hotel switchboard from unoccupied rooms, cold spots chilled the main parlor, and a spectral musician played the piano in the **Blossom Room**.

> **Everyone knows that Hollywood is the place to find celebrities – dead or alive.**

Like this Hollywood mural, Los Angeles is filled with movie stars, both living and dead.

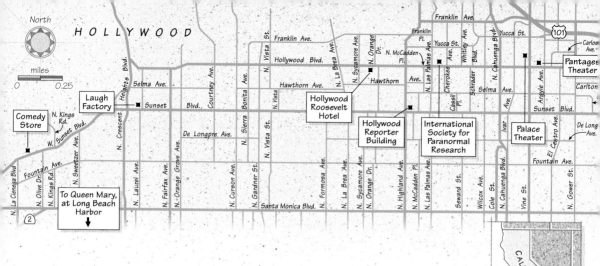

Here For Eternity

Strange as they were, these occurrences were less unsettling than certain activity reported on the ninth floor, particularly in and around **Room 928**. That room is said to be haunted by the ghost of the troubled and talented Montgomery Clift.

Clift became a respected star in the 1950s with superb performances in such classic films as *A Place in the Sun* and *From Here to Eternity*. He was in his last weeks of shooting the latter movie in 1952 when he checked into Room 928.

His career was flourishing at the time, but in his private life Clift was sliding deeper and deeper toward self-destruction. Under the pressure of trying to hide his homosexuality from the public, he'd begun drinking too much and experimenting with drugs. It was as though Clift's own unhappiness gave him a special understanding of Pvt. Robert E. Lee Prewitt, the

Montgomery Clift, who teamed with Frank Sinatra in the film *From Here to Eternity* (above), haunts Room 928 of the Hollywood Roosevelt Hotel (opposite).

brooding and doomed antihero who meets his fate in Hawaii the night after the Japanese bomb Pearl Harbor – the role he was playing in *From Here to Eternity*.

Unfortunately, Clift was drinking heavily off the set with co-star Frank Sinatra and with James Jones, author of the novel on which the film was based. Clift died in 1966.

Whether his stay at the Hollywood Roosevelt was associated with professional triumph or personal hell, Clift's shade is said to linger there. Guests in or near Room 928 have reported hearing loud monologues in the hallway, as though someone were rehearsing lines, only to peer out and find no one there. There have been sightings of a man who looks like Clift pacing the hall and then disappearing into Room 928, and guests have been known to bolt from the room because of sudden feelings of dread.

In 1992, Peter James, a Los Angeles-based psychic, spent a night in the room to investigate the claims. He says he sensed intense anger around the doorway, but it didn't keep him from falling asleep. In the middle of the night, however, he was awakened by the sensation that someone was lying on top of him. He struggled to move, he says, and the weight finally lifted. Later in the night he saw a man sitting in a chair in the corner. For a time the figure neither moved nor spoke, but it eventually stood up, walked toward the bathroom,

and disappeared. James felt that the visitor was Clift, whose uneasy spirit was somehow trapped in the hotel.

The Last Laugh

While Montgomery Clift's spirit inhabits the Hollywood Roosevelt, the late Groucho Marx reportedly visits the **Laugh Factory**, a Sunset Boulevard nightclub. The wisecracking, cigar-smoking leader of the zany Marx Brothers often used the building as an office in its preclub days. Jamie Masada, the Laugh Factory owner, reports witnessing evidence of Marx's visits. One evening, after locking up the club, Masada had to return to retrieve his house keys. He opened the door and found candles relit on tables and the stage spotlight turned on. A strong smell of cigar smoke permeated the room. On another occasion he arrived at the club one morning to find an image of Marx embossed on a wall.

Not to be outdone, another Sunset Boulevard club, the **Comedy Store**, claims to have its own ghost – though not a luminary like Groucho Marx.

At the Whaley House (above), a lingering cloud of smoke suggests the presence of a cigar-puffing ghost.

Groucho Marx (opposite) once quipped that he didn't want to belong to any club that would accept him as a member. Evidently, his ghost is not so particular: It haunts the Comedy Store nightclub.

Whaley House

The California legislature passed a law in 1998 outlawing smoking in all public places, but the statute goes unheeded at the **Whaley House** in San Diego, a unique brick structure and city landmark since 1856. Visitors to the house have reported smelling and even seeing cigar smoke wafting about the upper floor, though no smoker is visible.

Cigar smoking was the favored vice of the original owner of the house, Thomas Whaley, a New York blueblood who'd been drawn to California during the Gold Rush days. He fell in love with the climate and decided to settle permanently in the state. At the time, San Diego was a frontier outpost with little more than a handful of adobe houses – and the Whaley House. The Greek Revival home, with an attached granary, was the first European-style house in the city.

The house served several purposes: a comfortable residence where Thomas and his wife Anna raised a family, and a public building used by the city as a meeting house and as a hotel for such visiting notables as presidents Ulysses S. Grant and Benjamin Harrison. Whaley heirs lived there until 1953. The house was scheduled for demolition a few years later, but a civic group paid to have it restored and converted into a museum dedicated to San Diego history.

One ghost in the multiply haunted Whaley House is believed to be that of "Yankee" Jim Robinson, a one-time prospector who was lynched on the site in 1852 – before the house was built – for trying to steal a government boat moored in San Diego harbor. But Robinson appears less frequently than Whaley himself, who manifests his presence not only with cigar smoke but with the sound of footsteps emanating from the upper rooms. Some visitors have even reported seeing his apparition treading the stairway or strolling through the backyard gardens. Anna's spirit seems to remain as well, recognizable by a strong lavender scent and by the aroma of cooking that, during Christmas and other festive occasions, comes from an empty kitchen.

Unbelievers can scoff at all the ghostly reports, but the federal government doesn't: The U.S. Commerce Department has officially designated the Whaley House as haunted.

The Comedy Store has launched the careers of Garry Shandling, David Letterman, and Jerry Seinfeld, among others. A comic named Steve Lubetkin also once hoped to make it big there, but his career stubbornly refused to take off. One evening in June 1979, after a performance at the Comedy Store failed to get many laughs, Lubetkin resolved to kill himself. The following night he made his way to the roof of the Hyatt Hotel next door. After waiting until a crowd lined up to get into the Comedy Store, he jumped from the Hyatt in a final grisly performance.

After the suicide leap, Lubetkin's ghost began visiting the Comedy Store. It appears to be particularly attracted to the upstairs office, where it reportedly moves the furniture around and causes electrical malfunctions. The disturbances have happened so often that employees have taken to saying "There's Steve" when anything untoward occurs. Psychics who have visited the building have claimed to feel Lubetkin's presence; they sense a man with a broken neck or back.

Hoodlum Hauntings

Even before the Lubetkin incident, the building that houses the Comedy Store had a reputation for hauntings. In the 1940s and 1950s, it was the site of Ciro's, a popular nightspot where the stars went to see and be seen. Rumor had it that Ciro's was controlled by the mob, and if its walls could talk, they could describe all sorts of illicit doings. By some accounts, the walls do talk. Comedy Store employees have reported seeing a man in a bomber jacket cowering behind a desk as though hiding from an assault. They also say that the club's audience sometimes includes mysterious men dressed in expensive-looking suits tailored in the 1940s style – men who watch performances

The Pantages Theater (left), pictured during the 1959 Academy Awards ceremony, is haunted by famed industrialist and film producer Howard Hughes.

The *Queen Mary* (opposite) has found a permanent mooring in Long Beach Harbor, but some of its spectral passengers have refused to disembark.

and then suddenly fade into thin air.

An irritable lot, Comedy Store ghosts make their dissatisfaction known in several ways. Chairs and ashtrays have skidded across rooms of their own accord in ghostly protests against certain performers. The specters seemed to particularly dislike comic Sam Kinnison, whose act entailed a lot of screaming. Equipment seemed to fail whenever he took the stage. Kinnison died in 1997, but so far there have been no reports of his joining the ghostly company that haunts the club where he got his start.

The Revenant Reporter

Show business seems to be a common bond for many Los Angeles ghosts even when the apparitions were not, in life, stars themselves. William "Billy" Wilkerson, for example, made a living reporting on celebrities. Wilkerson was the founder and publisher of the *Hollywood Reporter*, a daily paper devoted to coverage of the entertainment industry. It was he who launched Lana Turner's career when he noticed the beautiful teenager walking out of Schwab's drugstore and urged her to

meet a producer friend of his.

Wilkerson died in 1962, and his ghost is said to still reside in the old **Hollywood Reporter** building on Sunset Boulevard even though the paper moved out in 1993. At that time, renovations began as the *LA Weekly*, another newspaper, prepared to take over the space. Construction crews became alarmed when tools started disappearing and a radio kept changing to a classical music station all by itself. Some workers fled after seeing what they believed to be an apparition. Wilkerson's former office was left largely intact, perhaps making his spirit feel secure, for employees of *LA Weekly* have reported no encounters with his ghost.

Spirits in Vogue

Even in fame-driven Hollywood, some ghosts are anonymous. A number of them seem to haunt the older section of town along Hollywood and Sunset boulevards, stretches of Art Deco buildings from the 1920s and 1930s. Though architecturally interesting, old Hollywood has been turning seedy since the 1970s despite efforts to revitalize it. Perhaps because so many of its buildings are now sad relics, the area seems to attract spirits searching for the more glamorous days.

Built in 1936, the **Vogue Theater** at 6675 Hollywood Boulevard was a movie house for decades. It now houses the offices of the **International Society for Paranormal Research**, a parapsychology group that investigates haunted houses and can take interested parties on ghost-hunting tours. One would expect ghost chasers to inhabit a specter-ridden headquarters, and so it seems in this case. Sensitives have felt the presence of several entities at the Vogue: There are cold spots throughout the building, and often doors slam and footsteps echo from empty rooms.

The Man in the Balcony

Similar phenomena occur at the nearby **Pantages Theater**. Another of old Hollywood's grand movie houses, this Art Deco masterpiece was owned and operated by theater magnate Alexander Pantages. In 1949, millionaire Howard Hughes bought all of Pantages' properties when he acquired RKO Pictures. He kept an office on the second floor of the theater until he sold RKO in the mid-1950s. The theater changed hands again in 1967, this time going to the Pacific Theater chain. It was transformed into a performance theater in the 1990s – and

that's when strange things started to happen.

Employees working in Hughes' former office often feel an angry presence in the room, along with odd temperature drops and cold drafts that persist even when the windows are closed. There have been sightings of a tall man who looks like Hughes and odors of cigarette smoke. Inside the theater, people have reported hearing a female voice singing, a voice that has been picked up by a microphone.

The **Palace**, at 1735 Vine near the fabled corner of Hollywood and Vine, is said to house several ghosts. The Palace opened in 1927 as the Hollywood Playhouse and has had many incarnations since then, including one as a television studio for programs such as *This is Your Life* and *The Merv Griffin Show*. It's now a nightclub, but some of its former denizens seem to return in insubstantial form in search of old Hollywood flair – ghosts that manifest themselves as eerie lights at night and as the sounds of phantom pianos

playing in empty rooms. A man in a tuxedo makes the rounds of the building on some nights, and a couple has been seen talking animatedly in a balcony, only to disappear when anyone approaches.

The Haunted Queen

Los Angeles is sometimes denigrated as a group of suburbs in search of a downtown, and some of its ghosts seem to have followed the city's restless outward sprawl. At **Long Beach Harbor**, for instance, in the southernmost reaches of the metropolitan area, a group of wayward spirits can be found – not in a building but on a ship, the *Queen Mary*.

Once the proud flagship of the Cunard-White Star Line fleet, the *Queen Mary* carried passengers between Europe and America for most of her 31-year career

San Diego Retreat

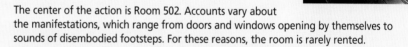

One of San Diego's most impressive landmarks is the **Hotel del Coronado**. This Victorian structure has been host to 14 American presidents and an assortment of royalty. It's also been the setting of several Hollywood films.

Erected on the Coronado peninsula in 1888, the hotel was the first building in California to have electric lights. After all these years, it's still one of the best hotels in San Diego – and a fine location for anyone in search of ghosts.

The center of the action is Room 502. Accounts vary about the manifestations, which range from doors and windows opening by themselves to sounds of disembodied footsteps. For these reasons, the room is rarely rented.

Hotel del Coronado
(below), one of the nation's grandest resorts, may be haunted by a woman who was abandoned by her con-man husband.

Actor Tyrone Power
(opposite) whispers to a friend at Ciro's, now home of the Comedy Store and spirits from various eras.

Legend has it that its manifestations are somehow linked to the sad fate of Kate Morgan. Kate and her husband, Tom Morgan, worked the western United States as con artists and professional gamblers. In November 1892, they were traveling in California when Kate announced that she was pregnant. Tom was not pleased and ordered her to have an abortion. Kate was unwilling, so the pair separated.

Kate checked into the Hotel del Coronado, and there she apparently aborted the child after all. Then she sent several telegrams from the hotel, trying to get her husband back, or at least to get money from him. Evidently, she didn't get the response she wanted. She went into San Diego one evening, bought a gun, and returned to the hotel. In the midst of a fierce storm, she made her way to an exterior staircase leading to the ocean and shot herself. She was found dead the next morning.

The Morgans had traveled under an assumed name, making it difficult for San Diego authorities to unravel the mystery of the suicide victim. After they did come up with an identity, a relative sent money to retrieve Kate's body. That was the last anyone heard of her, but it was just the beginning of the haunting.

A careful investigation of the story in the 1980s revealed that Kate Morgan did stay at the hotel, but not in Room 502 where all the phenomena take place. Whether it's her spirit or another, something in Room 502 causes unearthly disturbances.

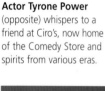

before being retired in 1967 and brought to Long Beach to become a permanently anchored hotel and resort. Several areas of the ship have a reputation for hauntings.

Some of the specters seem associated with a tragedy that occurred when the *Queen Mary* was pressed into service during World War II as a troop transport. On a voyage in 1942, she carried American troops across the Atlantic to England and was escorted by the *Coracoa*, a British destroyer that kept watch for German submarines. Miscommunication between the captains of the two ships caused a collision at sea. The *Coracoa* was sliced in half and sank in five minutes. The *Queen Mary* sustained a tear in her bow. Nearly all hands on the *Coracoa* were lost, since the *Queen Mary* was forbidden to stop and pick up survivors.

John Smith, the *Queen Mary*'s engineer who helped refit her into a hotel, made daily inspections of the hull when she was first moored in Long Beach to ensure that it wasn't taking on water. He never saw anything wrong, but whenever he went toward the bow, he heard water rushing and faint cries and moans. Each time he heard the sounds, Smith made a thorough inspection to see if there was damage. He never saw any signs of leakage and eventually ignored the mysterious sounds, figuring that something structural was causing them. After he learned more of the ship's history, however, he wasn't so sure.

Phantom Footprints

Some say the *Queen Mary*'s specters aren't confined to the human species. A number of the ship's passengers traveled with their pets, and the animals were kept in a kennel on the top deck. Especially memorable among them was an Irish setter that an Englishman took with him on a transatlantic voyage. The Englishman made a habit of retrieving his dog from the kennel every day and walking it along the decks. One night the setter started barking uncontrollably. Attendants couldn't calm it and decided to notify its owner, even though it was 3 a.m.

When a crewman checked the man's cabin, he found that the gentleman had died in his sleep. Some nights the dog's anguished cries still echo.

A ship built to cross the North Atlantic can't make too much use of a pool, but the *Queen Mary* had one in her first-class section. It's now kept only half full just to ward off cracking, but a phantom swimmer seems to take a refreshing dip in it anyway. Security guards and tourist guides have spotted a blond woman splashing around in it; they also say that sometimes wet footprints emerge from the pool and take several steps before disappearing.

Los Angeles may be the most populous city of the American West and a metaphor for rootless and restless modernity, but ghosts apparently congregate there as readily as they do in old New York, New Orleans, Charleston, or Philadelphia. Perhaps the length of its history is not all that makes spirits cling to a particular place. Perhaps the nature of the place – and its residents – counts, too.

TRAVEL TIPS

DETAILS

When to Go

With the exception of chronic smog, the area's weather is pleasant year-round. Winter temperatures may fall to 50°F; summer temperatures average 75°F but occasionally climb into the 90s.

How to Get There

The area is served by Los Angeles International Airport and Burbank Airport. Rental cars are available at both.

Getting Around

Buses are run by the Metropolitan Transit Authority, 323-626-4455.

INFORMATION

Greater Los Angeles Convention and Visitors Bureau

633 West 5th Street, Suite 600; Los Angeles, CA 90071; tel: 800-228-2452 or 323-624-7300.

Hollywood Visitor Information Center

Janes House, 6541 Hollywood Boulevard; Hollywood, CA 90028; tel: 323-689-8822.

San Diego Convention and Visitors Bureau

11 Horton Plaza; San Diego, CA 92101; tel: 619-236-1212.

HAUNTED PLACES

Comedy Store

8433 Sunset Boulevard West; Los Angeles, CA 90027; tel: 323-656-6225.

The ghost of a failed comedian is said to haunt this popular nightclub.

Hollywood Reporter Building

6715 Sunset Boulevard; Hollywood, CA 90028; tel: 323-465-9909

Now the site of the *LA Weekly* offices, the building allegedly houses the spirit of William Wilkerson, former owner of the *Hollywood Reporter*.

Hotel del Coronado

1500 Orange Avenue; Coronado, CA 92118; tel: 619-435-6611.

Strange disturbances in Room 502 of this famed hotel have unsettled many guests.

International Society for Paranormal Research

6675 Hollywood Boulevard; Hollywood, CA 90028; tel: 323-644-8866.

The ISPR recently renovated the historic Vogue Theater, built in 1936. Peculiar phenomena – cold spots, sounds of footsteps, mysterious presences – suffuse the building.

Laugh Factory

8001 Sunset Boulevard; Hollywood, CA 90027; tel: 323-656-1336.

Groucho Marx used this building as an office and now haunts the nightclub.

Palace Theater

1735 Vine Street; Hollywood, CA 90028; tel: 323-462-6031.

This nightclub, once the Hollywood Playhouse, effervesces with Tinseltown ghosts, including a phantom piano player.

Pantages Theater

6233 Hollywood Boulevard; Hollywood, CA 90028; tel: 323-468-1770.

The ghost of Howard Hughes reportedly visits his old office in this former movie house, now a performance theater.

Whaley House

2482 San Diego Avenue; San Diego, CA 92110; tel: 619-298-2482.

Ghosts at this museum include that of a man lynched on the site in 1852 and the original owner, Thomas Whaley, whose cigar smoke is regularly detected throughout the brick house.

LODGING

PRICE GUIDE – double occupancy

$ = up to $49 $$ = $50–$99
$$$ = $100–$149 $$$$ = $150+

Chateau Marmont

8221 Sunset Boulevard; West Hollywood, CA 90046.; tel: 800-242-8328 or 323-655-5311.

A seven-story neo-Gothic hotel with bungalows, the Chateau Marmont has 63 rooms, all with private baths. Built in 1927, it is well known for celebrity guests, including Greta Garbo, Jim Morrison, Howard Hughes, and John Belushi, who died here of a drug overdose. Rooms are spacious, and many have antiques. According to local legend, the person haunting the hotel is a somewhat amorous male who's been known to make fleeting appearances in the beds of female guests. A restaurant, workout facility, and outdoor pool are available. $$$$

Hotel *Queen Mary*

1126 Queen's Highway; Long Beach, CA 90802; tel: 800-437-2934 or 562-435-3511.

Built in the 1920s as a luxury liner, the *Queen Mary* is today a hotel with 365 rooms. Accommodations run the gamut from tiny cabins to large, elegant staterooms. Numerous ghosts have been seen by employees and guests over the years. Door 13 in Shaft Alley is said to be haunted by an 18-year-old crewman who was crushed to death nearby. Meanwhile, near the first-class swimming pool, two women – one in a 1930s costume and another in 1960s garb – have been spotted from time to time. Another kindred spirit, a bearded man in overalls, hangs around the engine room. Stores, restaurants, art galleries, and live entertainment are available. $$–$$$$

Radisson Hollywood Roosevelt Hotel

2247 Mason Street; Hollywood, CA 90028; tel: 800-833-3333 or 323-466-7000.

The Hollywood Roosevelt has long been the place to see and be seen. Built in 1927, the 12-story building underwent a face-lift some 60 years later; now every inch sparkles, including spectacular ceilings with hand-painted Spanish iron grillwork. The hotel's 335 rooms range in size from cozy to spacious. All have private baths and a refrigerator. As for the hotel's ghosts, Marilyn Monroe is still making appearances, this time in the hotel mirrors, where she's sometimes joined by Montgomery Clift, James Dean, and other Hollywood stars. Amenities include 65 cabanas, Olympic-sized swimming pool, workout room, and a Jacuzzi. $$$$

TOURS

Ghost Expeditions of Los Angeles

International Society for Paranormal Research; 6675 Hollywood Boulevard; Hollywood, CA 90028; tel: 323-644-8866.

Assist ISPR's team of paranormal researchers on investigations of haunted properties.

Graveline Tours

Tel: 323-469-4149.

Passengers are chauffeured in a customized hearse to some of Tinseltown's most notorious sites – some of them haunted.

Excursions

General Cinema

1815 Hawthorne Boulevard; Redondo Beach, CA 90278; tel: 310-793-7077.

The cinema is situated next to an old cemetery. Shadowy figures haunt the projection room, and many employees refuse to go near it. There's always a cold spot on the wall near the popcorn area, no matter how much heat the popcorn generates. The spot moves, sometimes within minutes. Other strange happenings: Cabinets locked up overnight are unlocked in the morning, supplies are transported to new locations, sudden breezes pick up inside the theater, and a gray-haired woman hangs around after closing and vanishes.

San Diego

La Casa de Estudillo, Old Town Historical Park; 4002 Wallace Avenue; San Diego, CA 92110; tel: 619-220-5422.

Villa Montezuma; 1925 K Street; San Diego, CA 92102; tel: 619-239-2211.

Built in 1829, La Casa de Estudillo served as a fort, orphanage, hotel, and church before becoming a museum. Employees report myriad hauntings – strange faces in mirrors, unaccountable music, dancing phantoms. Ghost investigators were forced out of the museum by supernatural forces in 1988; a photographer's camera lens shattered. Meanwhile, Villa Montezuma, a Victorian mansion built in 1887 by opera singer Jesse Shepard, registers curious sensations of its own. Shepard once held "musical séances" in the house, conjuring spirits with his voice. His presence is sometimes felt in the séance room. A somber apparition, possibly that of a servant who hanged himself in the cupola, occasionally is spotted there.

Stagecoach Inn

Ventu Park Road; Newbury Park, CA 91320; tel: 805-498-9441.

Two ghosts are associated with this museum, a replica of the 19th-century Grand Union Hotel. The first is a tall, female ghost who haunts the site of the old stagecoach stop, leaving behind the pungent scent of her perfume. The second ghost is of an unfortunate traveler who was murdered in his sleep. A séance was conducted in his room, revealing the spirit of Pierre Duvon, a mountain man who was killed in the hotel in 1885.

Hawaii

CHAPTER **20**

n July of 1975, geologist Jack Lockwood was flying with a fellow U.S. Geological Survey scientist over **Mauna Loa** on the **Big Island of Hawaii**. One of five volcanoes that make up the Big Island, Mauna Loa is the most massive mountain on Earth, more than 10 times the size of Washington State's Mount Rainier. At the time of Lockwood's flyover, it had been quiet for about a quarter of a century. On the other hand, **Kilauea**, its smaller sister mountain, had been erupting off and on for several years running, consistent with the two volcanoes' usual pattern of alternating eruptions.

◆　　Now it was Mauna Loa's turn. As Lockwood's partner snapped photographs, red curtains of molten lava shimmied in the air along the erupting fissure and flowed down the volcano's slope. After 18 hours the eruption stopped, only to be followed by a series of earthquakes. Making another aerial pass the next day, Lockwood was dismayed to see three hikers at the rest

Spirits divine and mundane are at home in the tropical lushness and volcanic fire of beautiful Hawaii.

cabin near **Mokuaweoweo**, the summit crater. The earthquakes and unpredictable emissions of choking sulfurous gas made the area exceedingly dangerous, and Lockwood alerted the National Park Service that a helicopter rescue was needed. He was told that to bring out three people, the helicopter would have to make two trips.　◆　　Later, however, the geologist learned that the chopper had made just one trip; only two people had been rescued. When asked about the third member of their party, the two were puzzled. No one else had been with them at the cabin. Hearing this, Lockwood was himself mystified. He checked with his flying companion: Had he imagined the other person, a woman, sitting on the porch?

Spectacular Kilauea, like other volcanoes in Hawaii, is watched over by the goddess Madame Pele, who warns potential victims of impending eruptions.

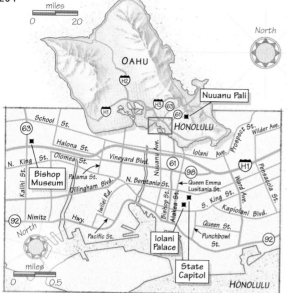

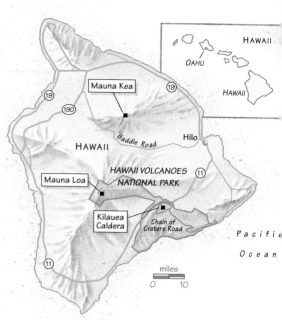

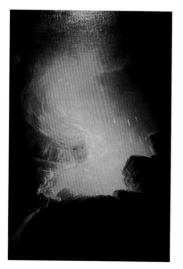

No, came the answer; her face hadn't been visible, but she'd definitely been there, a woman in a dress.

For island-born residents, the vanished woman presented no mystery: She was Madame Pele, in one of her more common forms, or *kinolau* ("many bodies"). She had doubtless come to warn the hikers, just as she has warned islanders of imminent eruptions for hundreds of years.

Of all the *akua*, or gods, in the Hawaiian pantheon, Pele, goddess of the volcano, is both the most familiar and most elusive. Her traditional home is **Halemaumau**, a crater within Kilauea crater. For most of the 19th century, Halemaumau was a lake of boiling lava, a sight so terrifying and otherworldly that Mark Twain, among others,

Madame Pele
(left), portrayed in this painting, manifests both a creative and destructive nature. The goddess is believed to reside at Kilauea (opposite).

likened it to the fiery pits of hell. Today, although it can still emit dangerous puffs of sulfur fumes, Halemaumau is quiet, for the goddess is spending time elsewhere, as is her wont.

Indeed, Pele is known to wander the entire island chain. Stories abound throughout the islands of drivers picking up an old woman or a beautiful young girl who rides with them for a time – and suddenly vanishes. Some believers advocate picking up the old woman, because failing to do so courts Pele's wrath. Others, too fearful of the goddess even to risk being in her presence, will speed past the old woman without looking at her. And others don't know what they've done until afterward.

The Vanishing Passenger

One Honolulu businessman had an unsettling encounter on the Big Island in 1987. The man – call him Darren – had a late meeting in Hilo on the Island's lush east coast and was scheduled for a meeting early the next morning in Kailua-Kona on the dry west side. The usual way to get from one side of the island to the other is to drive nearly all the way around the coast on a two-lane road, a trip that can take a couple of hours or more.

To be sure he'd make his 8 a.m. meeting, Darren decided to drive to Kona that night rather than the next morning. He also decided he'd take a slightly shorter route, across the saddle-shaped valley that dips between 13,677-foot Mauna Loa and 13,796-foot **Mauna Kea**. The ancient Hawaiians considered Mauna Kea the home of the snow goddess Poliahu, a spirit not on particularly good terms with Pele, her hot-tempered next-door neighbor on Mauna Loa. The lava scrub and open fields in the saddle between the peaks was often a battleground, and the Hawaiians tended to avoid it. But the U.S. military built a rough, narrow roadway, the Saddle Road, through the area during World War II. It was later paved, but it still has no lights or gas stations along its 50 miles. Not many local people take Saddle Road during the day, and fewer still drive it at night.

But Darren was from Honolulu. As he left Hilo and turned left from the coast into the ohia and fern forest at the Hilo end of Saddle Road, the night air was soft and the sky clear. Then, as the altitude changed, so did the weather. Just as he passed the last of the ohia, in the middle of nowhere, there was a downpour. Peering through the water streaming down the windshield, Darren saw a young girl on the side of the road.

She was drenched, so he pulled over to give her a ride. As she got in, with her long black hair dripping, he guessed her age as about 16, but a moment or two later, after she caught her breath and they began chatting, he realized that she was a very attractive 20- or 22-year-old.

Glancing over at her as he drove cautiously through the rain, he found the girl quite pleasant, and perhaps more mature than he'd originally judged: maybe 30 or so. He offered her a cigarette and a light, and as the flame lit her features he mentally added another few years to her age.

Soon the rain cleared, and a quarter moon lit the scrub on either side of the road. Darren commented on the scene's beauty, and he noticed a gravelly quality to her voice when she responded. He turned to look at her and found her staring back, the ember of the cigarette reflecting red in her eyes. Through the veil of smoke he saw a face suddenly withered – then suddenly gone.

What had Pele sought, if anything? One legend has her fleeing Tahiti after seducing her sister's husband: Had she meant to test her old charms on this unsuspecting motorist? More likely, her famed wanderlust had gripped her once again.

Temple of Sacrifice

The volcano goddess has been manifesting her dual nature, both destructive and creative, for more than 15 years. Since January 1983, lava has spewed virtually nonstop from Kilauea's Puu Oo crater. In this time, Pele has created more than 500 acres of new land even as she has destroyed houses and buried black sand beaches. The goddess even covered the ruins of Wahaula heiau, an ancient temple that had twice been spared the lava's onslaught – once in 1989 and again in 1990 – only to succumb at last in 1997.

Wahaula heiau, according to oral tradition, was the first temple of human sacrifice in Hawaii. The practice was introduced in the 13th century by Paao, a foreign priest from Tahiti or the Society Islands. Even the smoke from its altar fires was sacred, or *kapu*. Anyone unlucky enough to pass through the smoke was deemed to have broken the kapu and was put to death. For some 500 years, the stone altars of Wahaula ran with the blood of sacrificial victims until King Kamehameha II abolished the kapu system in 1819.

The Sacred Stones

The spirits of these victims accompanied the altar stones from the temple's ruins to **Honolulu** in the 1930s. Archaeologist John

Nuuanu Valley (opposite) as seen from 1,000-foot-high Nuuanu Pali, where voracious spirits allegedly steal pork from visitors.

Pork and the Pali

One of the first spooky stories Oahu-born children learn is that "bad things will happen if you take pork over the Pali at night."

The **Nuuanu Pali** is a sheer, 1,000-foot cliff at the head of **Nuuanu Valley**, a verdant, rainbow-garlanded valley tucked behind the bustle and sunny heat of Honolulu. As the valley narrows, the greenery on both sides of the highway grows denser, setting off the bright red flowers of the flame trees. The head of the valley is often shrouded with clouds that send down showers at unpredictable intervals. The rains feed surface streams high in the **Ko'olau Range**, and the streams become waterfalls at the edge of the cliff. Often the waterfalls are swept back up the cliff face by powerful winds. So strong are the winds of the Pali that they are said to have saved the life of a man; he had accidentally fallen and was blown back onto the edge of the cliff by the winds.

The "bad things" that happen on the Pali – the frequent accidents and many stalled cars – are said by some to be the spiteful doings of the *menehune*, the little people who work only at night and have a fondness for pork. Bringing pork to the Pali invites their unwanted attention.

Other traditions suggest that the ban on pork stems from a tumultuous affair between fiery Pele and the pig god Kamapua'a, who is associated with rain and the power of water to shape the earth. So violent was the single encounter between the two deities that Pele declared the ancient "right to separate domain." Pele and Kamapua'a agreed to live apart forever. To the pig god went all the rainy windward sides of the islands, while Pele controlled the dry leeward lands. To this day the division holds, and every island has a dry side and a wet side. Taking pork across the Pali is said to anger Pele, for it represents taking the body of Kamapua'a into her domain.

The third possible explanation for the pork prohibition is the ghostliest. In ancient times, travelers were warned against carrying food, especially pork, across the Pali because the cliff was haunted by restless, hungry spirits, waiting to attack visitors for their food.

Stokes put the stones on exhibit at the **Bishop Museum**. Founded in 1889, the museum honors Princess Bernice Pauahi Bishop, the last direct descendent of Kamehameha the Great. The original museum consisted of what is today called Hawaiian Hall, an imposing Victorian-style structure with an atrium and skylight.

When the stones from Wahaula had been formed into a model of the temple and put on exhibit in the center of the atrium, the mother of a young Hawaiian man who worked at the museum had a dream warning her of danger to her son. She begged him not to go to work, but he ignored her. No one knows exactly what happened, but other workers with him on the roof saw him fall through the skylight to his death – landing on the heiau stones. Some people said the temple had been consecrated by claiming its first sacrifice.

Perhaps not surprisingly, the museum's staff has experienced countless inexplicable occurrences over the years: windows that mysteriously close, locked doors that open, the sound of typing from an empty room. All of these happenings presumably are the work of some ghostly *uhane*, the animating spirit that is detached from the body at death.

Ghosts and Gum

Author and historian Glen Grant has reported his own eerie

Queen Liliuokalani's statue (left) may be less attached to its pedestal than it seems to be.

A head carved in stone (above) outside the Bishop Museum hints at shadowy curiosities within.

Iolani Palace (opposite), situated next to the capitol, is the only royal palace in the United States.

encounter with an uhane at the Bishop Museum. One night in the summer of 1987, Grant was on an after-hours tour of the museum for students training to be tour drivers. He'd struck up a conversation with a museum guard about spooky occurrences and was told to stay after the tour ended to witness some of the things that happen on nights when a lot of Hawaiian language is spoken in the museum. Hearing the native language apparently agitates the resident uhane.

As Grant and one of the students stood in the dark in the middle of Hawaiian Hall, Grant reproached the student for chewing bubble gum, which was not allowed. "I'm not chewing gum, Glen," the young man said. "You are."

The two confirmed that neither was guilty of gum chewing, despite the unmistakable scent of bubble gum. The guard said the fragrance indicated the presence of an old woman uhane, a frequent visitor, who wore a flower lei that smelled like bubble gum.

A Queen in the Capitol

Completed in 1969, Hawaii's five-story **State Capitol** in downtown Honolulu houses the state legislature and the governor's offices. The building – shaped like a volcano – not only embodies the spirit of Hawaii but may also be home to a number of Hawaiian spirits.

Visitors and workers alike have reported being inundated by inexplicable clouds of cigar smoke in a part of the building where Governor John Burns used to take his cigar breaks. Others speak of seeing the ghost of a beautiful, regal Hawaiian woman.

In one account, a legislative aide was working late one night in 1982 and called her husband to pick her up at 2 a.m. The man brought their young daughter with him. At first they waited outside, but after a while, they went into the building, he to get something to drink from a basement vending machine, the girl to bounce her ball in the basement hallway. A few minutes later, when the mother appeared, the daughter was nowhere to be found.

After half an hour of frantic searching, they heard the girl's ball bouncing behind a closed door in the basement stairwell. On opening the door, the parents found their daughter bouncing her ball as if in a trance; they had to shake her to get her to respond. The child said she'd been playing with a beautiful, barefoot Hawaiian woman in a black dress whose arms were draped with dozens of leis. When no such woman could be found, the mother simply assumed it was someone who'd come to distribute leis to the late-working legislators and had been kind enough to play with her daughter for a while.

Two weeks later, on April 10, the legislative aide and her daughter attended the unveiling of the statue of Queen Liliuokalani, Hawaii's last reigning monarch, which was to stand between the capitol and the queen's former residence, **Iolani Palace**. The hundreds of Hawaiians attending the ceremony that morning had brought leis to place around the statue's neck. But when the cloth was removed, they found that the statue was already wearing a *niho palaoa*, or whalebone pendant – a symbol of high rank that should not be covered with leis.

So on the first day of the statue's appearance in public, the queen wore dozens of leis – draped over her arms. Prior to the unveiling, the statue had been housed in a wooden crate near the stairwell in the basement of the capitol.

TRAVEL TIPS

DETAILS

When to Go

Hawaii enjoys subtropical weather with moderate humidity year-round. Temperatures range from the 70s to the 80s, and water temperature averages 75°F. Rainfall varies by location. Leeward, or west, sides of the islands are usually drier.

How to Get There

Major commercial airlines serve airports on Oahu and Hawaii. Traveling by air between islands is a simple matter: Hawaii has more than 30 airports and 15 heliports.

Getting Around

Car rentals are available at most airports. Mopeds and bicycles may be rented at most locations.

INFORMATION

Big Island Visitors Bureau

75-5719 West Alii Drive; Kailua-Kona, HI 96740; tel: 808-329-7787.

Hawaii Visitors and Convention Bureau

2270 Kalakaua Avenue, Suite 801; Honolulu, HI 96815; tel: 800-464-2924 or 808-923-1811.

Maui Visitors Bureau

P.O. Box 580; Wailuku, HI 96793; tel: 808-244-3530.

Oahu Visitors Bureau

737 Bishop Street, Suite 2860; Honolulu, HI 96813; tel: 808-523-8802.

HAUNTED PLACES

Bishop Museum

1525 Bernice Street; Honolulu, HI 96817; tel: 808-847-3511.

Sacred altar stones, removed from the ancient Wahaula temple, allegedly claimed the life of one worker at this museum. Peculiar occurrences abound in the museum, reportedly the result of an uhane, or spirit.

Mauna Loa

Hawaii Volcanoes National Park; P.O. Box 52; Hawaii National Park, HI 96718; tel: 808-967-7184.

Rising 13,677 feet above the sea, this volcano itself has a haunting aspect. Madame Pele, goddess of the volcano, was spotted here protecting two hikers during an eruption. According to legend, Pele lives within Kilauea crater, also in the park.

Nuuanu Pali

Oahu Visitors Bureau; 737 Bishop Street, Suite 2860; Honolulu, HI 96813; tel: 808-523-8802.

A picnic of ham sandwiches is definitely not a good idea around this sublime cliff in the Nuuanu Valley. Mishaps around the cliff are blamed on mysterious gnomes who are sent into a frenzy over pork. Some people speculate that ravenous spirits also have designs on the savory meat.

State Capitol

415 South Beretania Street; Honolulu, HI 96813; tel: 808-586-0178.

This volcano-shaped capitol is, aptly enough, inhabited by a cigar-puffing ghost. Those who've navigated through the haze of smoke believe that Gov. John Burns, known for his cigar breaks, haunts the building. The ghost of a lovely native woman moves throughout the capitol, while the spirit of Queen Liliuokalani has been spotted on the building's front stairway.

LODGING

PRICE GUIDE – double occupancy

$ = up to $49 $$ = $50–$99

$$$ = $100–$149 $$$$ = $150+

Hilton Hawaiian Village

2005 Kalia Road; Honolulu, HI 96815; tel: 800-445-8667 or 808-949-4321.

The ghost of a beautiful woman in a red dress wanders the halls of this hotel. Some say she is the spirit of a woman reportedly murdered in a tower room; others insist it is Madame Pele. Built on an ancient fishpond, the hotel has oceanfront acreage on Waikiki's best beach. The four modern towers contain more than 2,500 mid-sized rooms and 360 suites, all with private baths. Choose between ocean view, balcony, or garden view rooms. Amenities include restaurants, 20 acres of tropical gardens, shops, and a mini-golf course. $$$$

Ritz Carlton Kapalua

One Ritz Carlton Drive; Kapalua, Maui, HI 96761; tel: 800-262-8440 or 808-669-6200.

When excavation began for this hotel in the 1970s, human remains were unearthed. The entire hotel was redesigned and moved inland, and the burial grounds were preserved as a sacred site. Burials date from A.D. 610 to 1800, and there are other historic sites throughout the 1,500-acre resort. Several guests have reported seeing shadowy figures in the corridors, and some speculate that these phantoms may be the spirits of the dead who were disturbed by the construction. The hotel has some 600 rooms and suites. All have spacious lanais and most have ocean views. Three golf courses, tennis courts, snorkeling, scuba diving, a huge swimming pool, restaurants, and lounges are available. $$$$

Sheraton Moana Surfrider

2365 Kalakaua Avenue; Honolulu HI 96815; tel: 808-922-3111.

In addition to being situated at a former royal compound, this Oahu hotel was reportedly the site of a famous death. Jane Stanford, wife of university founder Leland Stanford, died under suspicious circumstances in this turn-of-the century hotel. The classic building features 793 spacious rooms and suites, all with private baths. Many rooms have ocean views. Amenities include a beachside cafe, banyan veranda, beach bar, tavern, and shiatsu massage. $$$$

Sheraton Princess Kaiulani

120 Kaiulani Avenue; Honolulu, HI 96815; tel: 808-922-5811.

Across the street from Waikiki Beach, this hotel sits on the former estate of Hawaii's last and most-beloved princess. Perhaps that's why some guests have reported seeing the spirit of a beautiful woman in the hallways. There are 1,147 mid-sized or spacious rooms. Some have ocean views; others have city views or overlook the pool. Restaurants featuring Japanese and Chinese cuisine are on the premises. A lounge, an international food court, a fitness room, and a swimming pool are available. $$$$

TOURS

Timewalks/Haunted Honolulu Walking Tour

2634 South King Street, Suite 3; Honolulu, HI; tel: 808-943-0371.

Noted historian and ghost-researcher Glen Grant has developed five popular tours to ghostly sites on the island of Oahu. Schedules and availability change. Call for information before planning your trip.

Excursions

Captain Cook Monument

Off Highway 11 on the west side of Hawaii, about 10 miles south of Kailua.

When Capt. James Cook first arrived in the Hawaiian Islands in early 1778, he was welcomed. But on a return voyage the next year, sentiment had turned against him. He was killed in a massacre at this site, and the entire area around the monument is said to bear an intense aura of horror and sadness. Despite the quiet pools and beautiful vistas, it is easy to sense the lingering spirits of a place where something went terribly wrong.

Old Federal Building

300 Ala Moana Boulevard; Honolulu, HI 96813.

The ghost of former federal employee Benedict L. Westkaemper is said to haunt this building. After committing suicide on Diamond Head in 1925, his spirit apparently returned to the building's basement, where a number of people claimed to have encountered him. Office workers sometimes see a man's shadow at night moving along the wall upstairs. The building has been blessed to put the spirit at ease, but sightings persist.

Highway H-3

Sixteen miles long, between Halawa and Kaneohe, on the island of Oahu.

The construction of this controversial highway destroyed or altered dozens of sites, including family homes, sacred burial grounds, and temples. The project was plagued with accidents and claimed the lives of two workers. It is believed that ancient Hawaiians built a vast religious complex in the valley traversed by the road. The complex, goes the story, was dedicated to the god Kane, associated with human sacrifice. In May 1992, the state realigned the freeway to avoid destroying the Hale O Papa and Laukini temples, but the Kukuiokane temple was buried under tons of concrete during construction. Many islanders avoid the highway. According to one native Hawaiian, "Every time somebody drives over it, they are driving over the bones."

SECTION FOUR

◆

Resource
Directory

FURTHER READING

Guides & References

A Dictionary of Ghost Lore, by Peter Haining (Prentice Hall, Inc., 1984).

The Donning International Encyclopedic Psychic Dictionary, by June G. Bletzer (Donning, 1986).

The Encyclopedia of Ghosts, by Daniel Cohen (Dodd, Mead & Company, 1984).

The Encyclopedia of Ghosts and Spirits, by John and Anne Spencer (Trafalagar Square, 1993).

The Encyclopedia of the Paranormal, by Gordon Stein, ed. (Prometheus Books, 1996).

The Ghost Hunters Handbook, by Troy Taylor (Whitechapel Productions, 1997).

Ghosts & How to See Them, by Peter Underwood (Anaya Publishers, 1993).

The Guidebook for the Study of Psychical Research, by Robert H. Ashby (Samuel Weiser, 1972).

Harper's Encyclopedia of Mystical and Paranormal Experience, by Rosemary Ellen Guiley (Harper, 1991).

Ghosts & the Paranormal

Apparitions, by Celia Green and Charles McCreery (St. Martin's Press, 1975).

Apparitions, by G. N. M. Tyrell (The Society for Psychical Research, 1973).

Apparitions and Haunted Houses, by Nathaniel Ernest Bennett (Faber & Faber Gryphon Books, 1971).

Apparitions and Survival after Death, by Raymond Bayless (Citadel Press, 1989).

Channeling: The Intuitive Connection, by William H. Kautz (Harper & Row, 1987).

Channeling: Investigations on Receiving Information from Paranormal Sources, by Jon Klimo (Jeremy P. Tarcher, 1987).

The Devil's Bride: Exorcism Past and Present, by Martin Ebon (Harper & Row, 1974).

The Edge of the Unknown, by Sir Arthur Conan Doyle (G. P. Putnam's Sons, 1930).

ESP, Hauntings and Poltergeists: A Parapsychologist's Handbook, by Loyd Auerbach (Warner Books, 1986).

A Gallery of Ghosts: An Anthology of Reported Experience, by Andrew MacKenzie (Arthur Baker Taplinger, 1972).

Ghosts and Hauntings, by Dennis Bardens (Taplinger Publishing Company, 1968).

Ghosts and Poltergeists, by Frank Smith (Doubleday, 1976).

Ghosts, Apparitions & Haunted Houses, by Arthur C. Clarke (P.C.A. Enterprise, 1991).

Ghosts, Hauntings, and Possessions: The Best of Hans Holzer, Book 1, by Hans Holzer & Raymond Buckland, eds. (Llewellyn Publications, 1991).

Ghosts in American Houses, by James Reynolds (Farrar, Straus and Cudahy, 1955).

Ghosts in Photographs, by Fred Gettings (Harmony Books, 1978).

Ghosts (Mysteries of Science), by Elaine Landau (Millbrook Press, 1995).

Ghosts: True Encounters with the World Beyond, by Hans Holzer (Aspera Ad Astra Inc., 1997).

Ghostwatch/The Institute for Psychical Research, by Colin B. Gardner, ed. (Foulsham, 1989).

The Ghost World, by T. F. Thiselton-Dyer (Ward & Downey, 1893).

Haunted Houses, by Charles G. Harper (Tower Books, 1971).

Haunted Houses, by Richard Winer and Nancy Osborn (Bantam Books, 1979).

Haunted Ladies, by Antoinette May (Chronicle Books, 1975).

Hauntings and Apparitions, by Andrew MacKenzie (Heinemann, 1982).

Incredible Tales of the Paranormal: Documented Accounts of Poltergeist, Levitations, Phantoms, and Other Phenomena, by Alexander Imich, ed. (Bramble Company, 1995).

In Defense of Ghosts, by Herbert B. Greenhouse (Simon and Schuster, Inc., 1970).

In Search of White Crows: Spiritualism, Parapsychology, and American Culture, by R. Laurence Moore (Oxford University Press, 1977).

The Journal of a Ghosthunter, by Simon Marsden (Cross River Press, 1994).

Mediums and the Development of Mediumship, by Rev. Robert G. Chaney (Books for Libraries Press, 1972).

The Medium, the Mystic, and the Physicist: Toward a General Theory of the Paranormal, by Lawrence LeShan (Viking Press, 1974).

Modern American Spiritualism, by Emma Hardinge (University Books, Inc., 1970).

Mysteries of the Unknown: Spirit Summonings, by the editors of Time-Life Books (Time-Life Books, 1989).

New Light on Old Ghosts, by Trevor H. Hall (Gerald Duckworth, 1965).

The Paranormal: A Guide to the Unexplained, by Anthony North (Sterling Publications, 1998).

Phantasms of the Living, by Eleanor M. Sidgwick et. al. (Ayer Publishing, 1975).

Poltergeist: A Study in Destructive Haunting, by Colin Wilson (Llewellyn Publications, 1993).

Poltergeists: Fact or Fancy, by Sachervell Sitwell (Dorset Press, 1988).

The Realm of Ghosts, by Eric Maple (A.S. Barnes, 1964).

Science and the Paranormal, George O. Abell and Barry Singer, eds. (Charles Scribner's Sons, 1981).

Science Confronts the Paranormal, by Kendrick Frazier, ed. (Prometheus Books, 1986).

The Seen and the Unseen, by Andrew MacKenzie (Weidenfeld and Nicolson, 1987).

A Skeptic's Handbook of Parapsychology, by Paul Kurtz, ed. (Prometheus Books, 1985).

True Experiences with Ghosts, by Martin Ebon (New American Library, 1968).

The Unexplained: Some Strange Cases in Psychical Research, by Andrew MacKenzie (Arthur Barker, 1966).

The Unquiet Dead: A Psychologist Treats Spirit Possession, by Edith Fiore (Doubleday, 1987).

Voices from the Tapes: Recordings from the Other World, by Peter Bander (Drake Publishers, 1973).

History

Appearances of the Dead: A Cultural History of Ghosts, by R. C. Finucane (Prometheus Books, 1984).

The Death-Blow to Spiritualism, by Reuben Briggs Davenport (Arno Press, 1976).

The Enigma of Daniel Home: Medium or Fraud?, by Trevor H. Hall (Prometheus Books, 1984).

Facts, Frauds, and Phantasms: A Survey of the Spiritualist Movement, by Georgess McHargue (Doubleday: 1972).

The Founders of Psychical Research, by Alan Gauld (Schocken Books, 1968).

Ghosts and Spirits in the Ancient World, by Eric John Dingwall (Keegan & Paul, 1930).

Ghosts: The Illustrated History, by Peter Haining (Macmillan Publishing, Co., Inc., 1975).

Harry Price: The Biography of a Ghost Hunter, by Paul Tabori (London, 1950).

The Heyday of Spiritualism, by Slater Brown (Hawthorn Books, 1970).

The History of Spiritualism Vol. I and II, by Sir Arthur Conan Doyle (Arno Press, 1975).

Holy Ghostbuster: A Parson's Encounters with the Paranormal, by J. Aelwyn Roberts (Element, 1996).

Houdini: The Untold Story, by Milbourne Christopher (Thomas Y. Crowell, 1976).

A Magician Among the Spirits, by Harry Houdini (Arno Press, 1972).

Margery, by Thomas R. Tietze (Harper & Row, 1973).

The Medium and the Scientist: The Story of Florence Cook and William Crookes (Prometheus Books, 1984).

The Other World: Spiritualism and Psychical Research in England, 1850-1914, by Janet Oppenheim (Cambridge University Press, 1985).

Paranormal People: The Famous, the Infamous and the Supernatural, by Paul Chambers (Sterling Publications, 1998).

Pioneers of the Unseen, by Paul Tabori (Taplinger, 1973).

Psychical Research: A Guide to Its History, Principles and Practices, by Ivor Grattan-Guinness (Aquarian Press, 1982).

Science and Parascience: A History of the Paranormal, 1914-1939, by Brian Inglis (Hodder and Stoughton, 1984.

The Shadow and the Light: A Defence of Daniel Dunglas Home, the Medium, by Elizabeth Jenkins (Hamish Hamilton 1982).

Sittings with Eusapia Palladino & Other Studies, by Everard Fielding (University Books, 1963).

The Society for Psychical Research 1882-1982: A History, by Renée Haynes (Macdonald, 1982).

The Spirit Rappers, Herbert G. Jackson, Jr. (Doubleday, 1972).

The Spiritualists, by Ruth Brandon (Alfred A. Knopf, 1983).

The Spiritualists, by Trevor H. Hall (Gerald Duckworth & Co. Ltd., 1962).

Ghost Stories

Animal Ghost Stories, by Nancy Roberts (August House Publications, 1995).

Battlefield Ghosts, by B. Keith Toney (Howell Press, 1997).

Best True Ghost Stories of the 20th Century, by David C. Knight (Prentice-Hall, Inc., 1984).

Ghostly Encounters: True Tales of the Ghouls, Spooks, & Spectres in the Lives of the Famous, by Astrid St. Aubyn, et. al. (Parkwest Publications, 1997).

Ghosts of the Air: True Stories of Aerial Hauntings, by Martin Caidin (Galde Press, Incorporated, 1994).

The Ghosts of War, by Daniel Cohen (G. P. Putnam's Sons, 1990).

The Haunted Reality: True Ghost Tales!, by Sharon A. Gill and Dave R. Oester (StarWest Images, 1996).

True Ghost Stories: A Psychic Researcher Hunts for Evidence of Hauntings, by Brad Steiger (Schiffer Publishing, 1997).

Regional Titles

Cape May Ghost Stories, by Charles J. Adams III and David J. Seibold (Exeter House Books, 1988).

Chicago Haunts: Ghostly Lore of the Windy City, by Ursula Bielski (Lake Claremont Press, 1997).

Eastern Ghosts: Haunting, Spine-Chilling Stories from New York, Pennsylvania, New Jersey, Delaware, Maryland, and the District of Columbia, by Martin H. Greenberg, ed. (Rutledge Hill Press, 1990).

Ghosts of New England, by Hans Holzer (Random House Value Publishing, Inc., 1997).

Ghosts of the West Coast: The Lost Souls of Alcatraz and Other Real-Life Hauntings, by Ted Wood (Walker & Company, 1999).

Ghost Stories from the American South, by W. K. McNeil, comp. and ed. (Dell, 1985).

Ghost Stories of the Delaware Coast, by Charles J. Adams III and David J. Seibold (Exeter House Books, 1990).

Ghosts: Washington's Most Famous Ghost Stories, by John Alexander (Washington Book Trading Company, 1988).

Gold Rush Ghosts, by Nancy Bradley and Vincent Gaddis (Borderland Sciences, 1990).

Haunted Alamo: A History of the Mission & Guide to Paranormal Activity, by Robert and Anne Powell Wlodarski (G-Host Publishing, 1998).

Haunted Alcatraz: A History of La Isla de los Alcatraces & Guide to Paranormal Activity, by Robert Wlodarski, et. al. (G-Host Publishing, 1998).

Haunted America, by Michael Norman and Beth Scott (Tor Books, 1994).

Haunted Heartland, by Beth Scott and Michael Norman (Warner Books, 1985).

Haunted Hotels: A Guide to American and Canadian Inns and Their Ghosts, by Robin Mead (Rutledge Hill Press, 1995).

Haunted Houses of California, by Antoinette May (Wide World Publishing/Tetra, 1997).

Haunted Houses, USA, by Dolores Riccio and Joan Bingham (Pocket Books, 1989).

The Haunted Southland: Where Ghosts Still Roam, by Nancy Roberts (University of South Carolina Press, 1992).

The Haunting of America, by Jean Anderson (Houghton Mifflin, 1973).

New York City Ghost Stories, by Charles J. Adams III (Exeter House Books, 1996).

Passing Strange: True Tales of New England Hauntings and Horrors, by Joseph A. Citro (Houghton Mifflin Company, 1997).

Pennsylvania Dutch Country Ghosts, Legends and Lore, by Charles J. Adams III (Exeter House Books, 1994).

ORGANIZATIONS

The American Ghost Society
515 East Third Street; Alton, IL 62002; tel: 618-465-1086.

California Society for Psychical Study, Inc.
Box 844; Berkeley, CA 94704; tel: 415-843-0307.

Center for Scientific Anomalies Research
P.O. Box 1052; Ann Arbor, MI 48103.

Ghost Research Society
P.O. Box 205; Oaklawn, IL 60454; tel: 708-425-5163.

Ghosts of the Prairie
515 East Third Street: Alton, IL 62002: tel: 618-465-1086.

Institute for Parapsychology
P.O. Box 6847, College Station; Durham, NC 27708.

Institute of Paranormal Investigations
P.O. Box 201203; San Antonio, TX 78220.

International Ghost Hunters Society
12885 Southwest North Rim Road; Crooked River Ranch, OR 97760; tel: 541-548-4418.

International Society for Paranormal Research
6675 Hollywood Boulevard; Hollywood, CA 90028; tel: 323-644-8866.

Society for Psychical Research
1 Adam and Eves Mewes; Kensington W8 6UG, England.

White Crow Society
314 West 231 Street, Suite 465; Riverdale, NY 10463; tel: 718-267-9723.

TOURISM INFORMATION

Arizona Office of Tourism
1100 West Washington Street; Phoenix, AZ 85007; tel: 800-842-8257 or 602-542-8687.

California State Division of Tourism
801 K Street, Suite 1600; Sacramento, CA 95814; tel: 800-462-2543 or 916-322-2881.

Georgia Tourism
285 Peachtree Center Avenue, Suite 1000; Atlanta, GA 30303; tel: 800-847-4842 or 404-656-3590.

Hawaii Visitors and Convention Bureau
2270 Kalakaua Avenue, Suite 801; Honolulu, HI 96815; tel: 800-464-2924 or 808-923-1811.

Illinois Tourism
James R. Thompson Center, 100 West Randolph, Suite 3-400; Chicago, IL 60601; tel: 800-223-0121 or 217-782-7139.

Louisiana Tourism
P.O. Box 94291; Baton Rouge, LA 70804-9291; tel: 800-633-6970 or 504-342-8119.

Maine Tourism
P.O. Box 2300; Hallowell, ME 04347; tel: 800-533-9595 or 207-623-0363.

Massachusetts Office of Travel and Tourism
100 Cambridge Street, 13th Floor; Boston, MA 02202; tel: 617-727-3201.

New York Tourism
1 Commerce Plaza; Albany, NY 12245; tel: 800-225-5697 or 518-474-4116.

Pennsylvania Travel
Room 453, Forum Building; Harrisburg, PA 17120; tel: 800-847-4872 or 717-787-5453.

South Carolina Division of Tourism
1205 Pendleton Street, Suite 104; Columbia, SC 29201; tel: 800-346-3643 or 843-734-0122.

Vermont Travel and Tourism
134 State Street; Montpelier, VT 05602; tel: 800-837-6668 or 802-828-3237.

Virginia Tourism
901 East Byrd, 19th Floor; Richmond, VA 23219; tel: 804-786-4484.

Washington Convention and Visitors Association
Department of Commerce Building, 1st Floor, 1450 Pennsylvania Avenue NW; Washington, D.C. 20005; tel: 202-789-7000.

PHOTO AND ILLUSTRATION CREDITS

Dan Abernathy 177B

Carlos Alejandro 2-3, 16

John Alves/Mystic Wanderer Images 189M, 189B

Ping Amranand 154T

Art Directors and Trip Photo Library 33T

Keith Baum 103M

Robert W. Bone 204, 209, 211B

John Bowden/Folio 185B

Nicole Buchenholz 99B

Paul J. Buklarewicz 205

Walter P. Calahan/Folio 118B

Camerique Stock Photography 166B, 195T

Luigi Ciufetteli 18B, 62T, 63, 66T, 66B, 87B, 90B

Richard Cummins/Viesti Collection 167T

Ted Curtin/Stock Boston 75

Cameron Davidson/Folio 111B

Detroit Institute of Arts 10-11

Dick Dietrich 74, 77, 161T

David A. Dobbs 128T, 128B

John Drew 175T

John Elk III 139T, 181B

Esbin-Anderson/Photo 20-20 176R

Everett Collection 24B, 80, 124, 125T, 165T, 192, 196, 199

J. Faircloth 135L, 135R, 136B

J. Faircloth/Transparencies 136T, 143B

Derek Fell 62B

Bryce Flynn/Stock Montage 76T

Lee Foster 161M

Mark E. Gibson/Photo 20-20 176L

Ralph Hall/Art Directors and Trip Photo Library 162

Harry Ransom Humanities Research Center, The University of Texas at Austin 36

Harvard College Library 12-13, 27

Robert Holmes 99T, 100, 150, 154B, 155B, 164, 168T, 182, 186T 186B, 190, 195B

Victoria Hurst/Tom Stack & Associates 127B

Images Colour Library 55

Independence National Historical Park Collection 121M

Index Stock Photography 67L, 206

James Randi Educational Foundation 45M

Mary Lou Janson 189T

Wolfgang Kaehler 139B, 149M

The Kobal Collection 24T, 56, 59B, 60B, 165B

Bob Krist 93B, 103T, 132, 137, 140, 144T, 144B, 146, 147T, 147B, 161B

Ken Laffal 143T

Tom Levy/Photo 20-20 184

G. Brad Lewis/Photo Resource Hawaii 202

Library of Congress 5T, 34T, 42, 76B, 87T, 88T, 89, 90T, 97T, 106T, 107, 109T, 110, 111T, 129, 142, 152, 177T

Robert Llewellyn 81B, 94, 114, 116, 117, 118T, 119T

Laurence Lowry/Stock Boston 78

M. Mackenzie/Art Directors and Trip Photo Library 104

Fred J. Maroon/Folio 26B, 109B

Simon Marsden 5B, 9T, 19, 20-21, 69, 212-213

Mary Evans Picture Library 1, 9B, 31B, 32T, 32B, 33B, 34B, 35, 37, 38, 40, 41T, 41B, 43T, 43B, 44, 50, 51T, 51M, 51B, 53B, 60T, 61, 68T, 68B

John Robert McCawley/Photri-Microstock 159

Moonlight Products 8T, 67R

Musées Royaux des Beaux-Arts de Belgique 26T

National Park Service 113T

Joseph Nettis 97B, 98, 101B, 103B

New England Stock 72, 79B

Jack Novak/Photri-Microstock 145

Terry Parke 134

Les Riess 45T, 153B, 155T, 157T, 157B, 158

Sam Roberts 201B

James P. Rowan 101T, 127T, 166T, 167B, 169, 171B

Mark Schechter/Photo Resource Hawaii 207

Jim Schwabel/New England Stock 121T

John Shaw 156

Kay Shaw 201T, 208T, 208B, 211T

John Skowronski/Folio 106B

Smithsonian Institution, National Anthropological Archives 179T, 179B

Lee Snider/The Image Works 91

Lee Snider/Photo Images 83T, 84, 113B, 121B, 131T, 131B, 149T, 149B

Stock Boston 79T

Stock Montage 25, 28, 30, 31T, 45B, 46-47, 52, 53T, 58T, 58B, 59T, 81T, 83B, 93T, 119BL, 119BR, 185T

Tom Till 113M, 122, 125B, 126, 171T

Tony Stone Images front cover

Allen J. Traber 153T

Michael Ventura/Folio 108

Ted Wood 4L, 6-7, 8L, 14-15, 18T, 22, 48, 54, 64, 70-71, 168B, 172, 175B, 178T, 178B, 181T, 187, 193, 194, 197, 198T, 198B

T. Zuidema/The Image Works 88B

Design by Mary Kay Garttmeier
Layout by Ingrid Hansen-Lynch
Maps by Karen Minot

Key: B = bottom; T = top; M = middle

INDEX